Amazon Kinesis Data Analytics Developer Guide

A catalogue record for this book is available from the Hong Kong Public Libraries.

Published in Hong Kong by Samurai Media Limited.

Email: info@samuraimedia.org

ISBN 9789888407682

Contents

What Is Amazon Kinesis Data Analytics?

With Amazon Kinesis Data Analytics, you can process and analyze streaming data using standard SQL. The service enables you to quickly author and run powerful SQL code against streaming sources to perform time series analytics, feed real-time dashboards, and create real-time metrics.

To get started with Kinesis Data Analytics, you create a Kinesis data analytics application that continuously reads and processes streaming data. The service supports ingesting data from Amazon Kinesis Data Streams and Amazon Kinesis Data Firehose streaming sources. Then, you author your SQL code using the interactive editor and test it with live streaming data. You can also configure destinations where you want Kinesis Data Analytics to send the results.

Kinesis Data Analytics supports Amazon Kinesis Data Firehose (Amazon S3, Amazon Redshift, and Amazon Elasticsearch Service), AWS Lambda, and Amazon Kinesis Data Streams as destinations.

When Should I Use Amazon Kinesis Data Analytics?

Amazon Kinesis Data Analytics enables you to quickly author SQL code that continuously reads, processes, and stores data in near real time. Using standard SQL queries on the streaming data, you can construct applications that transform and provide insights into your data. Following are some of example scenarios for using Kinesis Data Analytics:

- **Generate time-series analytics** – You can calculate metrics over time windows, and then stream values to Amazon S3 or Amazon Redshift through a Kinesis data delivery stream.
- **Feed real-time dashboards** – You can send aggregated and processed streaming data results downstream to feed real-time dashboards.
- **Create real-time metrics** – You can create custom metrics and triggers for use in real-time monitoring, notifications, and alarms.

For information about the SQL language elements that are supported by Kinesis Data Analytics, see Amazon Kinesis Data Analytics SQL Reference.

Are You a First-Time User of Amazon Kinesis Data Analytics?

If you are a first-time user of Amazon Kinesis Data Analytics, we recommend that you read the following sections in order:

1. **Read the How It Works section of this guide.** This section introduces various Kinesis Data Analytics components that you work with to create an end-to-end experience. For more information, see Amazon Kinesis Data Analytics: How It Works.

2. **Try the Getting Started exercises.** For more information, see Getting Started with Amazon Kinesis Data Analytics.

3. **Explore the streaming SQL concepts.** For more information, see Streaming SQL Concepts.

4. **Try additional examples.** For more information, see Example Applications.

Amazon Kinesis Data Analytics: How It Works

An *application* is the primary resource in Amazon Kinesis Data Analytics that you can create in your account. You can create and manage applications using the AWS Management Console or the Amazon Kinesis Data Analytics API. Kinesis Data Analytics provides API operations to manage applications. For a list of API operations, see Actions.

Amazon Kinesis data analytics applications continuously read and process streaming data in real time. You write application code using SQL to process the incoming streaming data and produce output. Then, Kinesis Data Analytics writes the output to a configured destination. The following diagram illustrates a typical application architecture.

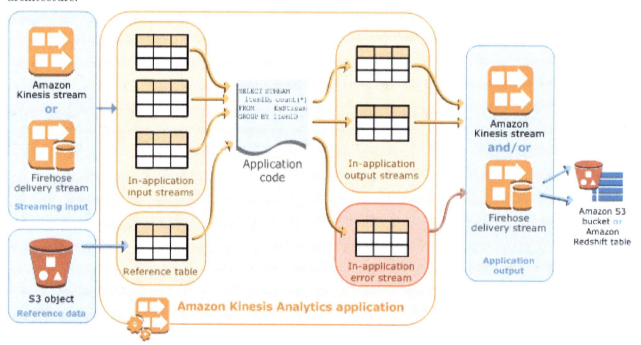

Each application has a name, description, version ID, and status. Amazon Kinesis Data Analytics assigns a version ID when you first create an application. This version ID is updated when you update any application configuration. For example, if you add an input configuration, add or delete a reference data source, or add or delete output configuration, or update application code, Kinesis Data Analytics updates the current application version ID. Kinesis Data Analytics also maintains time stamps for when an application was created and last updated.

In addition to these basic properties, each application consists of the following:

- **Input** – The streaming source for your application. You can select either a Kinesis data stream or a Kinesis Data Firehose data delivery stream as the streaming source. In the input configuration, you map the streaming source to an in-application input stream. The in-application stream is like a continuously updating table upon which you can perform the SELECT and INSERT SQL operations. In your application code you can create additional in-application streams to store intermediate query results.

  You can optionally partition a single streaming source in multiple in-application input streams to improve the throughput. For more information, see Limits and Configuring Application Input.

  Amazon Kinesis Data Analytics provides a time stamp column in each application stream called Timestamps and the ROWTIME Column. You can use this column in time-based windowed queries. For more

16

information, see Windowed Queries.

You can optionally configure a reference data source to enrich your input data stream within the application. It results in an in-application reference table. You must store your reference data as an object in your S3 bucket. When the application starts, Amazon Kinesis Data Analytics reads the Amazon S3 object and creates an in-application table. For more information, see Configuring Application Input.

- **Application code** – A series of SQL statements that process input and produce output. You can write SQL statements against in-application streams and reference tables, and you can write JOIN queries to combine data from both of these sources.

  For information about the SQL language elements that are supported by Kinesis Data Analytics, see Amazon Kinesis Data Analytics SQL Reference.

  In its simplest form, application code can be a single SQL statement that selects from a streaming input and inserts results into a streaming output. It can also be a series of SQL statements where output of one feeds into the input of the next SQL statement. Further, you can write application code to split an input stream into multiple streams and then apply additional queries to process these streams. For more information, see Application Code.

- **Output** – In application code, query results go to in-application streams. In your application code, you can create one or more in-application streams to hold intermediate results. You can then optionally configure application output to persist data in the in-application streams, that hold your application output (also referred to as in-application output streams), to external destinations. External destinations can be a Kinesis data delivery stream or a Kinesis data stream. Note the following about these destinations:

  - You can configure a Kinesis data delivery stream to write results to Amazon S3, Amazon Redshift, or Amazon Elasticsearch Service (Amazon ES).

  - You can also write application output to a custom destination, instead of Amazon S3 or Amazon Redshift. To do that, you specify a Kinesis data stream as the destination in your output configuration. Then, you configure AWS Lambda to poll the stream and invoke your Lambda function. Your Lambda function code receives stream data as input. In your Lambda function code, you can write the incoming data to your custom destination. For more information, see Using AWS Lambda with Amazon Kinesis Data Analytics.

  For more information, see Configuring Application Output.

In addition, note the following:

- Amazon Kinesis Data Analytics needs permissions to read records from a streaming source and write application output to the external destinations. You use IAM roles to grant these permissions.

- Kinesis Data Analytics automatically provides an in-application error stream for each application. If your application has issues while processing certain records, for example because of a type mismatch or late arrival, that record will be written to the error stream. You can configure application output to direct Kinesis Data Analytics to persist the error stream data to an external destination for further evaluation. For more information, see Error Handling.

- Amazon Kinesis Data Analytics ensures that your application output records are written to the configured destination. It uses an "at least once" processing and delivery model, even in the event of an application interruption for various reasons. For more information, see Delivery Model for Persisting Application Output to an External Destination.

Topics

- Configuring Application Input
- Application Code
- Configuring Application Output
- Error Handling
- Granting Amazon Kinesis Data Analytics Permissions to Access Streaming Sources (Creating an IAM Role)
- Automatically Scaling Applications to Increase Throughput

Configuring Application Input

Your Amazon Kinesis Data Analytics application can receive input from a single streaming source and, optionally, use one reference data source. For more information, see Amazon Kinesis Data Analytics: How It Works. The sections in this topic describe the application input sources.

Topics

- Configuring a Streaming Source
- Configuring a Reference Source
- Working with JSONPath
- Mapping Streaming Source Elements to SQL Input Columns
- Using the Schema Discovery Feature on Streaming Data
- Using the Schema Discovery Feature on Static Data
- Preprocessing Data Using a Lambda Function
- Parallelizing Input Streams for Increased Throughput

Configuring a Streaming Source

At the time that you create an application, you specify a streaming source. You can also modify an input after you create the application. Amazon Kinesis Data Analytics supports the following streaming sources for your application:

- A Kinesis data stream
- A Kinesis Data Firehose delivery stream

Kinesis Data Analytics continuously polls the streaming source for new data and ingests it in in-application streams according to the input configuration. Your application code can query the in-application stream. As part of input configuration you provide the following:

- **Streaming source** – You provide the Amazon Resource Name (ARN) of the stream and an IAM role that Kinesis Data Analytics can assume to access the stream on your behalf.

- **In-application stream name prefix** – When you start the application, Kinesis Data Analytics creates the specified in-application stream. In your application code, you access the in-application stream using this name.

  You can optionally map a streaming source to multiple in-application streams. For more information, see Limits. In this case, Amazon Kinesis Data Analytics creates the specified number of in-application streams with names as follows: *prefix*_001, *prefix*_002, and *prefix*_003. By default, Kinesis Data Analytics maps the streaming source to one in-application stream named *prefix*_001.

  There is a limit on the rate that you can insert rows in an in-application stream. Therefore, Kinesis Data Analytics supports multiple such in-application streams so that you can bring records into your application at a much faster rate. If you find that your application is not keeping up with the data in the streaming source, you can add units of parallelism to improve performance.

- **Mapping schema** – You describe the record format (JSON, CSV) on the streaming source. You also describe how each record on the stream maps to columns in the in-application stream that is created. This is where you provide column names and data types.

Note
Kinesis Data Analytics adds quotation marks around the identifiers (stream name and column names) when creating the input in-application stream. When querying this stream and the columns, you must specify them in quotation marks using the same casing (matching lowercase and uppercase letters exactly). For more information about identifiers, see Identifiers in the *Amazon Kinesis Data Analytics SQL Reference*.

You can create an application and configure inputs in the Amazon Kinesis Data Analytics console. The console then makes the necessary API calls. You can configure application input when you create a new application API or add input configuration to an existing application. For more information, see CreateApplication and AddApplicationInput. The following is the input configuration part of the `Createapplication` API request body:

```
1   "Inputs": [
2           {
3               "InputSchema": {
4                   "RecordColumns": [
5                       {
6                           "IsDropped": boolean,
7                           "Mapping": "string",
8                           "Name": "string",
9                           "SqlType": "string"
10                      }
11                  ],
12                  "RecordEncoding": "string",
13                  "RecordFormat": {
14                      "MappingParameters": {
15                          "CSVMappingParameters": {
16                              "RecordColumnDelimiter": "string",
17                              "RecordRowDelimiter": "string"
18                          },
19                          "JSONMappingParameters": {
20                              "RecordRowPath": "string"
21                          }
22                      },
23                      "RecordFormatType": "string"
24                  }
25              },
26              "KinesisFirehoseInput": {
27                  "ResourceARN": "string",
28                  "RoleARN": "string"
29              },
30              "KinesisStreamsInput": {
31                  "ResourceARN": "string",
32                  "RoleARN": "string"
33              },
34              "Name": "string"
35          }
36      ]
```

Configuring a Reference Source

You can also optionally add a reference data source to an existing application to enrich the data coming in from streaming sources. You must store reference data as an object in your Amazon S3 bucket. When the application starts, Amazon Kinesis Data Analytics reads the Amazon S3 object and creates an in-application reference table. Your application code can then join it with an in-application stream.

You store reference data in the Amazon S3 object using supported formats (CSV, JSON). For example, suppose that your application performs analytics on stock orders. Assume the following record format on the streaming source:

```
1 Ticker, SalePrice, OrderId
```

```
2
3  AMZN     $700         1003
4  XYZ      $250         1004
5  ...
```

In this case, you might then consider maintaining a reference data source to provide details for each stock ticker, such as company name.

```
1  Ticker, Company
2  AMZN, Amazon
3  XYZ, SomeCompany
4  ...
```

Amazon Kinesis Data Analytics provides the following API actions to manage reference data sources:

- AddApplicationReferenceDataSource
- UpdateApplication

Note

The Kinesis Data Analytics console does not support managing reference data sources for your applications. You can use the AWS Command Line Interface (AWS CLI) to add reference data source to your application. For an example, see Example: Adding Reference Data to a Kinesis Data Analytics Application.

Note the following:

- If the application is running, Kinesis Data Analytics creates an in-application reference table, and then loads the reference data immediately.
- If the application is not running (for example, it's in the ready state), Kinesis Data Analytics saves only the updated input configuration. When the application starts running, Kinesis Data Analytics loads the reference data in your application as a table.

Suppose that you want to refresh the data after Kinesis Data Analytics creates the in-application reference table. Perhaps you updated the Amazon S3 object, or you want to use a different Amazon S3 object. In this case, you must explicitly call the UpdateApplication. Kinesis Data Analytics does not refresh the in-application reference table automatically.

There is a limit on the size of the Amazon S3 object that you can create as a reference data source. For more information, see Limits. If the object size exceeds the limit, Kinesis Data Analytics can't load the data. The application state appears as running, but the data is not being read.

When you add a reference data source, you provide the following information:

- **S3 bucket and object key name** – In addition to the bucket name and object key, you also provide an IAM role that Kinesis Data Analytics can assume to read the object on your behalf.
- **In-application reference table name** – Kinesis Data Analytics creates this in-application table and populates it by reading the Amazon S3 object. This is the table name you specify in your application code.
- **Mapping schema** – You describe the record format (JSON, CSV), encoding of data stored in the Amazon S3 object. You also describe how each data element maps to columns in the in-application reference table.

The following shows the request body in the `AddApplicationReferenceDataSource` API request.

```
1  {
2      "applicationName": "string",
3      "CurrentapplicationVersionId": number,
4      "ReferenceDataSource": {
5          "ReferenceSchema": {
6              "RecordColumns": [
7                  {
8                      "IsDropped": boolean,
9                      "Mapping": "string",
```

```
10              "Name": "string",
11              "SqlType": "string"
12            }
13          ],
14        "RecordEncoding": "string",
15        "RecordFormat": {
16          "MappingParameters": {
17            "CSVMappingParameters": {
18              "RecordColumnDelimiter": "string",
19              "RecordRowDelimiter": "string"
20            },
21            "JSONMappingParameters": {
22              "RecordRowPath": "string"
23            }
24          },
25          "RecordFormatType": "string"
26        }
27      },
28      "S3ReferenceDataSource": {
29        "BucketARN": "string",
30        "FileKey": "string",
31        "ReferenceRoleARN": "string"
32      },
33      "TableName": "string"
34    }
35 }
```

Working with JSONPath

JSONPath is a standardized way to query elements of a JSON object. JSONPath uses path expressions to navigate elements, nested elements, and arrays in a JSON document. For more information about JSON, see Introducing JSON.

Accessing JSON Elements with JSONPath

Following, you can find how to use JSONPath expressions to access various elements in JSON-formatted data. For the examples in this section, assume that the source stream contains a JSON record in the following format.

```
1  {
2    "customerName":"John Doe",
3    "address":
4    {
5      "streetAddress":
6      [
7        "number":"123",
8        "street":"AnyStreet"
9      ],
10     "city":"Anytown"
11   }
12   "orders":
13   [
14     { "orderId":"23284", "itemName":"Widget", "itemPrice":"33.99" },
15     { "orderId":"63122", "itemName":"Gadget", "itemPrice":"22.50" },
16     { "orderId":"77284", "itemName":"Sprocket", "itemPrice":"12.00" }
17   ]
18 }
```

Accessing JSON Elements

To query an element in JSON data using JSONPath, use the following syntax. Here, $ represents the root of the data hierarchy and `elementName` is the name of the element node to query.

```
1  $.elementName
```

The following expression queries the `customerName` element in the preceding JSON example.

```
1  $.customerName
```

The preceding expression returns the following from the preceding JSON record.

```
1  John Doe
```

Note
Path expressions are case sensitive. The expression `$.Name` returns `null` from the preceding JSON example.

Note
If no element appears at the location where the path expression specifies, the expression returns `null`. The following expression returns `null` from the preceding JSON example, because there is no matching element.

```
1  $.customerId
```

Accessing Nested JSON Elements

To query a nested JSON element, use the following syntax.

```
1 $.parentElement.element
```

The following expression queries the `city` element in the preceding JSON example.

```
1 $.address.city
```

The preceding expression returns the following from the preceding JSON record.

```
1 Anytown
```

You can query further levels of subelements using the following syntax.

```
1 $.parentElement.element.subElement
```

The following expression queries the `street` element in the preceding JSON example.

```
1 $.address.streetAddress.street
```

The preceding expression returns the following from the preceding JSON record.

```
1 AnyStreet
```

Accessing Arrays

Arrays are queried using an array index expression inside square brackets (`[]`). Currently, the only index expression supported is `0:`, meaning that all the elements in the array are returned.

The format of the data returned depends on whether the array index expression is the last expression in the path:

- When the array index is the last expression in the path expression, all of the contents of the array are returned as a single field in a single data row.
- When there is a nested expression after the array index expression, the array is "flattened." In other words, each element in the array is returned as a separate data row.

To query the entire contents of an array as a single row, use the following syntax.

```
1 $.arrayObject[0:]
```

The following expression queries the entire contents of the `orders` element in the preceding JSON example. It returns the array contents in a single column in a single row.

```
1 $.orders[0:]
```

The preceding expression returns the following from the preceding JSON record.

```
1 [{"orderId":"23284","itemName":"Widget","itemPrice":"33.99"},{"orderId":"61322","itemName":"
    Gadget","itemPrice":"22.50"},{"orderId":"77284","itemName":"Sprocket","itemPrice":"12.00"}]
```

To query the individual elements in an array as separate rows, use the following syntax.

```
1 $.arrayObject[0:].element
```

The following expression queries the `orderId` elements in the preceding JSON example, and returns each array element as a separate row.

```
1 $.orders[0:].orderId
```

The preceding expression returns the following from the preceding JSON record, with each data item returned as a separate row.

23284
63122
77284

Note
If expressions that query nonarray elements are included in a schema that queries individual array elements, the nonarray elements are repeated for each element in the array. For example, suppose that a schema for the preceding JSON example includes the following expressions:
$.customerName $.orders[0:].orderId In this case, the returned data rows from the sample input stream element resemble the following, with the **name** element repeated for every **orderId** element.

John Doe	23284
John Doe	63122
John Doe	77284

Note
The following limitations apply to array expressions in Amazon Kinesis Data Analytics:
Only one level of dereferencing is supported in an array expression. The following expression format is not supported.

```
1 $.arrayObject[0:].element[0:].subElement
```

Only one array can be flattened in a schema. Multiple arrays can be referenced—returned as one row containing all of the elements in the array. However, only one array can have each of its elements returned as individual rows.
A schema containing elements in the following format is valid. This format returns the contents of the second array as a single column, repeated for every element in the first array.

```
1 $.arrayObjectOne[0:].element
2 $.arrayObjectTwo[0:]
```

A schema containing elements in the following format is not valid.

```
1 $.arrayObjectOne[0:].element
2 $.arrayObjectTwo[0:].element
```

Other Considerations

Additional considerations for working with JSONPath are as follows:

- If no arrays are accessed by an individual element in the JSONPath expression, then a single row is created for each JSON record processed. Every JSONPath expression corresponds to a single column.

- When an array is flattened, any missing elements result in a null value being created in the in-application stream.

- An array is always flattened to at least one row. If no values would be returned (that is, the array is empty or none of its elements are queried), a single row with all null values is returned.

The following expression returns records with null values from the preceding JSON example, because there is no matching element at the specified path.

```
1 $.orders[0:].itemId
```

The preceding expression returns the following from the preceding JSON example record.

[See the AWS documentation website for more details]

Related Topics

- Introducing JSON

Mapping Streaming Source Elements to SQL Input Columns

With Amazon Kinesis Data Analytics, you can process and analyze streaming data in either JSON or CSV formats using standard SQL.

- To process and analyze streaming CSV data, you assign column names and data types for the columns of the input stream. Your application imports one column from the input stream per column definition, in order.

  You don't have to include all of the columns in the application input stream, but you cannot skip columns from the source stream. For example, you can import the first three columns from an input stream containing five elements, but you cannot import only columns 1, 2, and 4.

- To process and analyze streaming JSON data, you use JSONPath expressions to map JSON elements from a streaming source to SQL columns in an input stream. For more information about using JSONPath with Amazon Kinesis Data Analytics, see Working with JSONPath. The columns in the SQL table have data types that are mapped from JSON types. For supported data types, see Data Types. For details about converting JSON data to SQL data, see Mapping JSON Data Types to SQL Data Types.

For more information about how to configure input steams, see Configuring Application Input.

Mapping JSON Data to SQL Columns

You can map JSON elements to input columns using the AWS Management Console or the Kinesis Data Analytics API.

- To map elements to columns using the console, see Working with the Schema Editor.
- To map elements to columns using the Kinesis Data Analytics API, see the following section.

To map JSON elements to columns in the in-application input stream, you need a schema with the following information for each column:

- **Source Expression:** The JSONPath expression that identifies the location of the data for the column.
- **Column Name:** The name that your SQL queries use to reference the data.
- **Data Type: **The SQL data type for the column.

Using the API

To map elements from a streaming source to input columns, you can use the Kinesis Data Analytics API CreateApplication action. To create the in-application stream, specify a schema to transform your data into a schematized version used in SQL. The CreateApplication action configures your application to receive input from a single streaming source. To map JSON elements or CSV columns to SQL columns, you create a RecordColumn object in the SourceSchema `RecordColumns` array. The RecordColumn object has the following schema:

```
1 {
2     "Mapping": "String",
3     "Name": "String",
4     "SqlType": "String"
5 }
```

The fields in the RecordColumn object have the following values:

- `Mapping`: The JSONPath expression that identifies the location of the data in the input stream record. This value is not present for an input schema for a source stream in CSV format.
- `Name`: The column name in the in-application SQL data stream.
- `SqlType`: The data type of the data in the in-application SQL data stream.

JSON Input Schema Example

The following example demonstrates the format of the InputSchema value for a JSON schema.

```
1  "InputSchema": {
2      "RecordColumns": [
3          {
4              "SqlType": "VARCHAR(4)",
5              "Name": "TICKER_SYMBOL",
6              "Mapping": "$.TICKER_SYMBOL"
7          },
8          {
9              "SqlType": "VARCHAR(16)",
10             "Name": "SECTOR",
11             "Mapping": "$.SECTOR"
12         },
13         {
14             "SqlType": "TINYINT",
15             "Name": "CHANGE",
16             "Mapping": "$.CHANGE"
17         },
18         {
19             "SqlType": "DECIMAL(5,2)",
20             "Name": "PRICE",
21             "Mapping": "$.PRICE"
22         }
23     ],
24     "RecordFormat": {
25         "MappingParameters": {
26             "JSONMappingParameters": {
27                 "RecordRowPath": "$"
28             }
29         },
30         "RecordFormatType": "JSON"
31     },
32     "RecordEncoding": "UTF-8"
33 }
```

CSV Input Schema Example

The following example demonstrates the format of the InputSchema value for a schema in comma-separated value (CSV) format.

```
1  "InputSchema": {
2      "RecordColumns": [
3          {
4              "SqlType": "VARCHAR(16)",
5              "Name": "LastName"
6          },
7          {
8              "SqlType": "VARCHAR(16)",
9              "Name": "FirstName"
10         },
11         {
12             "SqlType": "INTEGER",
```

```
13                "Name": "CustomerId"
14            }
15        ],
16        "RecordFormat": {
17            "MappingParameters": {
18                "CSVMappingParameters": {
19                    "RecordColumnDelimiter": ",",
20                    "RecordRowDelimiter": "\n"
21                }
22            },
23            "RecordFormatType": "CSV"
24        },
25        "RecordEncoding": "UTF-8"
26 }
```

Mapping JSON Data Types to SQL Data Types

JSON data types are converted to corresponding SQL data types according to the application's input schema. For information about supported SQL data types, see Data Types. Amazon Kinesis Data Analytics converts JSON data types to SQL data types according to the following rules.

Null Literal

A null literal in the JSON input stream (that is, "City":null) converts to a SQL null regardless of destination data type.

Boolean Literal

A Boolean literal in the JSON input stream (that is, "Contacted":true) converts to SQL data as follows:

- Numeric (DECIMAL, INT, and so on): true converts to 1; false converts to 0.
- Binary (BINARY or VARBINARY):
  - true: Result has lowest bit set and remaining bits cleared.
  - false: Result has all bits cleared.

  Conversion to VARBINARY results in a value 1 byte in length.

- BOOLEAN: Converts to the corresponding SQL BOOLEAN value.
- Character (CHAR or VARCHAR): Converts to the corresponding string value (true or false). The value is truncated to fit the length of the field.
- Datetime (DATE, TIME, or TIMESTAMP): Conversion fails and a coercion error is written to the error stream.

Number

A number literal in the JSON input stream (that is, "CustomerId":67321) converts to SQL data as follows:

- Numeric (DECIMAL, INT, and so on): Converts directly. If the converted value exceeds the size or precision of the target data type (that is, converting 123.4 to INT), conversion fails and a coercion error is written to the error stream.
- Binary (BINARY or VARBINARY): Conversion fails and a coercion error is written to the error stream.

29

- BOOLEAN:
  - 0: Converts to `false`.
  - All other numbers: Converts to `true`.
- Character (CHAR or VARCHAR): Converts to a string representation of the number.
- Datetime (DATE, TIME, or TIMESTAMP): Conversion fails and a coercion error is written to the error stream.

String

A string value in the JSON input stream (that is, `"CustomerName":"John Doe"`) converts to SQL data as follows:

- Numeric (DECIMAL, INT, and so on): Amazon Kinesis Data Analytics attempts to convert the value to the target data type. If the value cannot be converted, conversion fails and a coercion error is written to the error stream.

- Binary (BINARY or VARBINARY): If the source string is a valid binary literal (that is, `X'3F67A23A'`, with an even number of f), the value is converted to the target data type. Otherwise, conversion fails and a coercion error is written to the error stream.

- BOOLEAN: If the source string is `"true"`, converts to `true`. This comparison is case-insensitive. Otherwise, converts to `false`.

- Character (CHAR or VARCHAR): Converts to the string value in the input. If the value is longer than the target data type, it is truncated and no error is written to the error stream.

- Datetime (DATE, TIME, or TIMESTAMP): If the source string is in a format that can be converted to the target value, the value is converted. Otherwise, conversion fails and a coercion error is written to the error stream.

  Valid datetime formats include:

  - "1992-02-14"
  - "1992-02-14 18:35:44.0"

Array or Object

An array or object in the JSON input stream converts to SQL data as follows:

- Character (CHAR or VARCHAR): Converts to the source text of the array or object. See Accessing Arrays.
- All other data types: Conversion fails and a coercion error is written to the error stream.

For an example of a JSON array, see Working with JSONPath.

Related Topics

- Configuring Application Input
- Data Types
- Working with the Schema Editor
- CreateApplication
- RecordColumn
- SourceSchema

Using the Schema Discovery Feature on Streaming Data

Providing an input schema that describes how records on the streaming input map to an in-application stream can be cumbersome and error prone. You can use the DiscoverInputSchema API (called the *discovery API*) to infer a schema. Using random samples of records on the streaming source, the API can infer a schema (that is, column names, data types, and position of the data element in the incoming data).

Note
To use the Discovery API to generate a schema from a file stored in Amazon S3, see Using the Schema Discovery Feature on Static Data.

The console uses the Discovery API to generate a schema for a specified streaming source. Using the console, you can also update the schema, including adding or removing columns, changing column names or data types, and so on. However, make changes carefully to ensure that you do not create an invalid schema.

After you finalize a schema for your in-application stream, there are functions you can use to manipulate string and datetime values. You can use these functions in your application code when working with rows in the resulting in-application stream. For more information, see Example: Transforming DateTime Values.

Column Naming During Schema Discovery

During schema discovery, Amazon Kinesis Data Analytics tries to retain as much of the original column name as possible from the streaming input source, except in the following cases:

- The source stream column name is a reserved SQL keyword, such as `TIMESTAMP`, `USER`, `VALUES`, or `YEAR`.
- The source stream column name contains unsupported characters. Only letters, numbers, and the underscore character (_) are supported.
- The source stream column name begins with a number.
- The source stream column name is longer than 100 characters.

If a column is renamed, the renamed schema column name begins with `COL_`. In some cases, none of the original column name can be retained—for example, if the entire name is unsupported characters. In such a case, the column is named `COL_#`, with # being a number indicating the column's place in the column order.

After discovery completes, you can update the schema using the console to add or remove columns, or change column names, data types, or data size.

Examples of Discovery-Suggested Column Names

Source Stream Column Name	Discovery-Suggested Column Name
USER	COL_USER
USER@DOMAIN	COL_USERDOMAIN
@@	COL_0

Schema Discovery Issues

What happens if Kinesis Data Analytics does not infer a schema for a given streaming source?

Kinesis Data Analytics infers your schema for common formats, such as CSV and JSON, which are UTF-8 encoded. Kinesis Data Analytics supports any UTF-8 encoded records (including raw text like application logs and records) with a custom column and row delimiter. If Kinesis Data Analytics doesn't infer a schema, you can define a schema manually using the schema editor on the console (or using the API).

If your data does not follow a pattern (which you can specify using the schema editor), you can define a schema as a single column of type VARCHAR(N), where N is the largest number of characters you expect your record to include. From there, you can use string and date-time manipulation to structure your data after it is in an in-application stream. For examples, see Example: Transforming DateTime Values.

Using the Schema Discovery Feature on Static Data

The schema discovery feature can generate a schema from either the data in a stream or data in a static file that is stored in an Amazon S3 bucket. Suppose that you want to generate a schema for a Kinesis Data Analytics application for reference purposes or when live streaming data isn't available. You can use the schema discovery feature on a static file that contains a sample of the data in the expected format of your streaming or reference data. Kinesis Data Analytics can run schema discovery on sample data from a JSON or CSV file that's stored in an Amazon S3 bucket. Using schema discovery on a data file uses the DiscoverInputSchema API with the S3Configuration parameter specified.

To run discovery on a static file, you provide the API with an S3Configuration structure with the following information:

- **BucketARN:** The Amazon Resource Name (ARN) of the Amazon S3 bucket that contains the file. For the format of an Amazon S3 bucket ARN, see Amazon Resource Names (ARNs) and AWS Service Namespaces: Amazon Simple Storage Service (Amazon S3).
- **RoleARN:** The ARN of an IAM role with the AmazonS3ReadOnlyAccess policy. For information about how to add a policy to a role, see Modifying a Role.
- **FileKey**: The file name of the object.

Note
Generating a schema from a data file is currently not available in the AWS Management Console.

To generate a schema from an Amazon S3 object using the DiscoverInputSchema API

1. Make sure that you have the AWS CLI set up. For more information, see Step 2: Set Up the AWS Command Line Interface (AWS CLI) in the Getting Started section.

2. Create a file named data.csv with the following contents:

```
1  year,month,state,producer_type,energy_source,units,consumption
2  2001,1,AK,TotalElectricPowerIndustry,Coal,ShortTons,47615
3  2001,1,AK,ElectricGeneratorsElectricUtilities,Coal,ShortTons,16535
4  2001,1,AK,CombinedHeatandPowerElectricPower,Coal,ShortTons,22890
5  2001,1,AL,TotalElectricPowerIndustry,Coal,ShortTons,3020601
6  2001,1,AL,ElectricGeneratorsElectricUtilities,Coal,ShortTons,2987681
```

3. Sign in to the Amazon S3 console at https://console.aws.amazon.com/s3/.

4. Create an Amazon S3 bucket and upload the data.csv file you created. Note the ARN of the created bucket. For information about creating an Amazon S3 bucket and uploading a file, see Getting Started with Amazon Simple Storage Service.

5. Open the IAM console at https://console.aws.amazon.com/iam/. Create a role with the AmazonS3ReadOnlyAccess policy. Note the ARN of the new role. For information about creating a role, see Creating a Role to Delegate Permissions to an AWS Service. For information about how to add a policy to a role, see Modifying a Role.

6. Run the following DiscoverInputSchema command in the AWS CLI, substituting the ARNs for your Amazon S3 bucket and IAM role:

```
1  $aws kinesisanalytics discover-input-schema --s3-configuration '{ "RoleARN": "arn:aws:iam
       ::123456789012:role/service-role/your-IAM-role", "BucketARN": "arn:aws:s3:::your-bucket
       -name", "FileKey": "data.csv" }'
```

7. The response will look similar to the following:

```
1  {
2      "InputSchema": {
3          "RecordEncoding": "UTF-8",
```

```
4        "RecordColumns": [
5            {
6                "SqlType": "INTEGER",
7                "Name": "COL_year"
8            },
9            {
10               "SqlType": "INTEGER",
11               "Name": "COL_month"
12           },
13           {
14               "SqlType": "VARCHAR(4)",
15               "Name": "state"
16           },
17           {
18               "SqlType": "VARCHAR(64)",
19               "Name": "producer_type"
20           },
21           {
22               "SqlType": "VARCHAR(4)",
23               "Name": "energy_source"
24           },
25           {
26               "SqlType": "VARCHAR(16)",
27               "Name": "units"
28           },
29           {
30               "SqlType": "INTEGER",
31               "Name": "consumption"
32           }
33       ],
34       "RecordFormat": {
35           "RecordFormatType": "CSV",
36           "MappingParameters": {
37               "CSVMappingParameters": {
38                   "RecordRowDelimiter": "\r\n",
39                   "RecordColumnDelimiter": ","
40               }
41           }
42       }
43   },
44   "RawInputRecords": [
45       "year,month,state,producer_type,energy_source,units,consumption\r\n2001,1,AK,
             TotalElectricPowerIndustry,Coal,ShortTons,47615\r\n2001,1,AK,
             ElectricGeneratorsElectricUtilities,Coal,ShortTons,16535\r\n2001,1,AK,
             CombinedHeatandPowerElectricPower,Coal,ShortTons,22890\r\n2001,1,AL,
             TotalElectricPowerIndustry,Coal,ShortTons,3020601\r\n2001,1,AL,
             ElectricGeneratorsElectricUtilities,Coal,ShortTons,2987681"
46   ],
47   "ParsedInputRecords": [
48       [
49           null,
50           null,
51           "state",
52           "producer_type",
```

```
53          "energy_source",
54          "units",
55          null
56      ],
57      [
58          "2001",
59          "1",
60          "AK",
61          "TotalElectricPowerIndustry",
62          "Coal",
63          "ShortTons",
64          "47615"
65      ],
66      [
67          "2001",
68          "1",
69          "AK",
70          "ElectricGeneratorsElectricUtilities",
71          "Coal",
72          "ShortTons",
73          "16535"
74      ],
75      [
76          "2001",
77          "1",
78          "AK",
79          "CombinedHeatandPowerElectricPower",
80          "Coal",
81          "ShortTons",
82          "22890"
83      ],
84      [
85          "2001",
86          "1",
87          "AL",
88          "TotalElectricPowerIndustry",
89          "Coal",
90          "ShortTons",
91          "3020601"
92      ],
93      [
94          "2001",
95          "1",
96          "AL",
97          "ElectricGeneratorsElectricUtilities",
98          "Coal",
99          "ShortTons",
100         "2987681"
101     ]
102    ]
103 }
```

Preprocessing Data Using a Lambda Function

If the data in your stream needs format conversion, transformation, enrichment, or filtering, you can preprocess the data using an AWS Lambda function. You can do this before your application SQL code executes or before your application creates a schema from your data stream.

Using a Lambda function for preprocessing records is useful in the following scenarios:

- Transforming records from other formats (such as KPL or GZIP) into formats that Kinesis Data Analytics can analyze. Kinesis Data Analytics currently supports JSON or CSV data formats.
- Expanding data into a format that is more accessible for operations such as aggregation or anomaly detection. For instance, if several data values are stored together in a string, you can expand the data into separate columns.
- Data enrichment with other AWS services, such as extrapolation or error correction.
- Applying complex string transformation to record fields.
- Data filtering for cleaning up the data.

a.

Using a Lambda Function for Preprocessing Records

When creating your Kinesis Data Analytics application, you enable Lambda preprocessing in the **Connect to a Source** page.

To use a Lambda function to preprocess records in a Kinesis Data Analytics application

1. Sign in to the AWS Management Console and open the Kinesis Data Analytics console at https://console.aws.amazon.com/kinesisanalytics.

2. On the **Connect to a Source** page for your application, choose **Enabled** in the **Record pre-processing with AWS Lambda** section.

3. To use a Lambda function that you have already created, choose the function in the **Lambda function** drop-down list.

4. To create a new Lambda function from one of the Lambda preprocessing templates, choose the template from the drop-down list. Then choose **View in Lambda** to edit the function.

5. To create a new Lambda function, choose **Create new**. For information about creating a Lambda function, see Create a HelloWorld Lambda Function and Explore the Console.

6. Choose the version of the Lambda function to use. To use the latest version, choose **$LATEST**.

When you choose or create a Lambda function for record preprocessing, the records are preprocessed before your application SQL code executes or your application generates a schema from the records.

Lambda Preprocessing Permissions

To use Lambda preprocessing, the application's IAM role requires the following permissions policy:

```
1    {
2      "Sid": "UseLambdaFunction",
3      "Effect": "Allow",
4      "Action": [
5          "lambda:InvokeFunction",
6          "lambda:GetFunctionConfiguration"
7      ],
8      "Resource": "<FunctionARN>"
```

For more information about adding permissions policies, see Authentication and Access Control for Amazon Kinesis Data Analytics.

Lambda Preprocessing Metrics

You can monitor the number of Lambda invocations, bytes processed, successes and failures, and so on, using Amazon CloudWatch. For information about CloudWatch metrics that are emitted by Kinesis Data Analytics Lambda preprocessing, see Amazon Kinesis Analytics Metrics.

Data Preprocessing Event Input Data Model/ Record Response Model

To preprocess records, your Lambda function must be compliant with the required event input data and record response models.

Event Input Data Model

Kinesis Data Analytics continuously reads data from your Kinesis data stream or Kinesis Data Firehose delivery stream. For each batch of records it retrieves, the service manages how each batch gets passed to your Lambda function. Your function receives a list of records as input. Within your function, you iterate through the list and apply your business logic to accomplish your preprocessing requirements (such as data format conversion or enrichment).

The input model to your preprocessing function varies slightly, depending on whether the data was received from a Kinesis data stream or a Kinesis Data Firehose delivery stream.

If the source is a Kinesis Data Firehose delivery stream, the event input data model is as follows:

Kinesis Data Firehose Request Data Model

Field	Description
Field	Description
Field	Description
invocationId	The Lambda invocation Id (random GUID).
applicationArn	Kinesis Data Analytics application Amazon Resource Name (ARN)
streamArn	Delivery stream ARN
records [See the AWS documentation website for more details]	
recordId	record ID (random GUID)
kinesisFirehoseRecordMetadata	[See the AWS documentation website for more details]
data	Base64-encoded source record payload
approximateArrivalTimestamp	Delivery stream record approximate arrival time

If the source is a Kinesis data stream, the event input data model is as follows:

Kinesis Streams Request Data Model

Field	Description
Field	Description
Field	Description
invocationId	The Lambda invocation Id (random GUID).
applicationArn	Kinesis Data Analytics application ARN
streamArn	Delivery stream ARN
records [See the AWS documentation website for more details]	
recordId	record ID based off of Kinesis record sequence number
kinesisStreamRecordMetadata	[See the AWS documentation website for more details]
data	Base64-encoded source record payload
sequenceNumber	Sequence number from the Kinesis stream record
partitionKey	Partition key from the Kinesis stream record
shardId	ShardId from the Kinesis stream record
approximateArrivalTimestamp	Delivery stream record approximate arrival time

Record Response Model

All records returned from your Lambda preprocessing function (with record IDs) that are sent to the Lambda function must be returned. They must contain the following parameters, or Kinesis Data Analytics rejects them and treats it as a data preprocessing failure. The data payload part of the record can be transformed to accomplish preprocessing requirements.

Response Data Model

Field	Description
records [See the AWS documentation website for more details]	
recordId	The record ID is passed from Kinesis Data Analytics to Lambda during the invocation. The transformed record must contain the same record ID. Any mismatch between the ID of the original record and the ID of the transformed record is treated as a data preprocessing failure.
result	The status of the data transformation of the record. The possible values are: [See the AWS documentation website for more details]

Field	Description
data	The transformed data payload, after base64-encoding. Each data payload can contain multiple JSON documents if the application ingestion data format is JSON. Or each can contain multiple CSV rows (with a row delimiter specified in each row) if the application ingestion data format is CSV. The Kinesis Data Analytics service successfully parses and processes data with either multiple JSON documents or CSV rows within the same data payload.

Common Data Preprocessing Failures

The following are common reasons why preprocessing can fail.

- Not all records (with record IDs) in a batch that are sent to the Lambda function are returned back to the Kinesis Data Analytics service.
- The response is missing either the record ID, status, or data payload field. The data payload field is optional for a `Dropped` or `ProcessingFailed` record.
- The Lambda function timeouts are not sufficient to preprocess the data.
- The Lambda function response exceeds the response limits imposed by the AWS Lambda service.

In the case of data preprocessing failures, the Kinesis Data Analytics service continues to retry Lambda invocations on the same set of records until successful. You can monitor the following CloudWatch metrics to gain insight into failures.

- Kinesis Data Analytics Application `MillisBehindLatest`: Indicates how far behind an application is reading from the streaming source.
- Kinesis Data Analytics Application `InputPreprocessing` CloudWatch metrics: Indicates the number of successes and failures, among other statistics. For more information, see Amazon Kinesis Analytics Metrics.
- AWS Lambda function CloudWatch metrics and logs.

Creating Lambda Functions for Preprocessing

Your Amazon Kinesis Data Analytics application can use Lambda functions for preprocessing records as they are ingested into the application. Kinesis Data Analytics provides the following templates on the console to use as a starting point for preprocessing your data.

Topics

- Creating a Preprocessing Lambda Function in Node.js
- Creating a Preprocessing Lambda Function in Python
- Creating a Preprocessing Lambda Function in Java
- Creating a Preprocessing Lambda Function in .NET

Creating a Preprocessing Lambda Function in Node.js

The following templates for creating preprocessing Lambda function in Node.js are available on the Kinesis Data Analytics console:

Lambda Blueprint	Language and version	Description
General Kinesis Data Analytics Input Processing	Node.js 6.10	A Kinesis Data Analytics record preprocessor that receives JSON or CSV records as input and then returns them with a processing status. Use this processor as a starting point for custom transformation logic.
Compressed Input Processing	Node.js 6.10	A Kinesis Data Analytics record processor that receives compressed (GZIP or Deflate compressed) JSON or CSV records as input and returns decompressed records with a processing status.

Creating a Preprocessing Lambda Function in Python

The following templates for creating preprocessing Lambda function in Python are available on the console:

Lambda Blueprint	Language and version	Description
General Kinesis Analytics Input Processing	Python 2.7	A Kinesis Data Analytics record preprocessor that receives JSON or CSV records as input and then returns them with a processing status. Use this processor as a starting point for custom transformation logic.

Lambda Blueprint	Language and version	Description
KPL Input Processing	Python 2.7	A Kinesis Data Analytics record processor that receives Kinesis Producer Library (KPL) aggregates of JSON or CSV records as input and returns disaggregated records with a processing status.

Creating a Preprocessing Lambda Function in Java

To create a Lambda function in Java for preprocessing records, use the Java events classes.

The following code demonstrates a sample Lambda function that preprocesses records using Java:

```
public class LambdaFunctionHandler implements
        RequestHandler<KinesisAnalyticsStreamsInputPreprocessingEvent,
            KinesisAnalyticsInputPreprocessingResponse> {

    @Override
    public KinesisAnalyticsInputPreprocessingResponse handleRequest(
            KinesisAnalyticsStreamsInputPreprocessingEvent event, Context context) {
        context.getLogger().log("InvocatonId is : " + event.invocationId);
        context.getLogger().log("StreamArn is : " + event.streamArn);
        context.getLogger().log("ApplicationArn is : " + event.applicationArn);

        List<KinesisAnalyticsInputPreprocessingResponse.Record> records = new ArrayList<
            KinesisAnalyticsInputPreprocessingResponse.Record>();
        KinesisAnalyticsInputPreprocessingResponse response = new
            KinesisAnalyticsInputPreprocessingResponse(records);

        event.records.stream().forEach(record -> {
            context.getLogger().log("recordId is : " + record.recordId);
            context.getLogger().log("record aat is :" + record.kinesisStreamRecordMetadata.
                approximateArrivalTimestamp);
            // Add your record.data pre-processing logic here.
            // response.records.add(new Record(record.recordId,
                KinesisAnalyticsInputPreprocessingResult.Ok, <preprocessedrecordData>));
        });
        return response;
    }

}
```

Creating a Preprocessing Lambda Function in .NET

To create a Lambda function in .NET for preprocessing records, use the .NET events classes.

The following code demonstrates a sample Lambda function that preprocesses records using C#:

```
public class Function
    {
```

```
3    public KinesisAnalyticsInputPreprocessingResponse FunctionHandler(
         KinesisAnalyticsStreamsInputPreprocessingEvent evnt, ILambdaContext context)
4    {
5        context.Logger.LogLine($"InvocationId: {evnt.InvocationId}");
6        context.Logger.LogLine($"StreamArn: {evnt.StreamArn}");
7        context.Logger.LogLine($"ApplicationArn: {evnt.ApplicationArn}");
8
9        var response = new KinesisAnalyticsInputPreprocessingResponse
10       {
11           Records = new List<KinesisAnalyticsInputPreprocessingResponse.Record>()
12       };
13
14       foreach (var record in evnt.Records)
15       {
16           context.Logger.LogLine($"\tRecordId: {record.RecordId}");
17           context.Logger.LogLine($"\tShardId: {record.RecordMetadata.ShardId}");
18           context.Logger.LogLine($"\tPartitionKey: {record.RecordMetadata.PartitionKey}");
19           context.Logger.LogLine($"\tRecord ApproximateArrivalTime: {record.RecordMetadata
                 .ApproximateArrivalTimestamp}");
20           context.Logger.LogLine($"\tData: {record.DecodeData()}");
21
22           // Add your record preprocessig logic here.
23
24           var preprocessedRecord = new KinesisAnalyticsInputPreprocessingResponse.Record
25           {
26               RecordId = record.RecordId,
27               Result = KinesisAnalyticsInputPreprocessingResponse.OK
28           };
29           preprocessedRecord.EncodeData(record.DecodeData().ToUpperInvariant());
30           response.Records.Add(preprocessedRecord);
31       }
32       return response;
33   }
34 }
```

For more information about creating Lambda functions for preprocessing and destinations in .NET, see Amazon.Lambda.KinesisAnalyticsEvents.

Parallelizing Input Streams for Increased Throughput

Amazon Kinesis Data Analytics applications can support multiple in-application input streams, to scale an application beyond the throughput of a single in-application input stream. For more information on in-application input streams, see Amazon Kinesis Data Analytics: How It Works.

In almost all cases, Amazon Kinesis Data Analytics scales your application to handle the capacity of the Amazon Kinesis streams or Amazon Kinesis Data Firehose source streams that feed into your application. However, if your source stream's throughput exceeds the throughput of a single in-application input stream, you can explicitly increase the number of in-application input streams that your application uses. You do so with the `InputParallelism` parameter.

When the `InputParallelism` parameter is greater than one, Amazon Kinesis Data Analytics evenly splits the partitions of your source stream among the in-application streams. For instance, if your source stream has 50 shards, and you have set `InputParallelism` to 2, each in-application input stream receives the input from 25 source stream shards.

When you increase the number of in-application streams, your application must access the data in each stream explicitly. For information on accessing multiple in-application streams in your code, see Accessing Separate In-Application Streams in Your Amazon Kinesis Data Analytics Application.

Although Kinesis Data Analytics and Kinesis Data Firehose stream shards are both divided among in-application streams in the same way, they differ in the way they appear to your application:

- The records from a Kinesis Data Analytics stream include a `shard_id` field that can be used to identify the source shard for the record.
- The records from a Kinesis Data Firehose stream don't include a field that identifies the record's source shard or partition, because Kinesis Data Firehose abstracts this information away from your application.

Evaluating Whether to Increase Your Number of In-Application Input Streams

In most cases, a single in-application input stream can handle the throughput of a single source stream, depending on the complexity and data size of the input streams. To determine if you need to increase the number of in-application input streams, you can monitor the `MillisBehindLatest` metric in Amazon CloudWatch. If the `MillisBehindLatest` metric has either of the following characteristics, you should increase your application's `InputParallelism` setting:

- The `MillisBehindLatest` metric is gradually increasing, indicating that your application is falling behind the latest data in the stream.
- The `MillisBehindLatest` metric is consistently above 1000 (one second).

You don't need to increase your application's `InputParallelism` setting if the following are true:

- The `MillisBehindLatest` metric is gradually decreasing, indicating that your application is catching up to the latest data in the stream.
- The `MillisBehindLatest` metric is below 1000 (one second).

For more information on using CloudWatch, see the CloudWatch User Guide.

Implementing Multiple In-Application Input Streams

You can set the number of in-application input streams when an application is created using CreateApplication. You set this number after an application is created using UpdateApplication.

Note
You can only set the `InputParallelism` setting using the Amazon Kinesis Data Analytics API or the AWS CLI.

You cannot set this setting using the AWS Management Console. For information on setting up the CLI, see Step 2: Set Up the AWS Command Line Interface (AWS CLI).

Setting a New Application's Input Stream Count

The following example demonstrates how to use the `CreateApplication` API action to set a new application's input stream count to 2.

For more information on `CreateApplication`, see CreateApplication.

```
 1 {
 2    "ApplicationCode": "<The SQL code the new application will run on the input stream>",
 3    "ApplicationDescription": "<A friendly description for the new application>",
 4    "ApplicationName": "<The name for the new application>",
 5    "Inputs": [
 6      {
 7        "InputId": "ID for the new input stream",
 8        "InputParallelism": {
 9          "Count": 2
10      }],
11    "Outputs": [ ... ],
12      }]
13 }
```

Setting an Existing Application's Input Stream Count

The following example demonstrates how to use the `UpdateApplication` API action to set an existing application's input stream count to 2.

For more information on `Update_Application`, see UpdateApplication.

```
 1 {
 2    "InputUpdates": [
 3      {
 4        "InputId": "yourInputId",
 5        "InputParallelismUpdate": {
 6          "CountUpdate": 2
 7        }
 8      }
 9    ],
10 }
```

Accessing Separate In-Application Streams in Your Amazon Kinesis Data Analytics Application

To use multiple in-application input streams in your application, you must explicitly select from the different streams. The following code example demonstrates how to query multiple input streams in the application created in the Getting Started tutorial.

In the following example, each source stream is first aggregated using COUNT before being combined into a single in-application stream called `in_application_stream001`. Aggregating the source streams beforehand helps make sure that the combined in-application stream can handle the traffic from multiple streams without being overloaded.

Note
To run this example and get results from both in-application input streams, you need to update both the number of shards in your source stream and the `InputParallelism` parameter in your application.

```
1 CREATE OR REPLACE STREAM in_application_stream_001 (
2     ticker VARCHAR(64),
3     ticker_count INTEGER
4 );
5
6 CREATE OR REPLACE PUMP pump001 AS
7 INSERT INTO in_application_stream_001
8 SELECT STREAM ticker_symbol, COUNT(ticker_symbol)
9 FROM source_sql_stream_001
10 GROUP BY STEP(source_sql_stream_001.rowtime BY INTERVAL '60' SECOND),
11     ticker_symbol;
12
13 CREATE OR REPLACE PUMP pump002 AS
14 INSERT INTO in_application_stream_001
15 SELECT STREAM ticker_symbol, COUNT(ticker_symbol)
16 FROM source_sql_stream_002
17 GROUP BY STEP(source_sql_stream_002.rowtime BY INTERVAL '60' SECOND),
18     ticker_symbol;
```

The preceding code example produces output in `in_application_stream001` similar to the following:

ROWTIME	TICKER	TICKER_COUNT
2017-05-17 22:05:00.0	QAZ	15
2017-05-17 22:06:00.0	SAC	16
2017-05-17 22:06:00.0	PLM	10
2017-05-17 22:06:00.0	AMZN	15

Additional Considerations

When using multiple input streams, be aware of the following:

- The maximum number of in-application input streams is 64.
- The in-application input streams are distributed evenly among the shards of the application's input stream.
- The performance gains from adding in-application streams don't scale linearly. That is, doubling the number of in-application streams doesn't double throughput. With a typical row size, each in-application stream can achieve throughput of about 5,000 to 15,000 rows per second. By increasing the in-application stream count to 10, you can achieve a throughput of 20,000 to 30,000 rows per second. Throughput speed is dependent on the count, data types, and data size of the fields in the input stream.
- Some aggregate functions (such as AVG) can produce unexpected results when applied to input streams partitioned into different shards. Because you need to run the aggregate operation on individual shards before combining them into an aggregate stream, the results might be weighted toward whichever stream contains more records.
- If your application continues to experience poor performance (reflected by a high `MillisBehindLatest` metric) after you increase your number of input streams, you might have reached your limit of Kinesis

Processing Units (KPUs). For more information, see Automatically Scaling Applications to Increase Throughput.

Application Code

Application code is a series of SQL statements that process input and produce output. These SQL statements operate on in-application streams and reference tables. For more information, see Amazon Kinesis Data Analytics: How It Works.

For information about the SQL language elements that are supported by Kinesis Data Analytics, see Amazon Kinesis Data Analytics SQL Reference.

In relational databases, you work with tables, using INSERT statements to add records and the SELECT statement to query the data. In Amazon Kinesis Data Analytics, you work with streams. You can write a SQL statement to query these streams. The results of querying one in-application stream are always sent to another in-application stream. When performing complex analytics, you might create several in-application streams to hold the results of intermediate analytics. And then finally, you configure application output to persist results of the final analytics (from one or more in-application streams) to external destinations. In summary, the following is a typical pattern for writing application code:

- The SELECT statement is always used in the context of an INSERT statement. That is, when you select rows, you insert results into another in-application stream.
- The INSERT statement is always used in the context of a pump. That is, you use pumps to write to an in-application stream.

The following example application code reads records from one in-application (SOURCE_SQL_STREAM_001) stream and write it to another in-application stream (DESTINATION_SQL_STREAM). You can insert records to in-application streams using pumps, as shown following:

```
1 CREATE OR REPLACE STREAM "DESTINATION_SQL_STREAM" (ticker_symbol VARCHAR(4),
2                                                    change DOUBLE,
3                                                    price DOUBLE);
4 -- Create a pump and insert into output stream.
5 CREATE OR REPLACE PUMP "STREAM_PUMP" AS
6
7   INSERT INTO "DESTINATION_SQL_STREAM"
8     SELECT STREAM ticker_symbol, change,price
9     FROM   "SOURCE_SQL_STREAM_001";
```

The identifiers that you specify for stream names and column names follow standard SQL conventions. For example, if you put quotation marks around an identifier, it makes the identifier case sensitive. If you don't, the identifier defaults to uppercase. For more information about identifiers, see Identifiers in the *Amazon Kinesis Data Analytics SQL Reference*.

Your application code can consist of many SQL statements. For example:

- You can write SQL queries in a sequential manner where the result of one SQL statement feeds into the next SQL statement.
- You can also write SQL queries that run independent of each other. For example, you can write two SQL statements that query the same in-application stream, but send output into different in-applications streams. You can then query the newly created in-application streams independently.

You can create in-application streams to save intermediate results. You insert data in in-application streams using pumps. For more information, see In-Application Streams and Pumps.

If you add an in-application reference table, you can write SQL to join data in in-application streams and reference tables. For more information, see Example: Adding Reference Data to a Kinesis Data Analytics Application.

According to the application's output configuration, Amazon Kinesis Data Analytics writes data from specific in-application streams to the external destination according to the application's output configuration. Make sure that your application code writes to the in-application streams specified in the output configuration.

For more information, see the following topics:

- Streaming SQL Concepts
- Amazon Kinesis Data Analytics SQL Reference

Configuring Application Output

In your application code, you write the output of SQL statements to one or more in-application streams. You can optionally add output configuration to your application to persist everything written to an in-application stream to an external destination such as an Amazon Kinesis data stream, a Kinesis Data Firehose delivery stream, or an AWS Lambda function.

There is a limit on the number of external destinations you can use to persist an application output. For more information, see Limits.

Note
We recommend that you use one external destination to persist in-application error stream data so that you can investigate the errors.

In each of these output configurations, you provide the following:

- **In-application stream name** – The stream that you want to persist to an external destination.

  Amazon Kinesis Data Analytics looks for the in-application stream that you specified in the output configuration (note that the stream name is case sensitive and must match exactly). Make sure that your application code creates this in-application stream.

- **External destination** – You can persist data to a Kinesis data stream, a Kinesis Data Firehose delivery stream, or a Lambda function. You provide the Amazon Resource Name (ARN) of the stream or function, and an IAM role that Kinesis Data Analytics can assume to write to the stream or function on your behalf. You also describe the record format (JSON, CSV) to Kinesis Data Analytics to use when writing to the external destination.

If Amazon Kinesis Data Analytics can't write to the streaming or Lambda destination, the service continues to try indefinitely. This creates back pressure, causing your application to fall behind. If this is not resolved, your application eventually stops processing new data. You can monitor Amazon Kinesis Analytics Metrics and set alarms for failures. For more information about metrics and alarms, see Using Amazon CloudWatch Metrics and Creating Amazon CloudWatch Alarms.

You can configure the application output using the AWS Management Console. The console makes the API call to save the configuration.

Creating an Output Using the AWS CLI

This section describes how to create the `Outputs` section of the request body for a `CreateApplication` or `AddApplicationOutput` operation.

Creating a Kinesis Stream Output

The following JSON fragment shows the `Outputs` section in the `CreateApplication` request body for creating an Amazon Kinesis data stream destination.

```
1  "Outputs": [
2      {
3          "DestinationSchema": {
4              "RecordFormatType": "string"
5          },
6          "KinesisStreamsOutput": {
7              "ResourceARN": "string",
8              "RoleARN": "string"
9          },
10         "Name": "string"
```

```
11      }
12
13  ]
```

Creating a Kinesis Data Firehose Delivery Stream Output

The following JSON fragment shows the `Outputs` section in the `CreateApplication` request body for creating an Amazon Kinesis Data Firehose delivery stream destination.

```
1  "Outputs": [
2     {
3         "DestinationSchema": {
4             "RecordFormatType": "string"
5         },
6         "KinesisFirehoseOutput": {
7             "ResourceARN": "string",
8             "RoleARN": "string"
9         },
10        "Name": "string"
11    }
12 ]
```

Creating a Lambda Function Output

The following JSON fragment shows the `Outputs` section in the `CreateApplication` request body for creating an AWS Lambda function destination.

```
1  "Outputs": [
2     {
3         "DestinationSchema": {
4             "RecordFormatType": "string"
5         },
6         "LambdaOutput": {
7             "ResourceARN": "string",
8             "RoleARN": "string"
9         },
10        "Name": "string"
11    }
12 ]
```

Using a Lambda Function as Output

Using AWS Lambda as a destination allows you to more easily perform post-processing of your SQL results before sending them to a final destination. Common post-processing tasks include the following:

- Aggregating multiple rows into a single record
- Combining current results with past results to address late-arriving data
- Delivering to different destinations based on the type of information
- Record format translation (such as translating to Protobuf)
- String manipulation or transformation
- Data enrichment after analytical processing
- Custom processing for geospatial use cases
- Data encryption

Lambda functions can deliver analytic information to a variety of AWS services and other destinations, including the following:

- Amazon Simple Storage Service (Amazon S3)
- Custom APIs
- Amazon DynamoDB
- Apache Aurora
- Amazon Redshift
- Amazon Simple Notification Service (Amazon SNS)
- Amazon Simple Queue Service (Amazon SQS)
- Amazon CloudWatch

For more information about creating Lambda applications, see Getting Started with AWS Lambda.

Topics

- Lambda as Output Permissions
- Lambda as Output Metrics
- Lambda as Output Event Input Data Model and Record Response Model
- Lambda Output Invocation Frequency
- Adding a Lambda Function for Use as an Output
- Common Lambda as Output Failures
- Creating Lambda Functions for Application Destinations

Lambda as Output Permissions

To use Lambda as output, the application's Lambda output IAM role requires the following permissions policy:

```
{
    "Sid": "UseLambdaFunction",
    "Effect": "Allow",
    "Action": [
        "lambda:InvokeFunction",
        "lambda:GetFunctionConfiguration"
    ],
    "Resource": "FunctionARN"
}
```

Lambda as Output Metrics

You use Amazon CloudWatch to monitor the number of bytes sent, successes and failures, and so on. For information about CloudWatch metrics that are emitted by Kinesis Data Analytics using Lambda as output, see

Lambda as Output Event Input Data Model and Record Response Model

To send Kinesis Data Analytics output records, your Lambda function must be compliant with the required event input data and record response models.

Event Input Data Model

Kinesis Data Analytics continuously sends the output records from the application to the Lambda as output function with the following request model. Within your function, you iterate through the list and apply your business logic to accomplish your output requirements (such as data transformation before sending to a final destination).

Field	Description
Field	Description
Field	Description
invocationId	The Lambda invocation ID (random GUID).
applicationArn	The Kinesis data analytics application Amazon Resource Name (ARN).
records [See the AWS documentation website for more details]	
recordId	record ID (random GUID)
lambdaDeliveryRecordMetadata	[See the AWS documentation website for more details]
data	Base64-encoded output record payload
retryHint	Number of delivery retries

Note

The `retryHint` is a value that increases for every delivery failure. This value is not durably persisted, and resets if the application is disrupted.

Record Response Model

Each record sent to your Lambda as output function (with record IDs) must be acknowledged with either `Ok` or `DeliveryFailed` and must contain the following parameters. Otherwise, Kinesis Data Analytics treats them as a delivery failure.

Field	Description
records [See the AWS documentation website for more details]	
recordId	The record ID is passed from Kinesis Data Analytics to Lambda during the invocation. Any mismatch between the ID of the original record and the ID of the acknowledged record is treated as a delivery failure.

Field	Description
result	The status of the delivery of the record. The following are possible values: [See the AWS documentation website for more details]

Lambda Output Invocation Frequency

A Kinesis data analytics application buffers the output records and invokes the AWS Lambda destination function frequently.

- If records are emitted to the destination in-application stream within the data analytics application as a tumbling window, the AWS Lambda destination function is invoked per tumbling window trigger. For example, if a tumbling window of 60 seconds is used to emit the records to the destination in-application stream, the AWS Lambda function is invoked once every 60 seconds.
- If records are emitted to the destination in-application stream within the data analytics application as a continuous query or a sliding window, the AWS Lambda destination function is invoked approximately once per second.

Note
Per-Lambda function invoke request payload size limits apply. Exceeding those limits results in output records being split and sent across multiple Lambda function calls.

Adding a Lambda Function for Use as an Output

The following procedure demonstrates how to add a Lambda function as an output for an Amazon Kinesis data analytics application.

1. Sign in to the AWS Management Console and open the Kinesis Data Analytics console at https://console.aws.amazon.com/kinesisanalytics.

2. Choose the application in the list, and then choose **Application details**.

3. In the **Destination** section, choose **Connect new destination**.

4. For the **Destination** item, choose **AWS Lambda function**.

5. In the **Deliver records to AWS Lambda** section, either choose an existing Lambda function or choose **Create new**.

6. If you are creating a new Lambda function, do the following:

    1. Choose one of the templates provided. For more information, Creating Lambda Functions for Application Destinations.

    2. The **Create Function** page opens in a new browser tab. In the **Name** box, give the function a meaningful name (for example, **myLambdaFunction**).

    3. Update the template with post-processing functionality for your application. For information about creating a Lambda function, see Getting Started in the *AWS Lambda Developer Guide*.

    4. On the Kinesis Data Analytics console, in the **Lambda function** drop-down list, choose the Lambda function that you just created.

7. In the **In-application stream** section, choose **Choose an existing in-application stream**. For **In-application stream name**, choose your application's output stream. The results from the selected output stream are sent to the Lambda output function.

8. Leave the rest of the form with the default values, and choose **Save and continue**.

Your application now sends records from the in-application stream to your Lambda function. You can see the results of the default template in the Amazon CloudWatch console. Monitor the `AWS/KinesisAnalytics/LambdaDelivery.OkRecords` metric to see the number of records being delivered to the Lambda function.

Common Lambda as Output Failures

The following are common reasons why delivery to a Lambda function can fail.

- Not all records (with record IDs) in a batch that are sent to the Lambda function are returned to the Kinesis Data Analytics service.
- The response is missing either the record ID or the status field.
- The Lambda function timeouts are not sufficient to accomplish the business logic within the Lambda function.
- The business logic within the Lambda function does not catch all the errors, resulting in a timeout and backpressure due to unhandled exceptions. These are often referred as "poison pill" messages.

In the case of data delivery failures, Kinesis Data Analytics continues to retry Lambda invocations on the same set of records until successful. To gain insight into failures, you can monitor the following CloudWatch metrics:

- Kinesis Data Analytics application Lambda as Output CloudWatch metrics: Indicates the number of successes and failures, among other statistics. For more information, see Amazon Kinesis Analytics Metrics.
- AWS Lambda function CloudWatch metrics and logs.

Creating Lambda Functions for Application Destinations

Your Kinesis Data Analytics application can use AWS Lambda functions as an output. Kinesis Data Analytics provides templates for creating Lambda functions to use as a destination for your applications. Use these templates as a starting point for post-processing output from your application.

Topics

- Creating a Lambda Function Destination in Node.js
- Creating a Lambda Function Destination in Python
- Creating a Lambda Function Destination in Java
- Creating a Lambda Function Destination in .NET

Creating a Lambda Function Destination in Node.js

The following template for creating a destination Lambda function in Node.js is available on the console:

Lambda as Output Blueprint	Language and Version	Description
kinesis-analytics-output	Node.js 6.10	Deliver output records from a Kinesis Data Analytics application to a custom destination.

Creating a Lambda Function Destination in Python

The following templates for creating a destination Lambda function in Python are available on the console:

Lambda as Output Blueprint	Language and Version	Description
kinesis-analytics-output-sns	Python 2.7	Deliver output records from a Kinesis Data Analytics application to Amazon SNS.
kinesis-analytics-output-ddb	Python 2.7	Deliver output records from a Kinesis Data Analytics application to Amazon DynamoDB.

Creating a Lambda Function Destination in Java

To create a destination Lambda function in Java, use the Java events classes.

The following code demonstrates a sample destination Lambda function using Java:

```
public class LambdaFunctionHandler
        implements RequestHandler<KinesisAnalyticsOutputDeliveryEvent,
            KinesisAnalyticsOutputDeliveryResponse> {

    @Override
    public KinesisAnalyticsOutputDeliveryResponse handleRequest(
        KinesisAnalyticsOutputDeliveryEvent event,
            Context context) {
        context.getLogger().log("InvocatonId is : " + event.invocationId);
```

```
8     context.getLogger().log("ApplicationArn is : " + event.applicationArn);
9
10    List<KinesisAnalyticsOutputDeliveryResponse.Record> records = new ArrayList<
          KinesisAnalyticsOutputDeliveryResponse.Record>();
11    KinesisAnalyticsOutputDeliveryResponse response = new
          KinesisAnalyticsOutputDeliveryResponse(records);
12
13    event.records.stream().forEach(record -> {
14        context.getLogger().log("recordId is : " + record.recordId);
15        context.getLogger().log("record retryHint is :" + record.
              lambdaDeliveryRecordMetadata.retryHint);
16        // Add logic here to transform and send the record to final destination of your
              choice.
17        response.records.add(new Record(record.recordId,
              KinesisAnalyticsOutputDeliveryResult.Ok));
18    });
19    return response;
20  }
21
22 }
```

Creating a Lambda Function Destination in .NET

To create a destination Lambda function in .NET, use the .NET events classes.

The following code demonstrates a sample destination Lambda function using C#:

```
1  public class Function
2      {
3          public KinesisAnalyticsOutputDeliveryResponse FunctionHandler(
              KinesisAnalyticsOutputDeliveryEvent evnt, ILambdaContext context)
4          {
5              context.Logger.LogLine($"InvocationId: {evnt.InvocationId}");
6              context.Logger.LogLine($"ApplicationArn: {evnt.ApplicationArn}");
7
8              var response = new KinesisAnalyticsOutputDeliveryResponse
9              {
10                 Records = new List<KinesisAnalyticsOutputDeliveryResponse.Record>()
11             };
12
13             foreach (var record in evnt.Records)
14             {
15                 context.Logger.LogLine($"\tRecordId: {record.RecordId}");
16                 context.Logger.LogLine($"\tRetryHint: {record.RecordMetadata.RetryHint}");
17                 context.Logger.LogLine($"\tData: {record.DecodeData()}");
18
19                 // Add logic here to send to the record to final destination of your choice.
20
21                 var deliveredRecord = new KinesisAnalyticsOutputDeliveryResponse.Record
22                 {
23                     RecordId = record.RecordId,
24                     Result = KinesisAnalyticsOutputDeliveryResponse.OK
25                 };
26                 response.Records.Add(deliveredRecord);
```

```
27          }
28          return response;
29      }
30  }
```

For more information about creating Lambda functions for pre-processing and destinations in .NET, see Amazon.Lambda.KinesisAnalyticsEvents.

Delivery Model for Persisting Application Output to an External Destination

Amazon Kinesis Data Analytics uses an "at least once" delivery model for application output to the configured destinations. When an application is running, Kinesis Data Analytics takes internal checkpoints. These checkpoints are points in time when output records have been delivered to the destinations without data loss. The service uses the checkpoints as needed to ensure that your application output is delivered at least once to the configured destinations.

In a normal situation, your application processes incoming data continuously, and Kinesis Data Analytics writes the output to the configured destinations such as a Kinesis data stream or a Kinesis Data Firehose delivery stream. However, your application can be interrupted occasionally; for example:

- You choose to stop your application and restart it later.
- You delete the IAM role that Kinesis Data Analytics needs to write your application output to the configured destination. Without the IAM role, Kinesis Data Analytics does not have any permissions to write to the external destination on your behalf.
- A network outage or other internal service failures cause your application to stop running momentarily.

When your application restarts, Kinesis Data Analytics ensures that it continues to process and write output from a point before or equal to when the failure occurred. This helps ensure that it doesn't miss delivering any application output to the configured destinations.

Suppose that you configured multiple destinations from the same in-application stream. After the application recovers from failure, Kinesis Data Analytics resumes persisting output to the configured destinations from the last record that was delivered to the slowest destination. This might result in the same output record delivered more than once to other destinations. In this case, you must handle potential duplications in the destination externally.

Error Handling

Amazon Kinesis Data Analytics returns API or SQL errors directly to you. For more information about API operations, see Actions. For more information about handling SQL errors, see Amazon Kinesis Data Analytics SQL Reference.

Amazon Kinesis Data Analytics reports runtime errors using an in-application error stream called `error_stream`.

Reporting Errors Using an In-Application Error Stream

Amazon Kinesis Data Analytics reports runtime errors to the in-application error stream called `error_stream`. The following are examples of errors that might occur:

- A record read from the streaming source does not conform to the input schema.
- Your application code specifies division by zero.
- The rows are out of order (for example, a record appears on the stream with a `ROWTIME` value that a user modified that causes a record to go out of order).
- The data in the source stream can't be converted to the data type specified in the schema (Coercion error). For information about what data types can be converted, see Mapping JSON Data Types to SQL Data Types.

We recommend that you handle these errors programmatically in your SQL code or persist the data on the error stream to an external destination. This requires that you add an output configuration (see Configuring Application Output) to your application. For an example of how the in-application error stream works, see Example: Exploring the In-Application Error Stream.

Note
Your Kinesis data analytics application can't access or modify the error stream programmatically because the error stream is created using the system account. You must use the error output to determine what errors your application might encounter. You then write your application's SQL code to handle anticipated error conditions.

Error Stream Schema

The error stream has the following schema:

Field	Data Type	Notes
ERROR_TIME	TIMESTAMP	The time when the error occurred
ERROR_LEVEL	VARCHAR(10)	
ERROR_NAME	VARCHAR(32)	
MESSAGE	VARCHAR(4096)	
DATA_ROWTIME	TIMESTAMP	The row time of the incoming record
DATA_ROW	VARCHAR(49152)	The hex-encoded data in the original row
PUMP_NAME	VARCHAR(128)	The originating pump, as defined with `CREATE PUMP`

Granting Amazon Kinesis Data Analytics Permissions to Access Streaming Sources (Creating an IAM Role)

Amazon Kinesis Data Analytics needs permissions to read records from a streaming source that you specify in your application input configuration. Amazon Kinesis Data Analytics also needs permissions to write your application output to streams that you specify in your application output configuration.

You can grant these permissions by creating an IAM role that Amazon Kinesis Data Analytics can assume. Permissions that you grant to this role determine what Amazon Kinesis Data Analytics can do when the service assumes the role.

Note
The information in this section is useful if you want to create an IAM role yourself. When you create an application in the Amazon Kinesis Data Analytics console, the console can create an IAM role for you at that time. The console uses the following naming convention for IAM roles that it creates:

```
1 kinesis-analytics-ApplicationName
```

After the role is created, you can review the role and attached policies in the IAM console.

Each IAM role has two policies attached to it. In the trust policy, you specify who can assume the role. In the permissions policy (there can be one or more), you specify the permissions that you want to grant to this role. The following sections describe these policies, which you can use when you create an IAM role.

Trust Policy

To grant Amazon Kinesis Data Analytics permissions to assume a role, you can attach the following trust policy to an IAM role:

```
1  {
2    "Version": "2012-10-17",
3    "Statement": [
4      {
5        "Effect": "Allow",
6        "Principal": {
7          "Service": "kinesisanalytics.amazonaws.com"
8        },
9        "Action": "sts:AssumeRole"
10     }
11   ]
12 }
```

Permissions Policy

If you are creating an IAM role to allow Amazon Kinesis Data Analytics to read from an application's streaming source, you must grant permissions for relevant read actions. Depending on your streaming source (for example, an Kinesis stream or a Kinesis Data Firehose delivery stream), you can attach the following permissions policy.

Permissions Policy for Reading an Kinesis Stream

```
1  {
2    "Version": "2012-10-17",
3    "Statement": [
```

```
 4        {
 5            "Sid": "ReadInputKinesis",
 6            "Effect": "Allow",
 7            "Action": [
 8                "kinesis:DescribeStream",
 9                "kinesis:GetShardIterator",
10                "kinesis:GetRecords"
11            ],
12            "Resource": [
13                "arn:aws:kinesis:aws-region:aws-account-id:stream/inputStreamName"
14            ]
15        }
16    ]
17 }
```

Permissions Policy for Reading a Kinesis Data Firehose Delivery Stream

```
 1 {
 2    "Version": "2012-10-17",
 3    "Statement": [
 4        {
 5            "Sid": "ReadInputFirehose",
 6            "Effect": "Allow",
 7            "Action": [
 8                "firehose:DescribeDeliveryStream",
 9                "firehose:Get*"
10            ],
11            "Resource": [
12                "arn:aws:firehose:aws-region:aws-account-id:deliverystream/inputFirehoseName"
13            ]
14        }
15    ]
16 }
```

If you direct Amazon Kinesis Data Analytics to write output to external destinations in your application output configuration, you need to grant the following permission to the IAM role.

Permissions Policy for Writing to an Kinesis Stream

```
 1 {
 2    "Version": "2012-10-17",
 3    "Statement": [
 4        {
 5            "Sid": "WriteOutputKinesis",
 6            "Effect": "Allow",
 7            "Action": [
 8                "kinesis:DescribeStream",
 9                "kinesis:PutRecord",
10                "kinesis:PutRecords"
11            ],
12            "Resource": [
13                "arn:aws:kinesis:aws-region:aws-account-id:stream/output-stream-name"
14            ]
15        }
16    ]
```

```
17 }
```

Permissions Policy for Writing to a Firehose Delivery Stream

```
 1 {
 2     "Version": "2012-10-17",
 3     "Statement": [
 4         {
 5             "Sid": "WriteOutputFirehose",
 6             "Effect": "Allow",
 7             "Action": [
 8                 "firehose:DescribeDeliveryStream",
 9                 "firehose:PutRecord",
10                 "firehose:PutRecordBatch"
11             ],
12             "Resource": [
13                 "arn:aws:firehose:aws-region:aws-account-id:deliverystream/output-firehose-name"
14             ]
15         }
16     ]
17 }
```

Automatically Scaling Applications to Increase Throughput

Amazon Kinesis Data Analytics elastically scales your application to accommodate the data throughput of your source stream and your query complexity for most scenarios. Kinesis Data Analytics provisions capacity in the form of Kinesis Processing Units (KPU). A single KPU provides you with the memory (4 GB) and corresponding computing and networking.

The default limit for KPUs for your application is eight. For instructions on how to request an increase to this limit, see **To request a limit increase** in AWS Service Limits.

Note
The drop-down item that is used to select a limit increase for KPUs is not yet available. When requesting an increase, choose the following options on the support form:
Regarding: Service limit increase **Limit Type:** Kinesis Analytics **Region:** *Select your application's Region*
Limit: Number of applications limit **New limit value:** 100 **Use Case Description:** Provide your application prefix, and specify that you are requesting a limit increase for KPUs.

Getting Started with Amazon Kinesis Data Analytics

Following, you can find topics to help get you started using Amazon Kinesis Data Analytics. If you are new to Kinesis Data Analytics, we recommend that you review the concepts and terminology presented in Amazon Kinesis Data Analytics: How It Works before performing the steps in the Getting Started section.

Topics

- Step 1: Set Up an AWS Account and Create an Administrator User
- Step 2: Set Up the AWS Command Line Interface (AWS CLI)
- Step 3: Create Your Starter Amazon Kinesis Data Analytics Application
- Step 4 (Optional) Edit the Schema and SQL Code Using the Console

Step 1: Set Up an AWS Account and Create an Administrator User

Before you use Amazon Kinesis Data Analytics for the first time, complete the following tasks:

1. Sign Up for AWS
2. Create an IAM User

Sign Up for AWS

When you sign up for Amazon Web Services (AWS), your AWS account is automatically signed up for all services in AWS, including Amazon Kinesis Data Analytics. You are charged only for the services that you use.

With Kinesis Data Analytics, you pay only for the resources you use. If you are a new AWS customer, you can get started with Kinesis Data Analytics for free. For more information, see AWS Free Usage Tier.

If you already have an AWS account, skip to the next task. If you don't have an AWS account, perform the steps in the following procedure to create one.

To create an AWS account

1. Open https://aws.amazon.com/, and then choose **Create an AWS Account**. **Note**
   This might be unavailable in your browser if you previously signed into the AWS Management Console. In that case, choose **Sign in to a different account**, and then choose **Create a new AWS account**.

2. Follow the online instructions.

   Part of the sign-up procedure involves receiving a phone call and entering a PIN using the phone keypad.

Note your AWS account ID because you'll need it for the next task.

Create an IAM User

Services in AWS, such as Amazon Kinesis Data Analytics, require that you provide credentials when you access them so that the service can determine whether you have permissions to access the resources owned by that service. The console requires your password. You can create access keys for your AWS account to access the AWS CLI or API. However, we don't recommend that you access AWS using the credentials for your AWS account. Instead, we recommend that you use AWS Identity and Access Management (IAM). Create an IAM user, add the user to an IAM group with administrative permissions, and then grant administrative permissions to the IAM user that you created. You can then access AWS using a special URL and that IAM user's credentials.

If you signed up for AWS, but you haven't created an IAM user for yourself, you can create one using the IAM console.

The Getting Started exercises in this guide assume that you have a user (`adminuser`) with administrator privileges. Follow the procedure to create `adminuser` in your account.

To create an administrator user and sign in to the console

1. Create an administrator user called `adminuser` in your AWS account. For instructions, see Creating Your First IAM User and Administrators Group in the *IAM User Guide*.

2. A user can sign in to the AWS Management Console using a special URL. For more information, How Users Sign In to Your Account in the *IAM User Guide*.

For more information about IAM, see the following:

- AWS Identity and Access Management (IAM)
- Getting Started
- IAM User Guide

Next Step

Step 2: Set Up the AWS Command Line Interface (AWS CLI)

Step 2: Set Up the AWS Command Line Interface (AWS CLI)

Follow the steps to download and configure the AWS Command Line Interface (AWS CLI).

Important
You don't need the AWS CLI to perform the steps in the Getting Started exercise. However, some of the exercises in this guide use the AWS CLI. You can skip this step and go to Step 3: Create Your Starter Amazon Kinesis Data Analytics Application, and then set up the AWS CLI later when you need it.

To set up the AWS CLI

1. Download and configure the AWS CLI. For instructions, see the following topics in the *AWS Command Line Interface User Guide*:

    * Getting Set Up with the AWS Command Line Interface
    * Configuring the AWS Command Line Interface

2. Add a named profile for the administrator user in the AWS CLI config file. You use this profile when executing the AWS CLI commands. For more information about named profiles, see Named Profiles in the *AWS Command Line Interface User Guide*.

```
1 [profile adminuser]
2 aws_access_key_id = adminuser access key ID
3 aws_secret_access_key = adminuser secret access key
4 region = aws-region
```

    For a list of available AWS Regions, see Regions and Endpoints in the *Amazon Web Services General Reference*.

3. Verify the setup by entering the following help command at the command prompt:

```
1 aws help
```

Next Step

Step 3: Create Your Starter Amazon Kinesis Data Analytics Application

Step 3: Create Your Starter Amazon Kinesis Data Analytics Application

By following the steps in this section, you can create your first Amazon Kinesis data analytics application using the console.

Note
We suggest that you review Amazon Kinesis Data Analytics: How It Works before trying the Getting Started exercise.

For this Getting Started exercise, you can use the console to work with either the demo stream or templates with application code.

- If you choose to use the demo stream, the console creates a Kinesis data stream in your account that is called `kinesis-analytics-demo-stream`.

  A Kinesis data analytics application requires a streaming source. For this source, several SQL examples in this guide use the demo stream `kinesis-analytics-demo-stream`. The console also runs a script that continuously adds sample data (simulated stock trade records) to this stream, as shown following.

  You can use `kinesis-analytics-demo-stream` as the streaming source for your application in this exercise.
  Note
  The demo stream remains in your account. You can use it to test other examples in this guide. However, when you leave the console, the script that the console uses stops populating the data. When needed, the console provides the option to start populating the stream again.

- If you choose to use the templates with example application code, you use template code that the console provides to perform simple analytics on the demo stream.

You use these features to quickly set up your first application as follows:

1. **Create an application** – You only need to provide a name. The console creates the application and the service sets the application state to `READY`.

2. **Configure input** – First, you add a streaming source, the demo stream. You must create a demo stream

in the console before you can use it. Then, the console takes a random sample of records on the demo stream and infers a schema for the in-application input stream that is created. The console names the in-application stream SOURCE_SQL_STREAM_001.

The console uses the discovery API to infer the schema. If necessary, you can edit the inferred schema. For more information, see DiscoverInputSchema. Kinesis Data Analytics uses this schema to create an in-application stream.

When you start the application, Kinesis Data Analytics reads the demo stream continuously on your behalf and inserts rows in the SOURCE_SQL_STREAM_001 in-application input stream.

3. **Specify application code** – You use a template (called **Continuous filter**) that provides the following code:

```
1  CREATE OR REPLACE STREAM "DESTINATION_SQL_STREAM"
2    (symbol VARCHAR(4), sector VARCHAR(12), CHANGE DOUBLE, price DOUBLE);
3
4  -- Create pump to insert into output.
5  CREATE OR REPLACE PUMP "STREAM_PUMP" AS
6    INSERT INTO "DESTINATION_SQL_STREAM"
7      SELECT STREAM ticker_symbol, sector, CHANGE, price
8      FROM "SOURCE_SQL_STREAM_001"
9      WHERE sector SIMILAR TO '%TECH%';
```

The application code queries the in-application stream SOURCE_SQL_STREAM_001. The code then inserts the resulting rows in another in-application stream DESTINATION_SQL_STREAM, using pumps. For more information about this coding pattern, see Application Code.

For information about the SQL language elements that are supported by Kinesis Data Analytics, see Amazon Kinesis Data Analytics SQL Reference.

4. **Configuring output** – In this exercise, you don't configure any output. That is, you don't persist data in the in-application stream that your application creates to any external destination. Instead, you verify query results in the console. Additional examples in this guide show how to configure output. For one example, see Example: Creating Simple Alerts.

Important
The exercise uses the US East (N. Virginia) Region (us-east-1) to set up the application. You can use any of the supported AWS Regions.

Next Step
Step 3.1: Create an Application

Step 3.1: Create an Application

In this section, you create an Amazon Kinesis data analytics application. You configure application input in the next step.

To create a data analytics application

1. Sign in to the AWS Management Console and open the Kinesis Data Analytics console at https://console.aws.amazon.com/kinesisanalytics.

2. Choose **Create new application**.

3. On the **New application** page, type an application name, type a description, and then choose **Save and continue**.

Doing this creates a Kinesis data analytics application with a status of READY. The console shows the application hub where you can configure input and output. **Note**
To create an application, the CreateApplication operation requires only the application name. You can add input and output configuration after you create an application in the console.

In the next step, you configure input for the application. In the input configuration, you add a streaming data source to the application and discover a schema for an in-application input stream by sampling data on the streaming source.

Next Step
Step 3.2: Configure Input

Step 3.2: Configure Input

Your application needs a streaming source. To help you get started, the console can create a demo stream (called `kinesis-analytics-demo-stream`). The console also runs a script that populates records in the stream.

To add a streaming source to your application

1. On the application hub page in the console, choose **Connect to a source**.

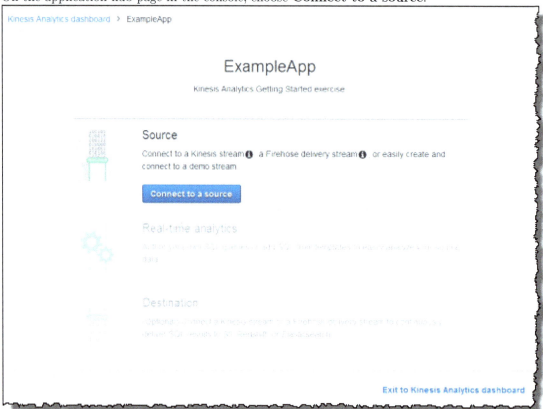

2. On the page that appears, review the following:

   - **Source** section, where you specify a streaming source for your application. You can select an existing stream source or create one. In this exercise, you create a new stream, the demo stream.

     By default the console names the in-application input stream that is created as `INPUT_SQL_STREAM_001`. For this exercise, keep this name as it appears.

     - **Stream reference name** – This option shows the name of the in-application input stream that is created, `SOURCE_SQL_STREAM_001`. You can change the name, but for this exercise, keep this name.

       In the input configuration, you map the demo stream to an in-application input stream that is created. When you start the application, Amazon Kinesis Data Analytics continuously reads the demo stream and insert rows in the in-application input stream. You query this in-application input stream in your application code.

- **Record pre-processing with AWS Lambda**: This option is where you specify an AWS Lambda expression that modifies the records in the input stream before your application code executes. In this exercise, leave the **Disabled** option selected. For more information about Lambda preprocessing, see Preprocessing Data Using a Lambda Function.

After you provide all the information on this page, the console sends an update request (see UpdateApplication) to add the input configuration the application.

3. On the **Source **page, choose **Configure a new stream**.

4. Choose **Create demo stream**. The console configures the application input by doing the following:

   - The console creates a Kinesis data stream called `kinesis-analytics-demo-stream`.
   - The console populates the stream with sample stock ticker data.
   - Using the DiscoverInputSchema input action, the console infers a schema by reading sample records on the stream. The schema that is inferred is the schema for the in-application input stream that is created. For more information, see Configuring Application Input.
   - The console shows the inferred schema and the sample data it read from the streaming source to infer the schema.

The console displays the sample records on the streaming source.

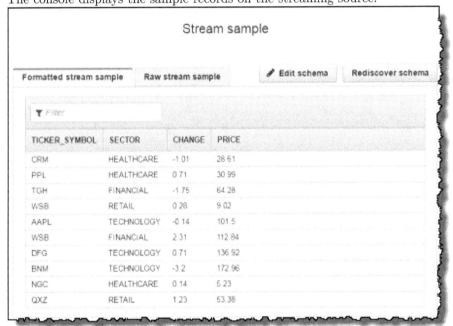

The following appear on the **Stream sample** console page:

- The **Raw stream sample** tab shows the raw stream records sampled by the DiscoverInputSchema API action to infer the schema.

- The **Formatted stream sample** tab shows the tabular version of the data in the **Raw stream sample** tab.

- If you choose **Edit schema**, you can edit the inferred schema. For this exercise, don't change the inferred schema. For more information about editing a schema, see Working with the Schema Editor.

  If you choose **Rediscover schema**, you can request the console to run DiscoverInputSchema again and infer the schema.

5. Choose **Save and continue**.

You now have an application with input configuration added to it. In the next step, you add SQL code to perform some analytics on the data in-application input stream.

Next Step
Step 3.3: Add Real-Time Analytics (Add Application Code)

Step 3.3: Add Real-Time Analytics (Add Application Code)

You can write your own SQL queries against the in-application stream, but for the following step you use one of the templates that provides sample code.

1. On the application hub page, choose **Go to SQL editor**.

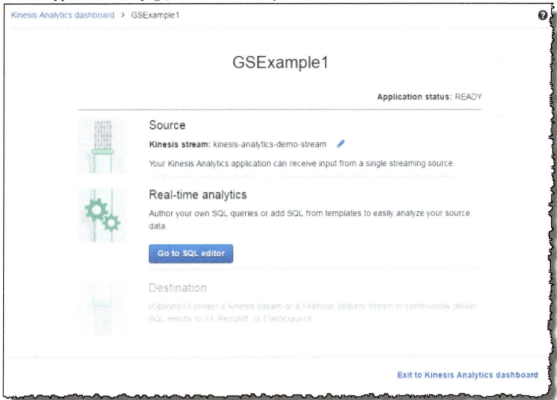

2. In the **Would you like to start running "GSExample1"?** dialog box, choose **Yes, start application**.

   The console sends a request to start the application (see StartApplication), and then the SQL editor page appears.

3. The console opens the SQL editor page. Review the page, including the buttons (**Add SQL from templates**, **Save and run SQL**) and various tabs.

4. In the SQL editor, choose **Add SQL from templates**.

5. From the available template list, choose **Continuous filter**. The sample code reads data from one in-application stream (the `WHERE` clause filters the rows) and inserts it in another in-application stream as follows:

   - It creates the in-application stream `DESTINATION_SQL_STREAM`.
   - It creates a pump `STREAM_PUMP`, and uses it to select rows from `SOURCE_SQL_STREAM_001` and insert them in the `DESTINATION_SQL_STREAM`.

6. Choose **Add this SQL to editor**.

7. Test the application code as follows:

   Remember, you already started the application (status is RUNNING). Therefore, Amazon Kinesis Data Analytics is already continuously reading from the streaming source and adding rows to the in-application stream `SOURCE_SQL_STREAM_001`.

1. In the SQL Editor, choose **Save and run SQL**. The console first sends update request to save the application code. Then, the code continuously executes.

2. You can see the results in the **Real-time analytics** tab.

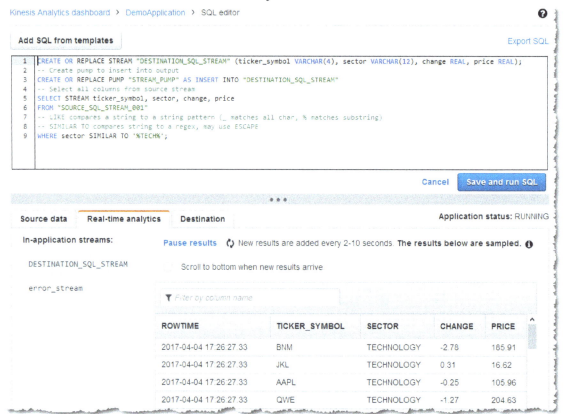

The SQL editor has the following tabs:

- The **Source data** tab shows an in-application input stream that is mapped to the streaming source. Choose the in-application stream, and you can see data coming in. Note the additional columns in the in-application input stream that weren't specified in the input configuration. These include the following time stamp columns:

  - **ROWTIME** – Each row in an in-application stream has a special column called ROWTIME. This column is the time stamp when Amazon Kinesis Data Analytics inserted the row in the first in-application stream (the in-application input stream that is mapped to the streaming source).

  - **Approximate_Arrival_Time** – Each Kinesis Data Analytics record includes a value called Approximate_Arrival_Time. This value is the approximate arrival time stamp that is set when the streaming source successfully receives and stores the record. When Kinesis Data Analytics reads records from a streaming source, it fetches this column into the in-application input stream.

  These time stamp values are useful in windowed queries that are time-based. For more information, see Windowed Queries.

- The **Real-time analytics** tab shows all the other in-application streams created by your application code. It also includes the error stream. Kinesis Data Analytics sends any rows it cannot process to the error stream. For more information, see Error Handling.

  Choose `DESTINATION_SQL_STREAM` to view the rows your application code inserted. Note the additional columns that your application code didn't create. These columns include the `ROWTIME` time stamp column. Kinesis Data Analytics simply copies these values from the source (`SOURCE_SQL_STREAM_001`).

- The **Destination** tab shows the external destination where Kinesis Data Analytics writes the query results. You haven't configured any external destination for your application output yet.

Next Step
Step 3.4: (Optional) Update the Application Code

Step 3.4: (Optional) Update the Application Code

In this step, you explore how to update the application code.

To update application code

1. Create another in-application stream as follows:

    - Create another in-application stream called `DESTINATION_SQL_STREAM_2`.
    - Create a pump, and then use it to insert rows in the newly created stream by selecting rows from the `DESTINATION_SQL_STREAM`.

    In the SQL editor, append the following code to the existing application code:

```
1  CREATE OR REPLACE STREAM "DESTINATION_SQL_STREAM_2"
2          (ticker_symbol VARCHAR(4),
3           change        DOUBLE,
4           price         DOUBLE);
5
6  CREATE OR REPLACE PUMP "STREAM_PUMP_2" AS
7    INSERT INTO "DESTINATION_SQL_STREAM_2"
8      SELECT STREAM ticker_symbol, change, price
9      FROM   "DESTINATION_SQL_STREAM";
```

   Save and run the code. Additional in-application streams appear on the **Real-time analytics** tab.

2. Create two in-application streams. Filter rows in the `SOURCE_SQL_STREAM_001` based on the stock ticker, and then insert them in to these separate streams.

    Append the following SQL statements to your application code:

```
1  CREATE OR REPLACE STREAM "AMZN_STREAM"
2          (ticker_symbol VARCHAR(4),
3           change        DOUBLE,
4           price         DOUBLE);
5
6  CREATE OR REPLACE PUMP "AMZN_PUMP" AS
7    INSERT INTO "AMZN_STREAM"
8      SELECT STREAM ticker_symbol, change, price
9      FROM   "SOURCE_SQL_STREAM_001"
10     WHERE  ticker_symbol SIMILAR TO '%AMZN%';
11
12 CREATE OR REPLACE STREAM "TGT_STREAM"
13         (ticker_symbol VARCHAR(4),
14          change        DOUBLE,
15          price         DOUBLE);
16
17 CREATE OR REPLACE PUMP "TGT_PUMP" AS
18   INSERT INTO "TGT_STREAM"
19     SELECT STREAM ticker_symbol, change, price
20     FROM   "SOURCE_SQL_STREAM_001"
21     WHERE  ticker_symbol SIMILAR TO '%TGT%';
```

   Save and run the code. Notice additional in-application streams on the **Real-time analytics** tab.

You now have your first working Amazon Kinesis data analytics application. In this exercise, you did the following:

- Created your first Kinesis data analytics application.

- Configured application input that identified the demo stream as the streaming source and mapped it to an in-application stream (SOURCE_SQL_STREAM_001) that is created. Kinesis Data Analytics continuously reads the demo stream and inserts records in the in-application stream.

- Your application code queried the SOURCE_SQL_STREAM_001 and wrote output to another in-application stream called DESTINATION_SQL_STREAM.

Now you can optionally configure application output to write the application output to an external destination. That is, you can configure the application output to write records in the DESTINATION_SQL_STREAM to an external destination. For this exercise, this is an optional step. To learn how to configure the destination, go to the next step.

Next Step
Step 4 (Optional) Edit the Schema and SQL Code Using the Console.

Step 4 (Optional) Edit the Schema and SQL Code Using the Console

Following, you can find information about how to edit an inferred schema and how to edit SQL code for Amazon Kinesis Data Analytics. You do so by working with the schema editor and SQL editor that are part of the Kinesis Data Analytics console.

Topics

- Working with the Schema Editor
- Working with the SQL Editor

Working with the Schema Editor

The schema for an Amazon Kinesis data analytics application's input stream defines how data from the stream is made available to SQL queries in the application.

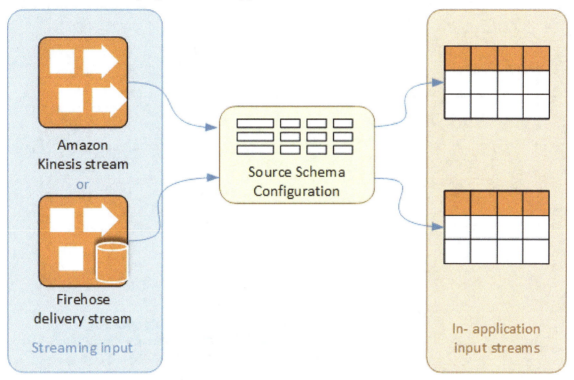

The schema contains selection criteria for determining what part of the streaming input is transformed into a data column in the in-application input stream. This input can be one of the following:

- A JSONPath expression for JSON input streams. JSONPath is a tool for querying JSON data.
- A column number for input streams in comma-separated values (CSV) format.
- A column name and a SQL data type for presenting the data in the in-application data stream. The data type also contains a length for character or binary data.

The console attempts to generate the schema using DiscoverInputSchema. If schema discovery fails or returns an incorrect or incomplete schema, you must edit the schema manually by using the schema editor.

Schema Editor Main Screen

The following screenshot shows the main screen for the Schema Editor.

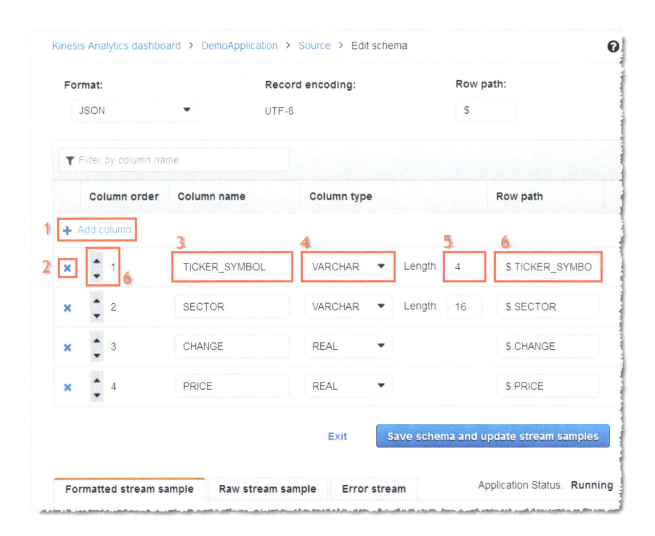

You can apply the following edits to the schema:

- Add a column (1): You might need to add a data column if a data item is not detected automatically.
- Delete a column (2): You can exclude data from the source stream if your application doesn't require it. This exclusion doesn't affect the data in the source stream. If data is excluded, that data simply isn't made available to the application.
- Rename a column (3). A column name can't be blank, must be longer than a single character, and must not contain reserved SQL keywords. The name must also meet naming criteria for SQL ordinary identifiers: The name must start with a letter and contain only letters, underscore characters, and digits.
- Change the data type (4) or length (5) of a column: You can specify a compatible data type for a column. If you specify an incompatible data type, the column is either populated with NULL or the in-application stream is not populated at all. In the latter case, errors are written to the error stream. If you specify a length for a column that is too small, the incoming data is truncated.
- Change the selection criteria of a column (6): You can edit the JSONPath expression or CSV column order used to determine the source of the data in a column. To change the selection criteria for a JSON schema, type a new value for the row path expression. A CSV schema uses the column order as selection criteria. To change the selection criteria for a CSV schema, change the order of the columns.

Editing the Schema for a Streaming Source

If you need to edit a schema for a streaming source, follow these steps.

To edit the schema for a streaming source

1. On the **Source** page, choose **Edit schema**.

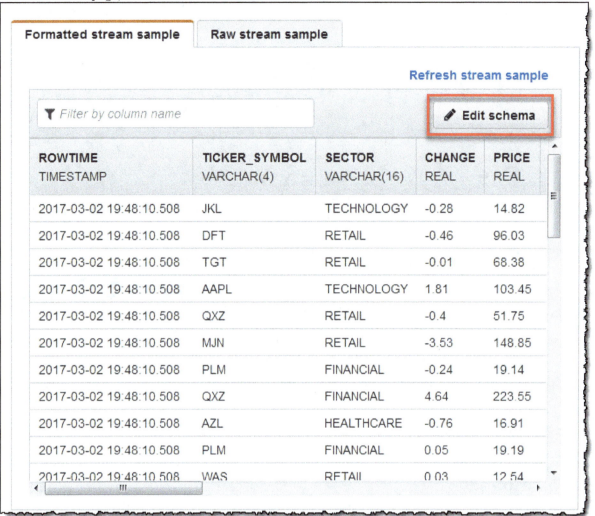

2. On the **Edit schema** page, edit the source schema.

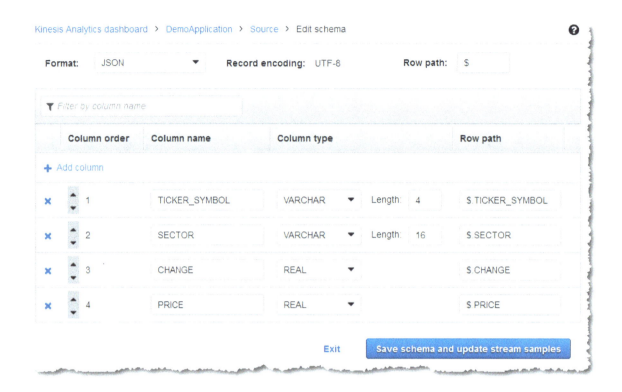

3. For **Format**, choose **JSON** or **CSV**. For JSON or CSV format, the supported encoding is ISO 8859-1. For further information on editing the schema for JSON or CSV format, see the procedures in the next sections.

Editing a JSON Schema

You can edit a JSON schema by using the following steps.

To edit a JSON schema

1. In the schema editor, choose **Add column** to add a column.

    A new column appears in the first column position. To change column order, choose the up and down arrows next to the column name.

    For a new column, provide the following information:

    - For **Column name**, type a name.

        A column name cannot be blank, must be longer than a single character, and must not contain reserved SQL keywords. It must also meet naming criteria for SQL ordinary identifiers: It must start with a letter and contain only letters, underscore characters, and digits.

    - For **Column type**, type an SQL data type.

        A column type can be any supported SQL data type. If the new data type is CHAR, VARBINARY, or VARCHAR, specify a data length for **Length**. For more information, see Data Types.

    - For **Row path**, provide a row path. A row path is a valid JSONPath expression that maps to a JSON element. **Note**
        The base **Row path** value is the path to the top-level parent that contains the data to be imported. This value is **$** by default. For more information, see `RecordRowPath` in JSONMappingParameters.

2. To delete a column, choose the **x** icon next to the column number.

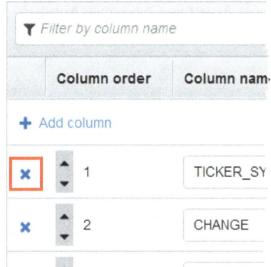

3. To rename a column, type a new name for **Column name**. The new column name cannot be blank, must be longer than a single character, and must not contain reserved SQL keywords. It must also meet naming criteria for SQL ordinary identifiers: It must start with a letter and contain only letters, underscore characters, and digits.

4. To change the data type of a column, choose a new data type for **Column type**. If the new data type is CHAR, VARBINARY, or VARCHAR, specify a data length for **Length**. For more information, see Data Types.

5. Choose **Save schema and update stream** to save your changes.

The modified schema appears in the editor and looks similar to the following.

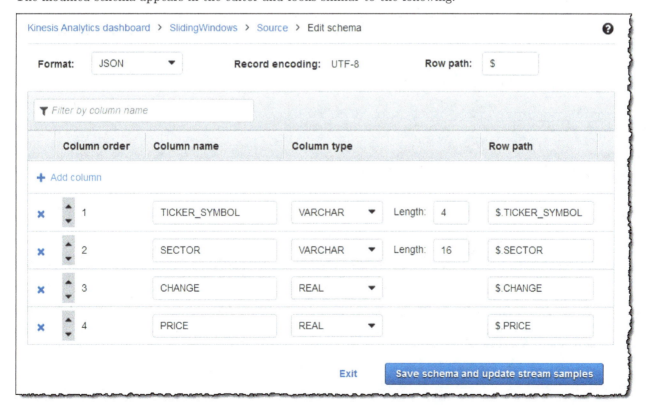

If your schema has many rows, you can filter the rows using **Filter by column name**. For example, to edit column names that start with P, such as a `Price` column, type P in the **Filter by column name** box.

Editing a CSV Schema

You can edit a CSV schema by using the following steps.

To edit a CSV schema

1. In the schema editor, for **Row delimiter**, choose the delimiter used by your incoming data stream. This is the delimiter between records of data in your stream, such as a newline character.

2. For **Column delimiter**, choose the delimiter used by your incoming data stream. This is the delimiter between fields of data in your stream, such as a comma.

3. To add a column, choose **Add column**.

   A new column appears in the first column position. To change column order, choose the up and down arrows next to the column name.

   For a new column, provide the following information:

   - For **Column name**, type a name.

     A column name cannot be blank, must be longer than a single character, and must not contain reserved SQL keywords. It must also meet naming criteria for SQL ordinary identifiers: It must start with a letter and contain only letters, underscore characters, and digits.

   - For **Column type**, type a SQL data type.

     A column type can be any supported SQL data type. If the new data type is CHAR, VARBINARY, or VARCHAR, specify a data length for **Length**. For more information, see Data Types.

4. To delete a column, choose the **x** icon next to the column number.

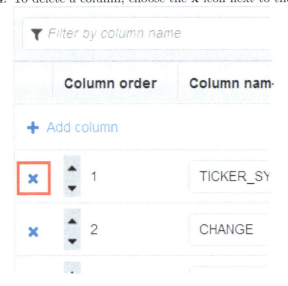

5. To rename a column, type a new name in **Column name**. The new column name cannot be blank, must be longer than a single character, and must not contain reserved SQL keywords. It must also meet naming criteria for SQL ordinary identifiers: It must start with a letter and contain only letters, underscore characters, and digits.

6. To change the data type of a column, choose a new data type for **Column type**. If the new data type is CHAR, VARBINARY, or VARCHAR, specify a data length for **Length**. For more information, see Data Types.

7. Choose **Save schema and update stream** to save your changes.

The modified schema appears in the editor and looks similar to the following.

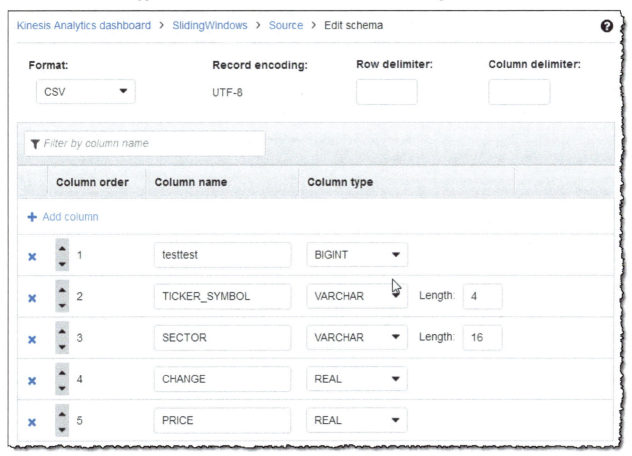

If your schema has many rows, you can filter the rows using **Filter by column name**. For example, to edit column names that start with P, such as a Price column, type P in the **Filter by column name** box.

Working with the SQL Editor

Following, you can find information about sections of the SQL editor and how each works. In the SQL editor, you can either author your own code yourself or choose **Add SQL from templates**. A SQL template gives you example SQL code that can help you write common Amazon Kinesis data analytics applications. The example applications in this guide use some of these templates. For more information, see Example Applications.

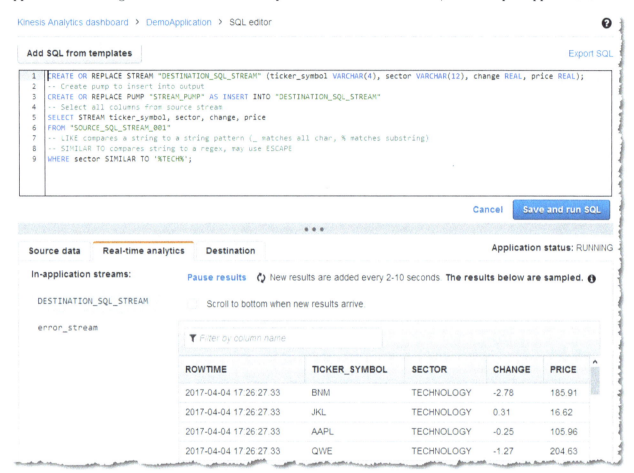

Source Data Tab

The **Source data** tab identifies a streaming source. It also identifies the in-application input stream that this source maps to and that provides the application input configuration.

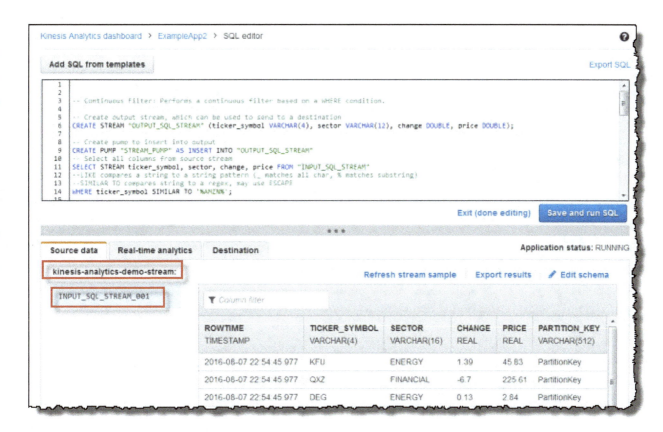

Amazon Kinesis Data Analytics provides the following time stamp columns, so that you don't need to provide explicit mapping in your input configuration:

- **ROWTIME** – Each row in an in-application stream has a special column called ROWTIME. This column is the time stamp for the point when Kinesis Data Analytics inserted the row in the first in-application stream.
- **Approximate_Arrival_Time** – Records on your streaming source include the Approximate_Arrival_Timestamp column. It is the approximate arrival time stamp that is set when the streaming source successfully receives and stores the related record. Kinesis Data Analytics fetches this column into the in-application input stream as Approximate_Arrival_Time. Amazon Kinesis Data Analytics provides this column only in the in-application input stream that is mapped to the streaming source.

These time stamp values are useful in windowed queries that are time-based. For more information, see Windowed Queries.

Real-Time Analytics Tab

The **Real-time analytics** tab shows all the in-application streams that your application code creates. This group of streams includes the error stream (error_stream) that Amazon Kinesis Data Analytics provides for all applications.

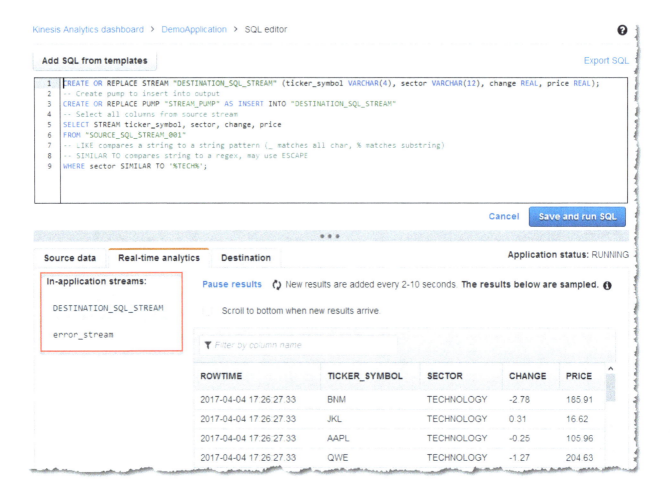

Destination Tab

The **Destination** tab enables you to configure application output, to persist in-application streams to external destinations. You can configure output to persist data in any of the in-application streams to external destinations. For more information, see Configuring Application Output.

Streaming SQL Concepts

Amazon Kinesis Data Analytics implements the ANSI 2008 SQL standard with extensions. These extensions enable you to process streaming data. The following topics cover key streaming SQL concepts.

Topics

- In-Application Streams and Pumps
- Timestamps and the ROWTIME Column
- Continuous Queries
- Windowed Queries
- Streaming Data Operations: Stream Joins

In-Application Streams and Pumps

When you configure application input, you map a streaming source to an in-application stream that is created. Data continuously flows from the streaming source into the in-application stream. An in-application stream works like a table that you can query using SQL statements, but it's called a stream because it represents continuous data flow.

Note
Do not confuse in-application streams with the Amazon Kinesis streams and Kinesis Data Firehose delivery streams. In-application streams exist only in the context of an Amazon Kinesis Data Analytics application. Amazon Kinesis streams and Kinesis Data Firehose delivery streams exist independent of your application, and you can configure them as a streaming source in your application input configuration or as a destination in output configuration.

You can also create additional in-application streams as needed to store intermediate query results. Creating an in-application stream is a two-step process. First, you create an in-application stream, and then you pump data into it. For example, suppose the input configuration of your application creates an in-application stream called `INPUTSTREAM`. In the following example, you create another stream (`TEMPSTREAM`), and then you pump data from `INPUTSTREAM` into it.

1. Create an in-application stream (`TEMPSTREAM`) with three columns, as shown following:

```
1 CREATE OR REPLACE STREAM "TEMPSTREAM" (
2    "column1" BIGINT NOT NULL,
3    "column2" INTEGER,
4    "column3" VARCHAR(64));
```

   The column names are specified in quotes, making them case-sensitive. For more information, see Identifiers in the Amazon Kinesis Data Analytics SQL Reference.

2. Insert data into the stream using a pump. A pump is a continuous insert query running that inserts data from one in-application stream to another in-application stream. The following statement creates a pump (`SAMPLEPUMP`) and inserts data into the `TEMPSTREAM` by selecting records from another stream (`INPUTSTREAM`).

```
1 CREATE OR REPLACE PUMP "SAMPLEPUMP" AS
2 INSERT INTO "TEMPSTREAM" ("column1",
3                           "column2",
4                           "column3")
5 SELECT STREAM inputcolumn1,
6               inputcolumn2,
7               inputcolumn3
8 FROM "INPUTSTREAM";
```

You can have multiple writers insert into an in-application stream, and there can be multiple readers selected from the stream. You can think of an in-application stream as implementing a publish/subscribe messaging paradigm in which the data row, including time of creation and time of receipt, can be processed, interpreted, and forwarded by a cascade of streaming SQL statements, without having to be stored in a traditional RDBMS.

After an in-application stream is created, you can perform normal SQL queries.

Note
When querying streams, most SQL statements are bound using a row-based or time-based window. For more information, see Windowed Queries.

You can also join streams. For examples of joining streams, see Streaming Data Operations: Stream Joins.

Timestamps and the ROWTIME Column

In-application streams include a special column called `ROWTIME`. It stores a timestamp when Amazon Kinesis Data Analytics inserts a row in the first in-application stream. `ROWTIME` reflects the timestamp at which Amazon Kinesis Data Analytics inserted a record into the first in-application stream after reading from the streaming source. This `ROWTIME` value is then maintained throughout your application.

Note
When you pump records from one in-application stream into another, you don't need to explicitly copy the `ROWTIME` column, Amazon Kinesis Data Analytics copies this column for you.

Amazon Kinesis Data Analytics guarantees that the `ROWTIME` values are monotonically increased. You use this timestamp in time-based windowed queries. For more information, see Windowed Queries.

You can access the ROWTIME column in your SELECT statement like any other columns in your in-application stream. For example:

```
1  SELECT STREAM ROWTIME,
2                 some_col_1,
3                 some_col_2
4  FROM  SOURCE_SQL_STREAM_001
```

Understanding Various Times in Streaming Analytics

In addition to `ROWTIME`, there are other types of times in real-time streaming applications. These are:

- **Event time** – The timestamp when the event occurred. This is also sometimes called the *client-side time*. It is often desirable to use this time in analytics because it is the time when an event occurred. However, many event sources, such as mobile phones and web clients, do not have reliable clocks, which can lead to inaccurate times. In addition, connectivity issues can lead to records appearing on a stream not in the same order the events occurred.

- **Ingest time** – The timestamp of when record was added to the streaming source. Amazon Kinesis Data Streams includes a field called `ApproximateArrivalTimeStamp` in every record that provides this timestamp. This is also sometimes referred to as the *server-side time*. This ingest time is often the close approximation of event time. If there is any kind of delay in the record ingestion to the stream, this can lead to inaccuracies, which are typically rare. Also, the ingest time is rarely out of order, but it can occur due to the distributed nature of streaming data. Therefore, Ingest time is a mostly accurate and in-order reflection of the event time.

- **Processing time** – The timestamp when Amazon Kinesis Data Analytics inserts a row in the first in-application stream. Amazon Kinesis Data Analytics provides this timestamp in the `ROWTIME` column that exists in each in-application stream. The processing time is always monotonically increasing, but it will not be accurate if your application falls behind (if an application falls behind, the processing time will not accurately reflect the event time). This `ROWTIME` is very accurate in relation to the wall clock, but it might not be the time when the event actually occurred.

As you can see from the preceding discussion, using each of these times in windowed queries that are time-based has advantages and disadvantages. We recommend you choose one or more of these times, and a strategy to deal with the relevant disadvantages based on your use case scenario.

Note
If you are using row-based windows, time is not an issue and you can ignore this section.

We recommend a two-window strategy that uses two time-based, both ROWTIME and one of the other times (ingest or event time).

- Use ROWTIME as the first window, which controls how frequently the query emits the results, as shown in the following example. It is not used as a logical time.
- Use one of the other times that is the logical time you want to associated with your analytics. This time represents when the event occurred. In the following example, the analytics goal is to group the records and return count by ticker.

The advantage of this strategy is that it can use a time that represents when the event occurred, and it can gracefully handle when your application falls behind or when events arrive out of order. If the application falls behind when bringing records into the in-application stream, they are still grouped by the logical time in the second window. The query uses ROWTIME to guarantee the order of processing. Any records that are late (ingest timestamp shows earlier value compared to the ROWTIME value) are processed successfully too.

Consider the following query against the demo stream used in the Getting Started Exercise. The query uses the GROUP BY clause and emits ticker count in a one-minute tumbling window.

```
1  CREATE OR REPLACE STREAM "DESTINATION_SQL_STREAM"
2      ("ingest_time"     timestamp,
3      "approximate_arrival_time" timestamp,
4      "ticker_symbol"   VARCHAR(12),
5      "symbol_count"         integer);
6
7
8  CREATE OR REPLACE PUMP "STREAM_PUMP" AS
9      INSERT INTO "DESTINATION_SQL_STREAM"
10     SELECT STREAM STEP("SOURCE_SQL_STREAM_001".ROWTIME BY INTERVAL '60' SECOND) AS "ingest_time
           ",
11         STEP("SOURCE_SQL_STREAM_001".Approximate_Arrival_Time BY INTERVAL '60' SECOND) AS "
               approximate_arrival_time",
12         "TICKER_SYMBOL",
13         COUNT(*) AS "symbol_count"
14     FROM "SOURCE_SQL_STREAM_001"
15     GROUP BY "TICKER_SYMBOL",
16         STEP("SOURCE_SQL_STREAM_001".ROWTIME BY INTERVAL '60' SECOND),
17         STEP("SOURCE_SQL_STREAM_001".Approximate_Arrival_Time BY INTERVAL '60' SECOND);
```

In GROUP BY, you first group the records based on ROWTIME in a one-minute window and then by Approximate_Arrival_Time.

Note that the timestamp values in the result are rounded down to the nearest 60 second interval. The first group result emitted by the query shows records in the first minute. The second group of results emitted shows records in the next minutes based on ROWTIME. The last record indicates that the application was late in bringing the record in the in-application stream (it shows a late ROWTIME value compared to the ingest timestamp).

```
1  ROWTIME                  INGEST_TIME       TICKER_SYMBOL  SYMBOL_COUNT
2
3  --First one minute window.
4  2016-07-19 17:05:00.0    2016-07-19 17:05:00.0    ABC      10
5  2016-07-19 17:05:00.0    2016-07-19 17:05:00.0    DEF      15
6  2016-07-19 17:05:00.0    2016-07-19 17:05:00.0    XYZ      6-
7  -Second one minute window.
8  2016-07-19 17:06:00.0    2016-07-19 17:06:00.0    ABC      11
9  2016-07-19 17:06:00.0    2016-07-19 17:06:00.0    DEF      11
10 2016-07-19 17:06:00.0    2016-07-19 17:05:00.0    XYZ      1    ***
11
12 ***late-arriving record, instead of appearing in the result of the
```

```
13 first 1-minute windows (based on ingest_time, it is in the result
14 of the second 1-minute window.
```

You can combine the results for a final accurate count per minute by pushing the results to a downstream database. For example, you can configure application output to persist the results to a Kinesis Data Firehose delivery stream that can write to an Amazon Redshift table. After results are in an Amazon Redshift table, you can query the Amazon Redshift table to compute the total count group by `Ticker_Symbol`. In the case of `XYZ`, the total is accurate (6+1) even though a record arrived late.

Continuous Queries

A query over a stream executes continuously over streaming data. This continuous execution enables scenarios, such as the ability for applications to continuously query a stream and generate alerts.

In the Getting Started exercise, you have an in-application stream called SOURCE_SQL_STREAM_001 that continuously receives stock prices from a demo stream (a Kinesis stream). Following is the schema:

```
1 (TICKER_SYMBOL VARCHAR(4),
2   SECTOR varchar(16),
3   CHANGE REAL,
4   PRICE REAL)
```

Suppose you are interested in stock price changes greater than 15%. You can use the following query in your application code. This query runs continuously and emits records when a stock price change greater than 1% is detected.

```
1 SELECT STREAM TICKER_SYMBOL, PRICE
2       FROM   "SOURCE_SQL_STREAM_001"
3       WHERE  (ABS((CHANGE / (PRICE-CHANGE)) * 100)) > 1
```

Use the following procedure to set up an Amazon Kinesis Data Analytics application and test this query.

To test the query

1. Set up an application by following the Getting Started Exercise.

2. Replace the **SELECT** statement in the application code with the preceding **SELECT** query. The resulting application code is shown following:

   ```
   1 CREATE OR REPLACE STREAM "DESTINATION_SQL_STREAM" (ticker_symbol VARCHAR(4),
   2                                                     price DOUBLE);
   3 -- CREATE OR REPLACE PUMP to insert into output
   4 CREATE OR REPLACE PUMP "STREAM_PUMP" AS
   5   INSERT INTO "DESTINATION_SQL_STREAM"
   6       SELECT STREAM TICKER_SYMBOL,
   7                     PRICE
   8       FROM   "SOURCE_SQL_STREAM_001"
   9       WHERE  (ABS((CHANGE / (PRICE-CHANGE)) * 100)) > 1;
   ```

Windowed Queries

SQL queries in your application code execute continuously over in-application streams. And, an in-application stream represents unbounded data that is flowing continuously through your application. Therefore, to get result sets from this continuously updating input, you often bound queries using a window defined in terms of time or rows. These are also called *windowed SQL*.

For a time-based windowed query, you specify the window size in terms of time (for example, a one-minute window). This requires a timestamp column in your in-application stream that is monotonically increasing (timestamp for a new row is greater than or equal to previous row). Amazon Kinesis Data Analytics provides such a timestamp column called `ROWTIME` for each in-application stream. You can use this column when specifying time-based queries. For your application, you might choose some other timestamp option. For more information, see Timestamps and the ROWTIME Column.

For a row-based windowed query, you specify window size in terms of the number of rows.

You can specify a query to process records in a tumbling window or sliding window manner, depending on your application needs. For more information, see the following topics:

- Tumbling Windows (Aggregations Using GROUP BY)
- Sliding Windows

Tumbling Windows (Aggregations Using GROUP BY)

When a windowed query processes each window in a non-overlapping manner, the window is referred to as a *tumbling window*. In this case, each record on an in-application stream belongs to a specific window, and it's processed only once (when the query processes the window to which the record belongs).

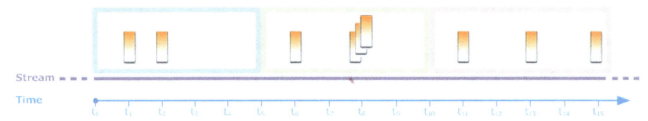

For example, an aggregation query using a GROUP BY clause processes rows in a tumbling window. The demo stream in the getting started exercise receives stock price data that is mapped to the in-application stream SOURCE_SQL_STREAM_001 in your application. This stream has the following schema.

```
1  (TICKER_SYMBOL VARCHAR(4),
2   SECTOR varchar(16),
3   CHANGE REAL,
4   PRICE REAL)
```

In your application code, suppose you want to find aggregate (min, max) prices for each ticker over a one-minute window. You can use the following query.

```
1  SELECT STREAM ROWTIME,
2               Ticker_Symbol,
3               MIN(Price) AS Price,
4               MAX(Price) AS Price
5  FROM    "SOURCE_SQL_STREAM_001"
6  GROUP BY Ticker_Symbol,
7           STEP("SOURCE_SQL_STREAM_001".ROWTIME BY INTERVAL '60' SECOND);
```

The preceding is an example of a windowed query that is time-based. The query groups records by ROWTIME values. For reporting on a per-minute basis, the STEP function rounds down the ROWTIME values to the nearest minute.

Note
You can also use the FLOOR function to group records into windows, but FLOOR can only round time values down to a whole time unit (hour, minute, second, and so on). STEP is recommended for grouping records into tumbling windows because it can round values down to an arbitrary interval, e.g. 30 seconds.

This query is an example of a nonoverlapping (tumbling) window. The GROUP BY clause groups records in a one-minute window, and each record belongs to a specific window (no overlapping). The query emits one output record per minute, providing the min/max ticker price recorded at the specific minute. This type of query is useful for generating periodic reports from the input data stream. In this example, reports are generated each minute.

To test the query

1. Set up an application by following the getting started exercise.

2. Replace the SELECT statement in the application code by the preceding SELECT query. The resulting application code is shown following:

```
1  CREATE OR REPLACE STREAM "DESTINATION_SQL_STREAM" (
2                            ticker_symbol VARCHAR(4),
3                            Min_Price     DOUBLE,
```

```
4                               Max_Price      DOUBLE);
5 -- CREATE OR REPLACE PUMP to insert into output
6 CREATE OR REPLACE PUMP "STREAM_PUMP" AS
7   INSERT INTO "DESTINATION_SQL_STREAM"
8     SELECT STREAM Ticker_Symbol,
9               MIN(Price) AS Min_Price,
10              MAX(Price) AS Max_Price
11    FROM    "SOURCE_SQL_STREAM_001"
12    GROUP BY Ticker_Symbol,
13             STEP("SOURCE_SQL_STREAM_001".ROWTIME BY INTERVAL '60' SECOND);
```

Sliding Windows

Instead of grouping records using `GROUP BY`, you can define a time-based or row-based window. You do this by adding an explicit `WINDOW` clause.

In this case, as the window slides with time, Amazon Kinesis Data Analytics emits an output when new records appear on the stream. Kinesis Data Analytics emits this output by processing rows in the window. Windows can overlap in this type of processing, and a record can be part of multiple windows and be processed with each window. The following example illustrates a sliding window.

Consider a simple query that counts records on the stream. We assume a 5-second window. In the following example stream, new records arrive at time t1, t2, t6, and t7, and three records arrive at time t8 seconds.

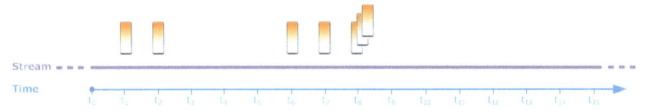

Keep the following in mind:

- We assume a 5-second window. The 5-second window slides continuously with time.
- For every row that enters a window, an output row is emitted by the sliding window. Soon after the application starts, you see the query emit output for every new record that appears on the stream, even though a 5-second window hasn't passed yet. For example, the query emits output when a record appears in the first second and second second. Later, the query processes records in the 5-second window.
- The windows slide with time. If an old record on the stream falls out of the window, the query doesn't emit output unless there is also a new record on the stream that falls within that 5-second window.

Suppose the query starts executing at t0. If so, the following occurs:

1. At the time t0, the query starts. The query doesn't emit output (count value) because there are no records at this time.

2. At time t1, a new record appears on the stream, and the query emits count value 1.

3. At time t2, another record appears, and the query emits count 2.

4. The 5-second window slides with time:

   - At t3, the sliding window t3 to t0
   - At t4 (sliding window t4 to t0)
   - At t5 the sliding window t5–t0

At all of these times, the 5-second window has the same records—there are no new records. Therefore, the query doesn't emit any output.

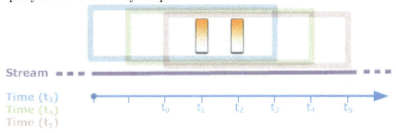

5. At time t6, the 5-second window is (t6 to t1). The query detects one new record at t6 so it emits output 2. The record at t1 is no longer in the window and doesn't count.

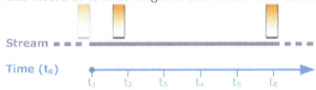

6. At time t7, the 5-second window is t7 to t2. The query detects one new record at t7 so it emits output 2. The record at t2 is no longer in the 5-second window, and therefore isn't counted.

7. At time t8, the 5-second window is t8 to t3. The query detects three new records, and therefore emits record count 5.

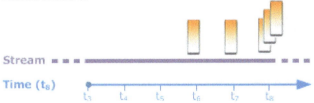

In summary, the window is a fixed size and slides with time. The query emits output when new records appear.

Note

We recommend that you use a sliding window no longer than one hour. If you use a longer window, the application takes longer to restart after regular system maintenance, because the source data needs to be read from the stream again.

The following are example queries that use the WINDOW clause to define windows and perform aggregates. Because the queries don't specify GROUP BY, the query uses the sliding window approach to process records on the stream.

Example 1: Process a Stream Using a 1-minute Sliding Window

Consider the demo stream in the Getting Started exercise that populates the in-application stream, SOURCE_SQL_STREAM_001. The following is the schema.

```
1 (TICKER_SYMBOL VARCHAR(4),
2  SECTOR varchar(16),
3  CHANGE REAL,
4  PRICE REAL)
```

Suppose that you want your application to compute aggregates using a sliding 1-minute window. That is, for each new record that appears on the stream, you want the application to emit an output by applying aggregates on records in the preceding 1-minute window.

You can use the following time-based windowed query. The query uses the WINDOW clause to define the 1-minute range interval. The PARTITION BY in the WINDOW clause groups records by ticker values within the sliding window.

```
1 SELECT STREAM ticker_symbol,
2               MIN(Price) OVER W1 AS Min_Price,
3               MAX(Price) OVER W1 AS Max_Price,
4               AVG(Price) OVER W1 AS Avg_Price
5 FROM   "SOURCE_SQL_STREAM_001"
6 WINDOW W1 AS (
7   PARTITION BY ticker_symbol
8   RANGE INTERVAL '1' MINUTE PRECEDING);
```

To test the query

1. Set up an application by following the Getting Started Exercise.

2. Replace the SELECT statement in the application code with the preceding SELECT query. The resulting application code is the following.

```
1 CREATE OR REPLACE STREAM "DESTINATION_SQL_STREAM" (
2                    ticker_symbol VARCHAR(10),
3                    Min_Price     double,
4                    Max_Price     double,
5                    Avg_Price     double);
6 CREATE OR REPLACE PUMP "STREAM_PUMP" AS
7   INSERT INTO "DESTINATION_SQL_STREAM"
8     SELECT STREAM ticker_symbol,
9               MIN(Price) OVER W1 AS Min_Price,
10              MAX(Price) OVER W1 AS Max_Price,
11              AVG(Price) OVER W1 AS Avg_Price
12    FROM   "SOURCE_SQL_STREAM_001"
13    WINDOW W1 AS (
14       PARTITION BY ticker_symbol
15       RANGE INTERVAL '1' MINUTE PRECEDING);
```

Example 2: Query Applying Aggregates on a Sliding Window

The following query on the demo stream returns the average of the percent change in the price of each ticker in a 10-second window.

```
1 SELECT STREAM Ticker_Symbol,
2               AVG(Change / (Price - Change)) over W1 as Avg_Percent_Change
3 FROM "SOURCE_SQL_STREAM_001"
4 WINDOW W1 AS (
5       PARTITION BY ticker_symbol
6       RANGE INTERVAL '10' SECOND PRECEDING);
```

To test the query

1. Set up an application by following the Getting Started Exercise.

2. Replace the SELECT statement in the application code with the preceding SELECT query. The resulting application code is the following.

```
1  CREATE OR REPLACE STREAM "DESTINATION_SQL_STREAM" (
2                               ticker_symbol VARCHAR(10),
3                               Avg_Percent_Change double);
4  CREATE OR REPLACE PUMP "STREAM_PUMP" AS
5     INSERT INTO "DESTINATION_SQL_STREAM"
6        SELECT STREAM Ticker_Symbol,
7                      AVG(Change / (Price - Change)) over W1 as Avg_Percent_Change
8        FROM "SOURCE_SQL_STREAM_001"
9        WINDOW W1 AS (
10               PARTITION BY ticker_symbol
11               RANGE INTERVAL '10' SECOND PRECEDING);
```

Example 3: Query Data from Multiple Sliding Windows on the Same Stream

You can write queries to emit output in which each column value is calculated using different sliding windows defined over the same stream.

In the following example, the query emits the output ticker, price, a2, and a10. It emits output for ticker symbols whose two-row moving average crosses the ten-row moving average. The a2 and a10 column values are derived from two-row and ten-row sliding windows.

```
1  CREATE OR REPLACE STREAM "DESTINATION_SQL_STREAM" (
2                               ticker_symbol      VARCHAR(12),
3                               price              double,
4                               average_last2rows  double,
5                               average_last10rows double);
6
7  CREATE OR REPLACE PUMP "myPump" AS INSERT INTO "DESTINATION_SQL_STREAM"
8  SELECT STREAM ticker_symbol,
9               price,
10              avg(price) over last2rows,
11              avg(price) over last10rows
12 FROM SOURCE_SQL_STREAM_001
13 WINDOW
14    last2rows AS (PARTITION BY ticker_symbol ROWS 2 PRECEDING),
15    last10rows AS (PARTITION BY ticker_symbol ROWS 10 PRECEDING);
```

To test this query against the demo stream, follow the test procedure described in Example 1.

Streaming Data Operations: Stream Joins

You can have multiple in-application streams in your application. You can write `JOIN` queries to correlate data arriving on these streams. For example, suppose you have the following in-application streams:

- **OrderStream** – Receives stock orders being placed.

```
1 (orderId SqlType, ticker SqlType, amount SqlType, ROWTIME TimeStamp)
```

- **TradeStream** – Receives resulting stock trades for those orders.

```
1 (tradeId SqlType, orderId SqlType, ticker SqlType, amount SqlType, ticker SqlType, amount
    SqlType, ROWTIME TimeStamp)
```

The following are `JOIN` query examples that correlate data on these streams.

Example 1: Report Orders Where There Are Trades Within One Minute of the Order Being Placed

In this example, your query joins both the `OrderStream` and `TradeStream`. However, because we want only trades placed one minute after the orders, the query defines the 1-minute window over the `TradeStream`. For information about windowed queries, see Sliding Windows.

```
1 SELECT STREAM
2     ROWTIME,
3     o.orderId, o.ticker, o.amount AS orderAmount,
4     t.amount AS tradeAmount
5 FROM OrderStream AS o
6 JOIN TradeStream OVER (RANGE INTERVAL '1' MINUTE PRECEDING) AS t
7 ON  o.orderId = t.orderId;
```

You can define the windows explicitly using the `WINDOW` clause and writing the preceding query as follows:

```
1 SELECT STREAM
2     ROWTIME,
3     o.orderId, o.ticker, o.amount AS orderAmount,
4     t.amount AS tradeAmount
5 FROM OrderStream AS o
6 JOIN TradeStream OVER t
7 ON o.orderId = t.orderId
8 WINDOW t AS
9     (RANGE INTERVAL '1' MINUTE PRECEDING)
```

When you include this query in your application code, the application code runs continuously. For each arriving record on the `OrderStream`, the application emits an output if there are trades within the 1-minute window following the order being placed.

The join in the preceding query is an inner join where the query emits records in `OrderStream` for which there is a matching record in `TradeStream` (and vice versa). Using an outer join you can create another interesting scenario. Suppose you want stock orders for which there are no trades within one minute of stock order being placed, and trades reported within the same window but for some other orders. This is example of an *outer join*.

```
1 SELECT STREAM
2     ROWTIME,
3     o.orderId, o.ticker, o.amount AS orderAmount,
4     t.ticker, t.tradeId, t.amount AS tradeAmount,
5 FROM OrderStream AS o
```

```
6 OUTER JOIN TradeStream OVER (RANGE INTERVAL '1' MINUTE PRECEDING) AS t
7 ON    o.orderId = t.orderId;
```

Example Applications

This section provides examples of creating and working with applications in Amazon Kinesis Data Analytics. They include example code and step-by-step instructions to help you create Kinesis data analytics applications and test your results.

Before you explore these examples, we recommend that you first review Amazon Kinesis Data Analytics: How It Works and Getting Started with Amazon Kinesis Data Analytics.

Topics

- Examples: Transforming Data
- Examples: Joins
- Examples: Machine Learning
- Examples: Alerts and Errors
- Examples: Solution Accelerators

Examples: Transforming Data

There are times when your application code must preprocess incoming records before performing any analytics in Amazon Kinesis Data Analytics. This can happen for various reasons, such as when records don't conform to the supported record formats, resulting in unnormalized columns in the in-application input streams.

This section provides examples of how to use the available string functions to normalize data, how to extract information that you need from string columns, and so on. The section also points to date time functions that you might find useful.

Preprocessing Streams with Lambda

For information about preprocessing streams with AWS Lambda, see Preprocessing Data Using a Lambda Function.

Topics

- Preprocessing Streams with Lambda
- Examples: Transforming String Values
- Example: Transforming DateTime Values
- Example: Transforming Multiple Data Types

Examples: Transforming String Values

Amazon Kinesis Data Analytics supports formats such as JSON and CSV for records on a streaming source. For details, see RecordFormat. These records then map to rows in an in-application stream as per the input configuration. For details, see Configuring Application Input. The input configuration specifies how record fields in the streaming source map to columns in an in-application stream.

This mapping works when records on the streaming source follow the supported formats, which results in an in-application stream with normalized data. But what if data on your streaming source does not conform to supported standards? For example, what if your streaming source contains data such as clickstream data, IoT sensors, and application logs?

Consider these examples:

- Streaming source contains application logs – The application logs follow the standard Apache log format, and are written to the stream using JSON format.

```
1 {
2    "Log":"192.168.254.30 - John [24/May/2004:22:01:02 -0700] "GET /icons/apache_pb.gif HTTP
        /1.1" 304 0"
3 }
```

  For more information about the standard Apache log format, see Log Files on the Apache website.

- Streaming source contains semi-structured data – The following example shows two records. The `Col_E_Unstructured` field value is a series of comma-separated values. There are five columns: the first four have string type values, and the last column contains comma-separated values.

```
1  { "Col_A" : "string",
2    "Col_B" : "string",
3    "Col_C" : "string",
4    "Col_D" : "string",
5    "Col_E_Unstructured" : "value,value,value,value"}
6
7  { "Col_A" : "string",
8    "Col_B" : "string",
9    "Col_C" : "string",
10   "Col_D" : "string",
11   "Col_E_Unstructured" : "value,value,value,value"}
```

- Records on your streaming source contain URLs, and you need a portion of the URL domain name for analytics.

```
1 { "referrer" : "http://www.amazon.com"}
2 { "referrer" : "http://www.stackoverflow.com" }
```

In such cases, the following two-step process generally works for creating in-application streams that contain normalized data:

1. Configure application input to map the unstructured field to a column of the `VARCHAR(N)` type in the in-application input stream that is created.

2. In your application code, use string functions to split this single column into multiple columns and then save the rows in another in-application stream. This in-application stream that your application code creates will have normalized data. You can then perform analytics on this in-application stream.

Amazon Kinesis Data Analytics provides the following string operations, standard SQL functions, and extensions to the SQL standard for working with string columns:

- **String operators** – Operators such as LIKE and SIMILAR are useful in comparing strings. For more information, see String Operators in the *Amazon Kinesis Data Analytics SQL Reference*.
- **SQL functions** – The following functions are useful when manipulating individual strings. For more information, see String and Search Functions in the *Amazon Kinesis Data Analytics SQL Reference*.
  - CHAR_LENGTH – Provides the length of a string.
  - INITCAP – Returns a converted version of the input string such that the first character of each space-delimited word is uppercase, and all other characters are lowercase.
  - LOWER/UPPER – Converts a string to lowercase or uppercase.
  - OVERLAY – Replaces a portion of the first string argument (the original string) with the second string argument (the replacement string).
  - POSITION – Searches for a string within another string.
  - REGEX_REPLACE – Replaces a substring with an alternative substring.
  - SUBSTRING – Extracts a portion of a source string starting at a specific position.
  - TRIM – Removes instances of the specified character from the beginning or end of the source string.
- **SQL extensions** – These are useful for working with unstructured strings such as logs and URIs. For more information, see Log Parsing Functions in the *Amazon Kinesis Data Analytics SQL Reference*.
  - FAST_REGEX_LOG_PARSER – Works similar to the regex parser, but it takes several shortcuts to ensure faster results. For example, the fast regex parser stops at the first match it finds (known as *lazy semantics*).
  - FIXED_COLUMN_LOG_PARSE – Parses fixed-width fields and automatically converts them to the given SQL types.
  - REGEX_LOG_PARSE – Parses a string based on default Java regular expression patterns.
  - SYS_LOG_PARSE – Parses entries commonly found in UNIX/Linux system logs.
  - VARIABLE_COLUMN_LOG_PARSE – Splits an input string into fields separated by a delimiter character or a delimiter string.
  - W3C_LOG_PARSE – Can be used for quickly formatting Apache logs.

For examples using these functions, see the following topics:

Topics

- Example: Extracting a Portion of a String (SUBSTRING Function)
- Example: Replacing a Substring using Regex (REGEX_REPLACE Function)
- Example: Parsing Log Strings Based on Regular Expressions (REGEX_LOG_PARSE Function)
- Example: Parsing Web Logs (W3C_LOG_PARSE Function)
- Example: Split Strings into Multiple Fields (VARIABLE_COLUMN_LOG_PARSE Function)

Example: Extracting a Portion of a String (SUBSTRING Function)

This example uses the `SUBSTRING` function to transform a string in Amazon Kinesis Data Analytics. The `SUBSTRING` function extracts a portion of a source string starting at a specific position. For more information, see SUBSTRING in the *Amazon Kinesis Data Analytics SQL Reference*.

In this example, you write the following records to an Amazon Kinesis data stream.

```
1 { "REFERRER" : "http://www.amazon.com" }
2 { "REFERRER" : "http://www.amazon.com"}
3 { "REFERRER" : "http://www.amazon.com"}
4 ...
```

You then create an Amazon Kinesis data analytics application on the console, using the Kinesis data stream as the streaming source. The discovery process reads sample records on the streaming source and infers an in-application schema with one column (`REFERRER`), as shown.

Then, you use the application code with the `SUBSTRING` function to parse the URL string to retrieve the company name. Then you insert the resulting data into another in-application stream, as shown following:

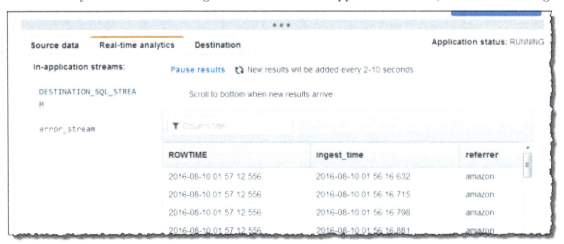

Topics

- Step 1: Create a Kinesis Data Stream
- Step 2: Create the Kinesis Data Analytics Application

Step 1: Create a Kinesis Data Stream

Create an Amazon Kinesis data stream and populate the log records as follows:

1. Sign in to the AWS Management Console and open the Kinesis console at https://console.aws.amazon.com/kinesis.

2. Choose **Data Streams** in the navigation pane.

3. Choose **Create Kinesis stream**, and create a stream with one shard. For more information, see Create a Stream in the *Amazon Kinesis Data Streams Developer Guide.*

4. Run the following Python code to populate sample log records. This simple code continuously writes the same log record to the stream.

```python
import json
import boto3
import random

kinesis = boto3.client('kinesis')
def getReferrer():
    data = {}
    data['REFERRER'] = 'http://www.amazon.com'
    return data

while True:
        data = json.dumps(getReferrer())
        print(data)
        kinesis.put_record(
                StreamName="teststreamforkinesisanalyticsapps",
                Data=data,
                PartitionKey="partitionkey")
```

Step 2: Create the Kinesis Data Analytics Application

Next, create an Amazon Kinesis data analytics application as follows:

1. Open the Kinesis Data Analytics console at https://console.aws.amazon.com/kinesisanalytics.

2. Choose **Create application**, type an application name, and choose **Create application**.

3. On the application details page, choose **Connect streaming data**.

4. On the **Connect to source** page, do the following:

   1. Choose the stream that you created in the preceding section.

   2. Choose the option to create an IAM role.

   3. Choose **Discover schema**. Wait for the console to show the inferred schema and samples records used to infer the schema for the in-application stream created. The inferred schema has only one column.

   4. Choose **Save and continue**.

5. On the application details page, choose **Go to SQL editor**. To start the application, choose **Yes, start application** in the dialog box that appears.

6. In the SQL editor, write the application code, and verify the results as follows:

    1. Copy the following application code and paste it into the editor.

```
1 -- CREATE OR REPLACE STREAM for cleaned up referrer
2 CREATE OR REPLACE STREAM "DESTINATION_SQL_STREAM" (
3     "ingest_time" TIMESTAMP,
4     "referrer" VARCHAR(32));
5
6 CREATE OR REPLACE PUMP "myPUMP" AS
7     INSERT INTO "DESTINATION_SQL_STREAM"
8         SELECT STREAM
9             "APPROXIMATE_ARRIVAL_TIME",
10            SUBSTRING("referrer", 12, (POSITION('.com' IN "referrer") - POSITION('www.' IN
                    "referrer") - 4))
11        FROM "SOURCE_SQL_STREAM_001";
```

    2. Choose **Save and run SQL**. On the **Real-time analytics **tab, you can see all the in-application streams that the application created and verify the data.

Example: Replacing a Substring using Regex (REGEX_REPLACE Function)

This example uses the `REGEX_REPLACE` function to transform a string in Amazon Kinesis Data Analytics. `REGEX_REPLACE` replaces a substring with an alternative substring. For more information, see REGEX_REPLACE in the *Amazon Kinesis Data Analytics SQL Reference*.

In this example, you write the following records to an Amazon Kinesis data stream:

```
1  { "REFERRER" : "http://www.amazon.com" }
2  { "REFERRER" : "http://www.amazon.com"}
3  { "REFERRER" : "http://www.amazon.com"}
4  ...
```

You then create an Amazon Kinesis data analytics application on the console, with the Kinesis data stream as the streaming source. The discovery process reads sample records on the streaming source and infers an in-application schema with one column (REFERRER) as shown.

Then, you use the application code with the `REGEX_REPLACE` function to convert the URL to use `https://` instead of `http://`. You insert the resulting data into another in-application stream, as shown following:

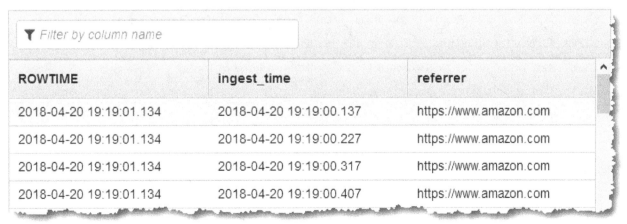

Topics

- Step 1: Create a Kinesis Data Stream
- Step 2: Create the Kinesis Data Analytics Application

Step 1: Create a Kinesis Data Stream

Create an Amazon Kinesis data stream and populate the log records as follows:

1. Sign in to the AWS Management Console and open the Kinesis console at https://console.aws.amazon.com/kinesis.

2. Choose **Data Streams** in the navigation pane.

3. Choose **Create Kinesis stream**, and create a stream with one shard. For more information, see Create a Stream in the *Amazon Kinesis Data Streams Developer Guide*.

4. Run the following Python code to populate the sample log records. This simple code continuously writes the same log record to the stream.

```python
import json
import boto3
import random

kinesis = boto3.client('kinesis')
def getReferrer():
    data = {}
    data['REFERRER'] = 'http://www.amazon.com'
    return data

while True:
        data = json.dumps(getReferrer())
        print(data)
        kinesis.put_record(
                StreamName="teststreamforkinesisanalyticsapps",
                Data=data,
                PartitionKey="partitionkey")
```

Step 2: Create the Kinesis Data Analytics Application

Next, create an Amazon Kinesis data analytics application as follows:

1. Open the Kinesis Data Analytics console at https://console.aws.amazon.com/kinesisanalytics.

2. Choose **Create application**, type an application name, and choose **Create application**.

3. On the application details page, choose **Connect streaming data**.

4. On the **Connect to source** page, do the following:

    1. Choose the stream that you created in the preceding section.

    2. Choose the option to create an IAM role.

    3. Choose **Discover schema**. Wait for the console to show the inferred schema and samples records used to infer the schema for the in-application stream created. The inferred schema has only one column.

    4. Choose **Save and continue**.

112

5. On the application details page, choose **Go to SQL editor**. To start the application, choose **Yes, start application** in the dialog box that appears.

6. In the SQL editor, write the application code and verify the results as follows:

   1. Copy the following application code, and paste it into the editor:

```
1  -- CREATE OR REPLACE STREAM for cleaned up referrer
2  CREATE OR REPLACE STREAM "DESTINATION_SQL_STREAM" (
3      "ingest_time" TIMESTAMP,
4      "referrer" VARCHAR(32));
5
6  CREATE OR REPLACE PUMP "myPUMP" AS
7    INSERT INTO "DESTINATION_SQL_STREAM"
8      SELECT STREAM
9        "APPROXIMATE_ARRIVAL_TIME",
10       REGEX_REPLACE("REFERRER", 'http://', 'https://', 1, 0)
11     FROM "SOURCE_SQL_STREAM_001";
```

   2. Choose **Save and run SQL**. On the **Real-time analytics **tab, you can see all the in-application streams that the application created and verify the data.

Example: Parsing Log Strings Based on Regular Expressions (REGEX_LOG_PARSE Function)

This example uses the `REGEX_LOG_PARSE` function to transform a string in Amazon Kinesis Data Analytics. `REGEX_LOG_PARSE` parses a string based on default Java regular expression patterns. For more information, see REGEX_LOG_PARSE in the *Amazon Kinesis Data Analytics SQL Reference.*

In this example, you write the following records to an Amazon Kinesis stream:

```
1 {"LOGENTRY": "203.0.113.24 - - [25/Mar/2018:15:25:37 -0700] \"GET /index.php HTTP/1.1\" 200 125
     \"-\" \"Mozilla/5.0 [en] Gecko/20100101 Firefox/52.0\""}
2 {"LOGENTRY": "203.0.113.24 - - [25/Mar/2018:15:25:37 -0700] \"GET /index.php HTTP/1.1\" 200 125
     \"-\" \"Mozilla/5.0 [en] Gecko/20100101 Firefox/52.0\""}
3 {"LOGENTRY": "203.0.113.24 - - [25/Mar/2018:15:25:37 -0700] \"GET /index.php HTTP/1.1\" 200 125
     \"-\" \"Mozilla/5.0 [en] Gecko/20100101 Firefox/52.0\""}
4 ...
```

You then create an Amazon Kinesis data analytics application on the console, with the Kinesis data stream as the streaming source. The discovery process reads sample records on the streaming source and infers an in-application schema with one column (LOGENTRY), as shown following.

ROWTIME TIMESTAMP	LOGENTRY VARCHAR(256)
2018-05-09 18:12:18.552	203.0.113.24 - - [25/Mar/2018:15:25:37 -0700] "GET /index.php HTTP/1.1"
2018-05-09 18:12:18.552	203.0.113.24 - - [25/Mar/2018:15:25:37 -0700] "GET /index.php HTTP/1.1"
2018-05-09 18:12:18.552	203.0.113.24 - - [25/Mar/2018:15:25:37 -0700] "GET /index.php HTTP/1.1"
2018-05-09 18:12:18.552	203.0.113.24 - - [25/Mar/2018:15:25:37 -0700] "GET /index.php HTTP/1.1"

Then, you use the application code with the `REGEX_LOG_PARSE` function to parse the log string to retrieve the data elements. You insert the resulting data into another in-application stream, as shown in the following screenshot:

ROWTIME	LOGENTRY	MATCH1	MATCH2
2018-05-09 18:16:11.616	203.0.113.24 - - [25/Mar	203.0.113.24 - - [25/Mar	125 "-" "Mozilla/5.0 [
2018-05-09 18:16:11.616	203.0.113.24 - - [25/Mar	203.0.113.24 - - [25/Mar	125 "-" "Mozilla/5.0 [
2018-05-09 18:16:11.616	203.0.113.24 - - [25/Mar	203.0.113.24 - - [25/Mar	125 "-" "Mozilla/5.0 [
2018-05-09 18:16:11.616	203.0.113.24 - - [25/Mar	203.0.113.24 - - [25/Mar	125 "-" "Mozilla/5.0 [

Topics

- Step 1: Create a Kinesis Data Stream

- Step 2: Create the Kinesis Data Analytics Application

Step 1: Create a Kinesis Data Stream

Create an Amazon Kinesis data stream and populate the log records as follows:

1. Sign in to the AWS Management Console and open the Kinesis console at https://console.aws.amazon. com/kinesis.

2. Choose **Data Streams** in the navigation pane.

3. Choose **Create Kinesis stream**, and create a stream with one shard. For more information, see Create a Stream in the *Amazon Kinesis Data Streams Developer Guide*.

4. Run the following Python code to populate sample log records. This simple code continuously writes the same log record to the stream.

```
1  import json
2  import boto3
3  import random
4
5  kinesis = boto3.client('kinesis')
6  def getReferrer():
7      data = {}
8      data['LOGENTRY'] = '203.0.113.24 - - [25/Mar/2018:15:25:37 -0700] "GET /index.php HTTP
          /1.1" 200 125 "-" "Mozilla/5.0 [en] Gecko/20100101 Firefox/52.0"'
9      return data
10
11 while True:
12         data = json.dumps(getReferrer())
13         print(data)
14         kinesis.put_record(
15             StreamName="teststreamforkinesisanalyticsapps",
16             Data=data,
17             PartitionKey="partitionkey")
```

Step 2: Create the Kinesis Data Analytics Application

Next, create an Amazon Kinesis data analytics application as follows:

1. Open the Kinesis Data Analytics console at https://console.aws.amazon.com/kinesisanalytics.

2. Choose **Create application**, and specify an application name.

3. On the application details page, choose **Connect streaming data**.

4. On the **Connect to source** page, do the following:

   1. Choose the stream that you created in the preceding section.

   2. Choose the option to create an IAM role.

   3. Choose **Discover schema**. Wait for the console to show the inferred schema and samples records used to infer the schema for the in-application stream created. The inferred schema has only one column.

   4. Choose **Save and continue**.

5. On the application details page, choose **Go to SQL editor**. To start the application, choose **Yes, start application** in the dialog box that appears.

6. In the SQL editor, write the application code, and verify the results as follows:

   1. Copy the following application code and paste it into the editor.

```
1 CREATE OR REPLACE STREAM "DESTINATION_SQL_STREAM" (logentry VARCHAR(24), match1 VARCHAR
      (24), match2 VARCHAR(24));
2
3 CREATE OR REPLACE PUMP "STREAM_PUMP" AS INSERT INTO "DESTINATION_SQL_STREAM"
4     SELECT STREAM T.LOGENTRY, T.REC.COLUMN1, T.REC.COLUMN2
5     FROM
6         (SELECT STREAM LOGENTRY,
7             REGEX_LOG_PARSE(LOGENTRY, '(\w.+) (\d.+) (\w.+) (\w.+)') AS REC
8             FROM SOURCE_SQL_STREAM_001) AS T;
```

   2. Choose **Save and run SQL**. On the **Real-time analytics **tab, you can see all the in-application streams that the application created and verify the data.

Example: Parsing Web Logs (W3C_LOG_PARSE Function)

This example uses the `W3C_LOG_PARSE` function to transform a string in Amazon Kinesis Data Analytics. You can use `W3C_LOG_PARSE` to format Apache logs quickly. For more information, see W3C_LOG_PARSE in the *Amazon Kinesis Data Analytics SQL Reference.*

In this example, you write log records to an Amazon Kinesis data stream. Example logs are shown following:

```
1 {"Log":"192.168.254.30 - John [24/May/2004:22:01:02 -0700] "GET /icons/apache_pba.gif HTTP/1.1"
    304 0"}
2 {"Log":"192.168.254.30 - John [24/May/2004:22:01:03 -0700] "GET /icons/apache_pbb.gif HTTP/1.1"
    304 0"}
3 {"Log":"192.168.254.30 - John [24/May/2004:22:01:04 -0700] "GET /icons/apache_pbc.gif HTTP/1.1"
    304 0"}
4 ...
```

You then create an Amazon Kinesis data analytics application on the console, with the Kinesis data stream as the streaming source. The discovery process reads sample records on the streaming source and infers an in-application schema with one column (log), as shown following:

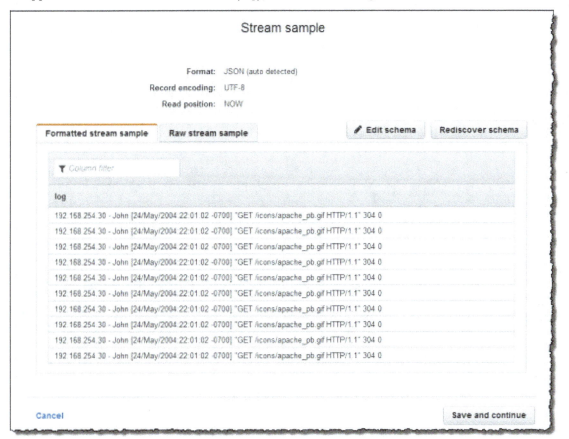

Then, you use the application code with the `W3C_LOG_PARSE` function to parse the log, and create another in-application stream with various log fields in separate columns, as shown following:

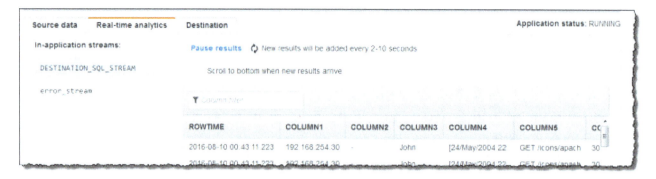

Topics

- Step 1: Create a Kinesis Data Stream
- Step 2: Create the Kinesis Data Analytics Application

Step 1: Create a Kinesis Data Stream

Create an Amazon Kinesis data stream, and populate the log records as follows:

1. Sign in to the AWS Management Console and open the Kinesis console at https://console.aws.amazon.com/kinesis.

2. Choose **Data Streams** in the navigation pane.

3. Choose **Create Kinesis stream**, and create a stream with one shard. For more information, see Create a Stream in the *Amazon Kinesis Data Streams Developer Guide*.

4. Run the following Python code to populate the sample log records. This simple code continuously writes the same log record to the stream.

```
1 import json
2 from boto import kinesis
3 import random
4
5 kinesis = kinesis.connect_to_region("us-east-1")
6 def getHighHeartRate():
7     data = {}
8     data['log'] = '192.168.254.30 - John [24/May/2004:22:01:02 -0700] "GET /icons/apache_pb
          .gif HTTP/1.1" 304 0'
9     return data
10
11 while True:
12         data = json.dumps(getHighHeartRate())
13         print data
14         kinesis.put_record("stream-name", data, "partitionkey")
```

Step 2: Create the Kinesis Data Analytics Application

Create an Amazon Kinesis data analytics application as follows:

1. Open the Kinesis Data Analytics console at https://console.aws.amazon.com/kinesisanalytics.

2. Choose **Create application**, type an application name, and choose **Create application**.

3. On the application details page, choose **Connect streaming data**.

4. On the **Connect to source** page, do the following:

    1. Choose the stream that you created in the preceding section.

    2. Choose the option to create an IAM role.

    3. Choose **Discover schema**. Wait for the console to show the inferred schema and samples records used to infer the schema for the in-application stream created. The inferred schema has only one column.

    4. Choose **Save and continue**.

5. On the application details page, choose **Go to SQL editor**. To start the application, choose **Yes, start application** in the dialog box that appears.

6. In the SQL editor, write the application code, and verify the results as follows:

    1. Copy the following application code and paste it into the editor.

```
1  CREATE OR REPLACE STREAM "DESTINATION_SQL_STREAM" (
2  column1 VARCHAR(16),
3  column2 VARCHAR(16),
4  column3 VARCHAR(16),
5  column4 VARCHAR(16),
6  column5 VARCHAR(16),
7  column6 VARCHAR(16),
8  column7 VARCHAR(16));
9
10 CREATE OR REPLACE PUMP "myPUMP" AS
11 INSERT INTO "DESTINATION_SQL_STREAM"
12        SELECT STREAM
13            l.r.COLUMN1,
14            l.r.COLUMN2,
15            l.r.COLUMN3,
16            l.r.COLUMN4,
17            l.r.COLUMN5,
18            l.r.COLUMN6,
19            l.r.COLUMN7
20        FROM (SELECT STREAM W3C_LOG_PARSE("log", 'COMMON')
21            FROM "SOURCE_SQL_STREAM_001") AS l(r);
```

    2. Choose **Save and run SQL**. On the **Real-time analytics **tab, you can see all the in-application streams that the application created and verify the data.

119

Example: Split Strings into Multiple Fields (VARIABLE_COL-UMN_LOG_PARSE Function)

This example uses the `VARIABLE_COLUMN_LOG_PARSE` function to manipulate strings in Kinesis Data Analytics. `VARIABLE_COLUMN_LOG_PARSE` splits an input string into fields separated by a delimiter character or a delimiter string. For more information, see VARIABLE_COLUMN_LOG_PARSE in the *Amazon Kinesis Data Analytics SQL Reference*.

In this example, you write semi-structured records to an Amazon Kinesis data stream. The example records are as follows:

```
1 { "Col_A" : "string",
2   "Col_B" : "string",
3   "Col_C" : "string",
4   "Col_D_Unstructured" : "value,value,value,value"}
5 { "Col_A" : "string",
6   "Col_B" : "string",
7   "Col_C" : "string",
8   "Col_D_Unstructured" : "value,value,value,value"}
```

You then create an Amazon Kinesis data analytics application on the console, using the Kinesis stream as the streaming source. The discovery process reads sample records on the streaming source and infers an in-application schema with four columns, as shown following:

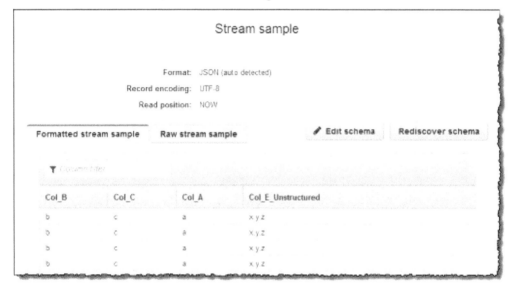

Then, you use the application code with the `VARIABLE_COLUMN_LOG_PARSE` function to parse the comma-separated values, and insert normalized rows in another in-application stream, as shown following:

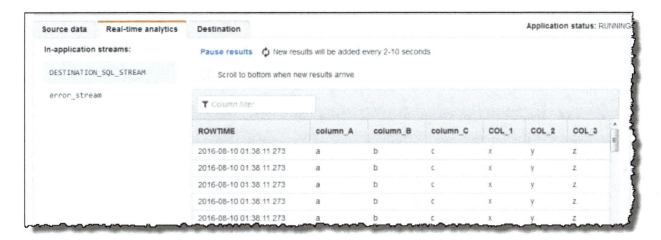

Topics

- Step 1: Create a Kinesis Data Stream
- Step 2: Create the Kinesis Data Analytics Application

Step 1: Create a Kinesis Data Stream

Create an Amazon Kinesis data stream and populate the log records as follows:

1. Sign in to the AWS Management Console and open the Kinesis console at https://console.aws.amazon.com/kinesis.

2. Choose **Data Streams** in the navigation pane.

3. Choose **Create Kinesis stream**, and create a stream with one shard. For more information, see Create a Stream in the *Amazon Kinesis Data Streams Developer Guide*.

4. Run the following Python code to populate the sample log records. This simple code continuously writes the same log record to the stream.

```python
import json
from boto import kinesis
import random

kinesis = kinesis.connect_to_region("us-east-1")
def getHighHeartRate():
    data = {}
    data['Col_A'] = 'a'
    data['Col_B'] = 'b'
    data['Col_C'] = 'c'
    data['Col_E_Unstructured'] = 'x,y,z'
    return data

while True:
        data = json.dumps(getHighHeartRate())
        print data
        kinesis.put_record("teststreamforkinesisanalyticsapps", data, "partitionkey")
```

Step 2: Create the Kinesis Data Analytics Application

Create an Amazon Kinesis data analytics application as follows:

1. Open the Kinesis Data Analytics console at https://console.aws.amazon.com/kinesisanalytics.

2. Choose **Create application**, type an application name, and choose **Create application**.

3. On the application details page, choose **Connect streaming data**.

4. On the **Connect to source** page, do the following:

    1. Choose the stream that you created in the preceding section.

    2. Choose the option to create an IAM role.

    3. Choose **Discover schema**. Wait for the console to show the inferred schema and samples records used to infer the schema for the in-application stream created. Note that the inferred schema has only one column.

    4. Choose **Save and continue**.

5. On the application details page, choose **Go to SQL editor**. To start the application, choose **Yes, start application** in the dialog box that appears.

6. In the SQL editor, write application code, and verify the results:

    1. Copy the following application code and paste it into the editor:

```
 1 CREATE OR REPLACE STREAM "DESTINATION_SQL_STREAM"(
 2          "column_A" VARCHAR(16),
 3          "column_B" VARCHAR(16),
 4          "column_C" VARCHAR(16),
 5          "COL_1" VARCHAR(16),
 6          "COL_2" VARCHAR(16),
 7          "COL_3" VARCHAR(16));
 8
 9 CREATE OR REPLACE PUMP "SECOND_STREAM_PUMP" AS
10 INSERT INTO "DESTINATION_SQL_STREAM"
11    SELECT STREAM  t."Col_A", t."Col_B", t."Col_C",
12                   t.r."COL_1", t.r."COL_2", t.r."COL_3"
13    FROM (SELECT STREAM
14          "Col_A", "Col_B", "Col_C",
15          VARIABLE_COLUMN_LOG_PARSE ("Col_E_Unstructured",
16                               'COL_1 TYPE VARCHAR(16), COL_2 TYPE VARCHAR(16),
                                       COL_3 TYPE VARCHAR(16)',
17                               ',') AS r
18        FROM "SOURCE_SQL_STREAM_001") as t;
```

    2. Choose **Save and run SQL**. On the **Real-time analytics **tab, you can see all the in-application streams that the application created and verify the data.

Example: Transforming DateTime Values

Amazon Kinesis Data Analytics supports converting columns to time stamps. For example, you might want to use your own time stamp as part of a GROUP BY clause as another time-based window, in addition to the ROWTIME column. Kinesis Data Analytics provides operations and SQL functions for working with date and time fields.

- **Date and time operators** – You can perform arithmetic operations on dates, times, and interval data types. For more information, see Date, Timestamp, and Interval Operators in the *Amazon Kinesis Data Analytics SQL Reference*.

- **SQL Functions** – These include the following. For more information, see Date and Time Functions in the *Amazon Kinesis Data Analytics SQL Reference*.

  - EXTRACT() – Extracts one field from a date, time, time stamp, or interval expression.
  - CURRENT_TIME – Returns the time when the query executes (UTC).
  - CURRENT_DATE – Returns the date when the query executes (UTC).
  - CURRENT_TIMESTAMP – Returns the time stamp when the query executes (UTC).
  - LOCALTIME – Returns the current time when the query executes as defined by the environment on which Kinesis Data Analytics is running (UTC).
  - LOCALTIMESTAMP – Returns the current time stamp as defined by the environment on which Kinesis Data Analytics is running (UTC).

- **SQL Extensions** – These include the following. For more information, see Date and Time Functions and Datetime Conversion Functions in the *Amazon Kinesis Data Analytics SQL Reference*.

  - CURRENT_ROW_TIMESTAMP – Returns a new time stamp for each row in the stream.
  - TSDIFF – Returns the difference of two time stamps in milliseconds.
  - CHAR_TO_DATE – Converts a string to a date.
  - CHAR_TO_TIME – Converts a string to time.
  - CHAR_TO_TIMESTAMP – Converts a string to a time stamp.
  - DATE_TO_CHAR – Converts a date to a string.
  - TIME_TO_CHAR – Converts a time to a string.
  - TIMESTAMP_TO_CHAR – Converts a time stamp to a string.

Most of the preceding SQL functions use a format to convert the columns. The format is flexible. For example, you can specify the format yyyy-MM-dd hh:mm:ss to convert an input string 2009-09-16 03:15:24 into a time stamp. For more information, Char To Timestamp(Sys) in the *Amazon Kinesis Data Analytics SQL Reference*.

Example: Transforming Dates

In this example, you write the following records to an Amazon Kinesis data stream.

```
1 {"EVENT_TIME": "2018-05-09T12:50:41.337510", "TICKER": "AAPL"}
2 {"EVENT_TIME": "2018-05-09T12:50:41.427227", "TICKER": "MSFT"}
3 {"EVENT_TIME": "2018-05-09T12:50:41.520549", "TICKER": "INTC"}
4 {"EVENT_TIME": "2018-05-09T12:50:41.610145", "TICKER": "MSFT"}
5 {"EVENT_TIME": "2018-05-09T12:50:41.704395", "TICKER": "AAPL"}
6 ...
```

You then create an Amazon Kinesis data analytics application on the console, with the Kinesis stream as the streaming source. The discovery process reads sample records on the streaming source and infers an in-application schema with two columns (`EVENT_TIME` and `TICKER`) as shown.

ROWTIME	EVENT_TIME TIMESTAMP	TICKER VARCHAR(4)	PARTITION_KEY	SEQUENCE
2018-05-09 21:48:06.198	2018-05-09 14:48:05.169	INTC	partitionkey	4958385475
2018-05-09 21:48:06.198	2018-05-09 14:48:05.259	TBV	partitionkey	4958385475
2018-05-09 21:48:06.198	2018-05-09 14:48:05.348	INTC	partitionkey	4958385475
2018-05-09 21:48:06.198	2018-05-09 14:48:05.436	MSFT	partitionkey	4958385475

Then, you use the application code with SQL functions to convert the `EVENT_TIME` time stamp field in various ways. You then insert the resulting data into another in-application stream, as shown in the following screenshot:

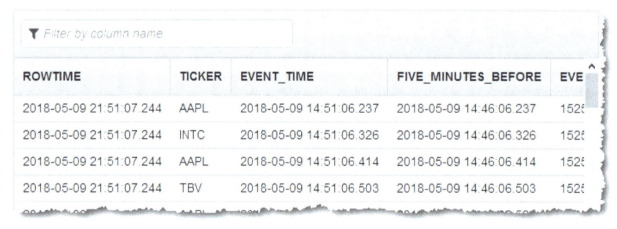

ROWTIME	TICKER	EVENT_TIME	FIVE_MINUTES_BEFORE	EVE
2018-05-09 21:51:07.244	AAPL	2018-05-09 14:51:06.237	2018-05-09 14:46:06.237	1525
2018-05-09 21:51:07.244	INTC	2018-05-09 14:51:06.326	2018-05-09 14:46:06.326	1525
2018-05-09 21:51:07.244	AAPL	2018-05-09 14:51:06.414	2018-05-09 14:46:06.414	1525
2018-05-09 21:51:07.244	TBV	2018-05-09 14:51:06.503	2018-05-09 14:46:06.503	1525

Step 1: Create a Kinesis Data Stream

Create an Amazon Kinesis data stream and populate it with event time and ticker records as follows:

1. Sign in to the AWS Management Console and open the Kinesis console at https://console.aws.amazon. com/kinesis.

2. Choose **Data Streams** in the navigation pane.

3. Choose **Create Kinesis stream**, and create a stream with one shard.

4. Run the following Python code to populate the stream with sample data. This simple code continuously writes a record with a random ticker symbol and the current time stamp to the stream.

```
1 import json
2 import boto3
3 import random
4 import datetime
5
```

```
 6 kinesis = boto3.client('kinesis')
 7 def getReferrer():
 8     data = {}
 9     now = datetime.datetime.now()
10     str_now = now.isoformat()
11     data['EVENT_TIME'] = str_now
12     data['TICKER'] = random.choice(['AAPL', 'AMZN', 'MSFT', 'INTC', 'TBV'])
13     return data
14
15 while True:
16         data = json.dumps(getReferrer())
17         print(data)
18         kinesis.put_record(
19                 StreamName="teststreamforkinesisanalyticsapps",
```

Step 2: Create the Amazon Kinesis Data Analytics Application

Create an application as follows:

1. Open the Kinesis Data Analytics console at https://console.aws.amazon.com/kinesisanalytics.

2. Choose **Create application**, type an application name, and choose **Create application**.

3. On the application details page, choose **Connect streaming data** to connect to the source.

4. On the **Connect to source** page, do the following:

   1. Choose the stream that you created in the preceding section.

   2. Choose to create an IAM role.

   3. Choose **Discover schema**. Wait for the console to show the inferred schema and the sample records that are used to infer the schema for the in-application stream created. The inferred schema has two columns.

   4. Choose **Edit Schema**. Change the **Column type** of the **EVENT_TIME** column to TIMESTAMP.

   5. Choose **Save schema and update stream samples**. After the console saves the schema, choose **Exit**.

   6. Choose **Save and continue**.

5. On the application details page, choose **Go to SQL editor**. To start the application, choose **Yes, start application** in the dialog box that appears.

6. In the SQL editor, write the application code and verify the results as follows:

   1. Copy the following application code and paste it into the editor.

```
 1 CREATE OR REPLACE STREAM "DESTINATION_SQL_STREAM" (
 2     TICKER VARCHAR(4),
 3     event_time TIMESTAMP,
 4     five_minutes_before TIMESTAMP,
 5     event_unix_timestamp BIGINT,
 6     event_timestamp_as_char VARCHAR(50),
 7     event_second INTEGER);
 8
 9 CREATE OR REPLACE PUMP "STREAM_PUMP" AS INSERT INTO "DESTINATION_SQL_STREAM"
10
11 SELECT STREAM
```

```
12      TICKER,
13      EVENT_TIME,
14      EVENT_TIME - INTERVAL '5' MINUTE,
15      UNIX_TIMESTAMP(EVENT_TIME),
16      TIMESTAMP_TO_CHAR('yyyy-MM-dd hh:mm:ss', EVENT_TIME),
17      EXTRACT(SECOND FROM EVENT_TIME)
18 FROM "SOURCE_SQL_STREAM_001"
```

2. Choose **Save and run SQL**. On the **Real-time analytics **tab, you can see all the in-application streams that the application created and verify the data.

Example: Transforming Multiple Data Types

A common requirement in extract, transform, and load (ETL) applications is to process multiple record types on a streaming source. You can create Amazon Kinesis data analytics applications to process these kinds of streaming sources. The process is as follows:

1. First, you map the streaming source to an in-application input stream, similar to all other Kinesis data analytics applications.

2. Then, in your application code, you write SQL statements to retrieve rows of specific types from the in-application input stream. You then insert them into separate in-application streams. (You can create additional in-application streams in your application code.)

In this exercise, you have a streaming source that receives records of two types (`Order` and `Trade`). These are stock orders and corresponding trades. For each order, there can be zero or more trades. Example records of each type are shown following:

Order record

```
1 {"RecordType": "Order", "Oprice": 9047, "Otype": "Sell", "Oid": 3811, "Oticker": "AAAA"}
```

Trade record

```
1 {"RecordType": "Trade", "Tid": 1, "Toid": 3812, "Tprice": 2089, "Tticker": "BBBB"}
```

When you create an application using the AWS Management Console, the console displays the following inferred schema for the in-application input stream created. By default, the console names this in-application stream `SOURCE_SQL_STREAM_001`.

When you save the configuration, Amazon Kinesis Data Analytics continuously reads data from the streaming source and inserts rows in the in-application stream. You can now perform analytics on data in the in-application stream.

In the application code in this example, you first create two additional in-application streams, `Order_Stream` and `Trade_Stream`. You then filter the rows from the SOURCE_SQL_STREAM_001 stream based on the record type and insert them in the newly created streams using pumps. For information about this coding pattern, see Application Code.

1. Filter order and trade rows into separate in-application streams:

    1. Filter the order records in the SOURCE_SQL_STREAM_001, and save the orders in the `Order_Stream`.

       ```
        1 --Create Order_Stream.
        2 CREATE OR REPLACE STREAM "Order_Stream"
        3            (
        4                order_id     integer,
        5                order_type   varchar(10),
        6                ticker       varchar(4),
        7                order_price  DOUBLE,
        8                record_type  varchar(10)
        9            );
       10
       11 CREATE OR REPLACE PUMP "Order_Pump" AS
       12    INSERT INTO "Order_Stream"
       13       SELECT STREAM oid, otype,oticker, oprice, recordtype
       14       FROM   "SOURCE_SQL_STREAM_001"
       15       WHERE  recordtype = 'Order';
       ```

    2. Filter the trade records in the SOURCE_SQL_STREAM_001, and save the orders in the `Trade_Stream`.

       ```
        1 --Create Trade_Stream.
        2 CREATE OR REPLACE STREAM "Trade_Stream"
        3            (trade_id     integer,
        4             order_id     integer,
        5             trade_price  DOUBLE,
        6             ticker       varchar(4),
        7             record_type  varchar(10)
        8            );
        9
       10 CREATE OR REPLACE PUMP "Trade_Pump" AS
       11    INSERT INTO "Trade_Stream"
       12       SELECT STREAM tid, toid, tprice, tticker, recordtype
       13       FROM   "SOURCE_SQL_STREAM_001"
       14       WHERE  recordtype = 'Trade';
       ```

2. Now you can perform additional analytics on these streams. In this example, you count the number of trades by the ticker in a one-minute tumbling window and save the results to yet another stream, DESTINATION_SQL_STREAM.

   ```
    1 --do some analytics on the Trade_Stream and Order_Stream.
    2 -- To see results in console you must write to OPUT_SQL_STREAM.
    3
    4 CREATE OR REPLACE STREAM "DESTINATION_SQL_STREAM" (
    5            ticker  varchar(4),
    6            trade_count   integer
    7            );
    8
    9 CREATE OR REPLACE PUMP "Output_Pump" AS
   10    INSERT INTO "DESTINATION_SQL_STREAM"
   11       SELECT STREAM ticker, count(*) as trade_count
   ```

```
12        FROM    "Trade_Stream"
13        GROUP BY ticker,
14                    FLOOR("Trade_Stream".ROWTIME TO MINUTE);
```

You see the result, as shown following:

Topics

- Step 1: Prepare the Data
- Step 2: Create the Application

Next Step

Step 1: Prepare the Data

Step 1: Prepare the Data

Before you create an Amazon Kinesis data analytics application for this example, you create a Kinesis data stream to use as the streaming source for your application. You also run Python code to write simulated blood pressure data to the stream.

Topics

- Step 1.1: Create a Kinesis Data Stream
- Step 1.2: Write Sample Records to the Input Stream

Step 1.1: Create a Kinesis Data Stream

In this section, you create a Kinesis data stream named `ExampleInputStream`. You can create this data stream using the AWS Management Console or the AWS CLI.

- To use the console:

    1. Sign in to the AWS Management Console and open the Kinesis console at https://console.aws.amazon.com/kinesis.

    2. Choose **Data Streams** in the navigation pane. Then choose **Create Kinesis stream**.

    3. For the name, type **ExampleInputStream**. For the number of shards, type **1**.

- Alternatively, to use the AWS CLI to create the data stream, run the following command:

```
1 $ aws kinesis create-stream --stream-name ExampleInputStream --shard-count 1
```

Step 1.2: Write Sample Records to the Input Stream

In this step, you run Python code to continuously generate sample records and write them to the data stream that you created.

1. Install Python and pip.

   For information about installing Python, see Python.

   You can install dependencies using pip. For information about installing pip, see Installation in the pip documentation.

2. Run the following Python code. You can change the Region to the one you want to use for this example. The `put-record` command in the code writes the JSON records to the stream.

```
1 import json
2 from boto import kinesis
3 import random
4
5 kinesis = kinesis.connect_to_region("us-east-1")
6
7 # Generate normal blood pressure with a 0.995 probability
8 def getNormalBloodPressure():
9     data = {}
10    data['Systolic'] = random.randint(90, 120)
11    data['Diastolic'] = random.randint(60, 80)
12    data['BloodPressureLevel'] = 'NORMAL'
13    return data
14
```

```
15 # Generate high blood pressure with probability 0.005
16 def getHighBloodPressure():
17     data = {}
18     data['Systolic'] = random.randint(130, 200)
19     data['Diastolic'] = random.randint(90, 150)
20     data['BloodPressureLevel'] = 'HIGH'
21     return data
22
23 # Generate low blood pressure with probability 0.005
24 def getLowBloodPressure():
25     data = {}
26     data['Systolic'] = random.randint(50, 80)
27     data['Diastolic'] = random.randint(30, 50)
28     data['BloodPressureLevel'] = 'LOW'
29     return data
30
31 while True:
32     rnd = random.random()
33     if (rnd < 0.005):
34         data = json.dumps(getLowBloodPressure())
35         print(data)
36         kinesis.put_record("BloodPressureExampleInputStream", data, "partitionkey")
37     elif (rnd > 0.995):
38         data = json.dumps(getHighBloodPressure())
39         print(data)
40         kinesis.put_record("BloodPressureExampleInputStream", data, "partitionkey")
41     else:
42         data = json.dumps(getNormalBloodPressure())
43         print(data)
44         kinesis.put_record("BloodPressureExampleInputStream", data, "partitionkey")
```

The previous code writes to `ExampleInputStream` records similar to the following examples:

```
1  {"Systolic": 109, "Diastolic": 64, "BloodPressureLevel": "NORMAL"}
2  {"Systolic": 99, "Diastolic": 72, "BloodPressureLevel": "NORMAL"}
3  {"Systolic": 159, "Diastolic": 100, "BloodPressureLevel": "HIGH"}
4  {"Systolic": 94, "Diastolic": 75, "BloodPressureLevel": "NORMAL"}
5  {"Systolic": 91, "Diastolic": 78, "BloodPressureLevel": "NORMAL"}
6  {"Systolic": 91, "Diastolic": 74, "BloodPressureLevel": "NORMAL"}
7  {"Systolic": 102, "Diastolic": 75, "BloodPressureLevel": "NORMAL"}
8  {"Systolic": 50, "Diastolic": 31, "BloodPressureLevel": "LOW"}
9  {"Systolic": 100, "Diastolic": 66, "BloodPressureLevel": "NORMAL"}
10 {"Systolic": 115, "Diastolic": 65, "BloodPressureLevel": "NORMAL"}
11 {"Systolic": 99, "Diastolic": 74, "BloodPressureLevel": "NORMAL"}
```

Next Step
Step 2: Create an Analytics Application

Step 2: Create the Application

In this section, you create an Amazon Kinesis data analytics application. You then update the application by adding input configuration that maps the streaming source you created in the preceding section to an in-application input stream.

1. Open the Kinesis Data Analytics console at https://console.aws.amazon.com/kinesisanalytics.

2. Choose **Create application**. This example uses the application name **ProcessMultipleRecordTypes**.

3. On the application details page, choose **Connect streaming data** to connect to the source.

4. On the **Connect to source** page, do the following:

   1. Choose the stream that you created in Step 1: Prepare the Data.

   2. Choose to create an IAM role.

   3. Wait for the console to show the inferred schema and samples records that are used to infer the schema for the in-application stream created.

   4. Choose **Save and continue**.

5. On the application hub, choose **Go to SQL editor**. To start the application, choose **Yes, start application** in the dialog box that appears.

6. In the SQL editor, write the application code and verify the results:

   1. Copy the following application code and paste it into the editor.

```
1  --Create Order_Stream.
2  CREATE OR REPLACE STREAM "Order_Stream"
3           (
4               "order_id"     integer,
5               "order_type"   varchar(10),
6               "ticker"       varchar(4),
7               "order_price"  DOUBLE,
8               "record_type"  varchar(10)
9               );
10
11 CREATE OR REPLACE PUMP "Order_Pump" AS
12    INSERT INTO "Order_Stream"
13       SELECT STREAM "Oid", "Otype","Oticker", "Oprice", "RecordType"
14       FROM   "SOURCE_SQL_STREAM_001"
15       WHERE  "RecordType" = 'Order';
16 --*******************************************
17 --Create Trade_Stream.
18 CREATE OR REPLACE STREAM "Trade_Stream"
19           ("trade_id"     integer,
20            "order_id"     integer,
21            "trade_price"  DOUBLE,
22            "ticker"       varchar(4),
23            "record_type"  varchar(10)
24            );
25
26 CREATE OR REPLACE PUMP "Trade_Pump" AS
27    INSERT INTO "Trade_Stream"
28       SELECT STREAM "Tid", "Toid", "Tprice", "Tticker", "RecordType"
29       FROM   "SOURCE_SQL_STREAM_001"
30       WHERE  "RecordType" = 'Trade';
```

```
31 --***************************************************************
32 --do some analytics on the Trade_Stream and Order_Stream.
33 CREATE OR REPLACE STREAM "DESTINATION_SQL_STREAM" (
34             "ticker"  varchar(4),
35             "trade_count"   integer
36             );
37
38 CREATE OR REPLACE PUMP "Output_Pump" AS
39   INSERT INTO "DESTINATION_SQL_STREAM"
40      SELECT STREAM "ticker", count(*) as trade_count
41      FROM   "Trade_Stream"
42      GROUP BY "ticker",
43              FLOOR("Trade_Stream".ROWTIME TO MINUTE);
```

2. Choose **Save and run SQL**. Choose the **Real-time analytics** tab to see all of the in-application streams that the application created and verify the data.

Next Step

You can configure application output to persist results to an external destination, such as another Kinesis stream or a Kinesis Data Firehose data delivery stream.

Examples: Joins

This section provides examples of Amazon Kinesis data analytics applications that use join queries. Each example provides step-by-step instructions for setting up and testing your Kinesis data analytics application.

Topics

- Example: Adding Reference Data to a Kinesis Data Analytics Application

Example: Adding Reference Data to a Kinesis Data Analytics Application

In this exercise, you add reference data to an existing Amazon Kinesis data analytics application. For information about reference data, see the following topics:

- Amazon Kinesis Data Analytics: How It Works
- Configuring Application Input

In this exercise, you add reference data to the application you created in the Kinesis Data Analytics Getting Started exercise. The reference data provides the company name for each ticker symbol; for example:

```
1 Ticker, Company
2 AMZN,Amazon
3 ASD, SomeCompanyA
4 MMB, SomeCompanyB
5 WAS,  SomeCompanyC
```

First, complete the steps in the Getting Started exercise to create a starter application. Then follow these steps to set up and add reference data to your application:

1. **Prepare the data**

    - Store the preceding reference data as an object in Amazon Simple Storage Service (Amazon S3).
    - Create an IAM role that Kinesis Data Analytics can assume to read the Amazon S3 object on your behalf.

2. **Add the reference data source to your application. **

    Kinesis Data Analytics reads the Amazon S3 object and creates an in-application reference table that you can query in your application code.

3. **Test the code.**

    In your application code, you write a join query to join the in-application stream with the in-application reference table, to get the company name for each ticker symbol.

Note
The Kinesis Data Analytics console does not support managing reference data sources for your applications. In this exercise, you use the AWS CLI to add a reference data source to your application. If you haven't already done so, set up the AWS CLI.

Topics

- Step 1: Prepare
- Step 2: Add the Reference Data Source to the Application Configuration
- Step 3: Test: Query the In-Application Reference Table

Step 1: Prepare

In this section, you store sample reference data as an object in an Amazon S3 bucket. You also create an IAM role that Kinesis Data Analytics can assume to read the object on your behalf.

Store Reference Data as an Amazon S3 Object

In this step, you store the sample reference data as an Amazon S3 object.

1. Open a text editor, add the following data, and save the file as `TickerReference.csv`.

```
1 Ticker, Company
2 AMZN,Amazon
3 ASD, SomeCompanyA
4 MMB, SomeCompanyB
5 WAS,  SomeCompanyC
```

2. Upload the `TickerReference.csv` file to your S3 bucket. For instructions, see Uploading Objects into Amazon S3 in the *Amazon Simple Storage Service Console User Guide.*

Create an IAM Role

Next, create an IAM role that Kinesis Data Analytics can assume and read the Amazon S3 object.

1. In AWS Identity and Access Management (IAM), create an IAM role named **KinesisAnalytics-ReadS3Object**. To create the role, follow the instructions in Creating a Role for an AWS Service (AWS Management Console) in the *IAM User Guide.*

    On the IAM console, specify the following:

    - For **Select Role Type**, choose **AWS Lambda**. After creating the role, you will change the trust policy to allow Kinesis Data Analytics (not AWS Lambda) to assume the role.
    - Do not attach any policy on the **Attach Policy** page.

2. Update the IAM role policies:

    1. On the IAM console, choose the role that you created.

    2. On the **Trust Relationships** tab, update the trust policy to grant Kinesis Data Analytics permissions to assume the role. The trust policy is shown following:

    ```
 1 {
 2    "Version": "2012-10-17",
 3    "Statement": [
 4      {
 5        "Effect": "Allow",
 6        "Principal": {
 7          "Service": "kinesisanalytics.amazonaws.com"
 8        },
 9        "Action": "sts:AssumeRole"
10      }
11    ]
12 }
    ```

    3. On the **Permissions** tab, attach an AWS managed policy called **AmazonS3ReadOnlyAccess**. This grants the role permissions to read an Amazon S3 object. This policy is shown following:

    ```
 1 {
 2    "Version": "2012-10-17",
 3    "Statement": [
 4      {
 5        "Effect": "Allow",
 6        "Action": [
 7          "s3:Get*",
 8          "s3:List*"
 9        ],
10        "Resource": "*"
11      }
12    ]
    ```

```
13 }
```

Step 2: Add the Reference Data Source to the Application Configuration

In this step, you add a reference data source to your application configuration. To begin, you need the following information:

- Your Amazon Kinesis data analytics application name and current application version ID
- Your S3 bucket name and object key name
- The IAM role Amazon Resource Name (ARN)

Use the AWS CLI to complete the step:

1. Run the `describe-application` operation to get the application description, as shown following:

```
1 $ aws kinesisanalytics describe-application \
2 --region us-east-1 \
3 --application-name application-name
```

2. Note the current application version ID.

   Each time you change your application, the current version is updated. So ensure that you have the current application version ID.

3. Use the following JSON to add the reference data source:

```
1 {
2     "TableName":"CompanyName",
3     "S3ReferenceDataSource":{
4         "BucketARN":"arn:aws:s3:::bucket-name",
5         "FileKey":"TickerReference.csv",
6         "ReferenceRoleARN":"arn:aws:iam::aws-account-id:role/IAM-role-name"
7     },
8     "ReferenceSchema":{
9         "RecordFormat":{
10             "RecordFormatType":"CSV",
11             "MappingParameters":{
12                 "CSVMappingParameters":{
13                     "RecordRowDelimiter":"\n",
14                     "RecordColumnDelimiter":","
15                 }
16             }
17         },
18         "RecordEncoding":"UTF-8",
19         "RecordColumns":[
20             {
21                 "Name":"Ticker",
22                 "SqlType":"VARCHAR(64)"
23             },
24             {
25                 "Name":"Company",
26                 "SqlType":"VARCHAR(64)"
27             }
28         ]
29     }
30 }
```

Run the `add-application-reference-data-source` command using the preceding reference data configuration information. Provide your bucket name, object key name, IAM role name, and AWS account ID.

```
1 $ aws kinesisanalytics add-application-reference-data-source  \
2 --endpoint https://kinesisanalytics.aws-region.amazonaws.com \
3 --region us-east-1 \
4 --application-name DemoStreamBasedGettingStarted \
5 --debug \
6 --reference-data-source '{"TableName":"CompanyName","S3ReferenceDataSource":{"BucketARN":"
      arn:aws:s3:::bucket-name","FileKey":"TickerReference.csv",
7 "ReferenceRoleARN":"arn:aws:iam::aws-account-id:role/IAM-role-name"},"ReferenceSchema":{ "
      RecordFormat":{"RecordFormatType":"CSV", "MappingParameters":{"CSVMappingParameters":{"
      RecordRowDelimiter":"\n","RecordColumnDelimiter":","} }},"RecordEncoding":"UTF-8","
      RecordColumns":[{"Name":"Ticker","SqlType":"VARCHAR(64)"},{ "Name":"Company","SqlType
      ":"VARCHAR(64)"}]}}' \
8 --current-application-version-id 10
```

4. Verify that the reference data was added to the application by using the `describe-application` operation to get the application description.

Step 3: Test: Query the In-Application Reference Table

You can now query the in-application reference table, `CompanyName`. You can use the reference information to enrich your application by joining the ticker price data with the reference table. The result shows the company name.

1. Replace your application code with the following. The query joins the in-application input stream with the in-application reference table. The application code writes the results to another in-application stream, `DESTINATION_SQL_STREAM`.

```
1 CREATE OR REPLACE STREAM "DESTINATION_SQL_STREAM" (ticker_symbol VARCHAR(4), "Company"
      varchar(20), sector VARCHAR(12), change DOUBLE, price DOUBLE);
2
3 CREATE OR REPLACE PUMP "STREAM_PUMP" AS INSERT INTO "DESTINATION_SQL_STREAM"
4   SELECT STREAM ticker_symbol, "c"."Company", sector, change, price
5   FROM "SOURCE_SQL_STREAM_001" LEFT JOIN "CompanyName" as "c"
6   ON "SOURCE_SQL_STREAM_001".ticker_symbol = "c"."Ticker";
```

2. Verify that the application output appears in the **SQLResults** tab. Make sure that some of the rows show company names (your sample reference data does not have all company names).

Examples: Machine Learning

This section provides examples of Amazon Kinesis Data Analytics applications that use machine learning queries. Machine learning queries perform complex analysis on data, relying on the history of the data in the stream to find unusual patterns. The examples provide step-by-step instructions to set up and test your Kinesis data analytics application.

Topics

- Example: Detecting Data Anomalies on a Stream (RANDOM_CUT_FOREST Function)
- Example: Detecting Data Anomalies and Getting an Explanation (RANDOM_CUT_FOR-EST_WITH_EXPLANATION Function)
- Example: Detecting Hotspots on a Stream (HOTSPOTS Function)

Example: Detecting Data Anomalies on a Stream (RANDOM_CUT_FOREST Function)

Amazon Kinesis Data Analytics provides a function (`RANDOM_CUT_FOREST`) that can assign an anomaly score to each record based on values in the numeric columns. For more information, see RANDOM_CUT_FOREST Function in the *Amazon Kinesis Data Analytics SQL Reference.*

In this exercise, you write application code to assign an anomaly score to records on your application's streaming source. To set up the application, you do the following:

1. **Set up a streaming source** – You set up a Kinesis data stream and write sample `heartRate` data, as shown following:

```
1 {"heartRate": 60, "rateType":"NORMAL"}
2 ...
3 {"heartRate": 180, "rateType":"HIGH"}
```

   The procedure provides a Python script for you to populate the stream. The `heartRate` values are randomly generated, with 99 percent of the records having `heartRate` values between 60 and 100, and only 1 percent of `heartRate` values between 150 and 200. Thus, the records that have `heartRate` values between 150 and 200 are anomalies.

2. **Configure input** – Using the console, you create a Kinesis Data Analytics application and configure the application input by mapping the streaming source to an in-application stream (`SOURCE_SQL_STREAM_001`). When the application starts, Kinesis Data Analytics continuously reads the streaming source and inserts records into the in-application stream.

3. **Specify application code** – The example uses the following application code:

```
1  --Creates a temporary stream.
2  CREATE OR REPLACE STREAM "TEMP_STREAM" (
3          "heartRate"        INTEGER,
4          "rateType"         varchar(20),
5          "ANOMALY_SCORE"    DOUBLE);
6
7  --Creates another stream for application output.
8  CREATE OR REPLACE STREAM "DESTINATION_SQL_STREAM" (
9          "heartRate"        INTEGER,
10         "rateType"         varchar(20),
11         "ANOMALY_SCORE"    DOUBLE);
12
13 -- Compute an anomaly score for each record in the input stream
14 -- using Random Cut Forest
15 CREATE OR REPLACE PUMP "STREAM_PUMP" AS
16    INSERT INTO "TEMP_STREAM"
17      SELECT STREAM "heartRate", "rateType", ANOMALY_SCORE
18      FROM TABLE(RANDOM_CUT_FOREST(
19             CURSOR(SELECT STREAM * FROM "SOURCE_SQL_STREAM_001")));
20
21 -- Sort records by descending anomaly score, insert into output stream
22 CREATE OR REPLACE PUMP "OUTPUT_PUMP" AS
23    INSERT INTO "DESTINATION_SQL_STREAM"
24      SELECT STREAM * FROM "TEMP_STREAM"
25      ORDER BY FLOOR("TEMP_STREAM".ROWTIME TO SECOND), ANOMALY_SCORE DESC;
```

The code reads rows in the `SOURCE_SQL_STREAM_001`, assigns an anomaly score, and writes the resulting rows to another in-application stream (`TEMP_STREAM`). The application code then sorts the records in the

`TEMP_STREAM` and saves the results to another in-application stream (`DESTINATION_SQL_STREAM`). You use pumps to insert rows in in-application streams. For more information, see In-Application Streams and Pumps.

4. **Configure output** – You configure the application output to persist data in the `DESTINATION_SQL_STREAM` to an external destination, which is another Kinesis data stream. Reviewing the anomaly scores that are assigned to each record and determining what score indicates an anomaly (and that you need to be alerted) is external to the application. You can use an AWS Lambda function to process these anomaly scores and configure alerts.

The exercise uses the US East (N. Virginia) (`us-east-1`) AWS Region to create these streams and your application. If you use any other Region, you must update the code accordingly.

Topics

- Step 1: Prepare
- Step 2: Create an Application
- Step 3: Configure Application Output
- Step 4: Verify Output

Next Step

Step 1: Prepare

Step 1: Prepare

Before you create an Amazon Kinesis data analytics application for this exercise, you must create two Kinesis data streams. Configure one of the streams as the streaming source for your application, and the other stream as the destination where Kinesis Data Analytics persists your application output.

Topics

- Step 1.1: Create the Input and Output Data Streams
- Step 1.2: Write Sample Records to the Input Stream

Step 1.1: Create the Input and Output Data Streams

In this section, you create two Kinesis streams: `ExampleInputStream` and `ExampleOutputStream`. You can create these streams using the AWS Management Console or the AWS CLI.

- To use the console:

    1. Sign in to the AWS Management Console and open the Kinesis console at https://console.aws.amazon.com/kinesis.

    2. Choose **Create data stream**. Create a stream with one shard named `ExampleInputStream`. For more information, see Create a Stream in the *Amazon Kinesis Data Streams Developer Guide*.

    3. Repeat the previous step, creating a stream with one shard named `ExampleOutputStream`.

- To use the AWS CLI:

    1. Use the following Kinesis `create-stream` AWS CLI command to create the first stream (`ExampleInputStream`).

```
1 $ aws kinesis create-stream \
2 --stream-name ExampleInputStream \
3 --shard-count 1 \
4 --region us-east-1 \
5 --profile adminuser
```

    2. Run the same command, changing the stream name to `ExampleOutputStream`. This command creates the second stream that the application will use to write output.

Step 1.2: Write Sample Records to the Input Stream

In this step, you run Python code to continuously generate sample records and write these records to the `ExampleInputStream` stream.

```
1 {"heartRate": 60, "rateType":"NORMAL"}
2 ...
3 {"heartRate": 180, "rateType":"HIGH"}
```

1. Install Python and `pip`.

    For information about installing Python, see the Python website.

    You can install dependencies using pip. For information about installing pip, see Installation on the pip website.

2. Run the following Python code. The `put-record` command in the code writes the JSON records to the stream.

```
 1 import json
 2 from boto import kinesis
 3 import random
 4
 5 kinesis = kinesis.connect_to_region("us-east-1")
 6 # generate normal heart rate with probability .99
 7 def getNormalHeartRate():
 8     data = {}
 9     data['heartRate'] = random.randint(60, 100)
10     data['rateType'] = "NORMAL"
11     return data
12 # generate high heart rate with probability .01 (very few)
13 def getHighHeartRate():
14     data = {}
15     data['heartRate'] = random.randint(150, 200)
16     data['rateType'] = "HIGH"
17     return data
18
19 while True:
20     rnd = random.random()
21     if (rnd < 0.01):
22         data = json.dumps(getHighHeartRate())
23         print data
24         kinesis.put_record("ExampleInputStream", data, "partitionkey")
25     else:
26         data = json.dumps(getNormalHeartRate())
27         print data
28         kinesis.put_record("ExampleInputStream", data, "partitionkey")
```

Next Step
Step 2: Create an Application

Step 2: Create an Application

In this section, you create an Amazon Kinesis data analytics application as follows:

- Configure the application input to use the Kinesis data stream that you created in Step 1: Prepare as the streaming source.
- Use the **Anomaly Detection** template on the console.

To create an application

1. Follow steps 1, 2, and 3 in the Kinesis Data Analytics **Getting Started** exercise (see Step 3.1: Create an Application) to create an application.

    - In the source configuration, do the following:
        - Specify the streaming source that you created in the preceding section.
        - After the console infers the schema, edit the schema, and set the `heartRate` column type to `INTEGER`.
          Most of the heart rate values are normal, and the discovery process will most likely assign the `TINYINT` type to this column. But a small percentage of values show a high heart rate. If these high values don't fit in the `TINYINT` type, Kinesis Data Analytics sends these rows to an error stream. Update the data type to `INTEGER` so that it can accommodate all the generated heart rate data.
    - Use the **Anomaly Detection** template on the console. You then update the template code to provide the appropriate column name.

2. Update the application code by providing column names. The resulting application code is shown following (paste this code into the SQL editor):

```
1  --Creates a temporary stream.
2  CREATE OR REPLACE STREAM "TEMP_STREAM" (
3         "heartRate"        INTEGER,
4         "rateType"         varchar(20),
5         "ANOMALY_SCORE"    DOUBLE);
6
7  --Creates another stream for application output.
8  CREATE OR REPLACE STREAM "DESTINATION_SQL_STREAM" (
9         "heartRate"        INTEGER,
10        "rateType"         varchar(20),
11        "ANOMALY_SCORE"    DOUBLE);
12
13 -- Compute an anomaly score for each record in the input stream
14 -- using Random Cut Forest
15 CREATE OR REPLACE PUMP "STREAM_PUMP" AS
16    INSERT INTO "TEMP_STREAM"
17      SELECT STREAM "heartRate", "rateType", ANOMALY_SCORE
18      FROM TABLE(RANDOM_CUT_FOREST(
19              CURSOR(SELECT STREAM * FROM "SOURCE_SQL_STREAM_001")));
20
21 -- Sort records by descending anomaly score, insert into output stream
22 CREATE OR REPLACE PUMP "OUTPUT_PUMP" AS
23    INSERT INTO "DESTINATION_SQL_STREAM"
24      SELECT STREAM * FROM "TEMP_STREAM"
25      ORDER BY FLOOR("TEMP_STREAM".ROWTIME TO SECOND), ANOMALY_SCORE DESC;
```

3. Run the SQL code and review the results in the Kinesis Data Analytics console:

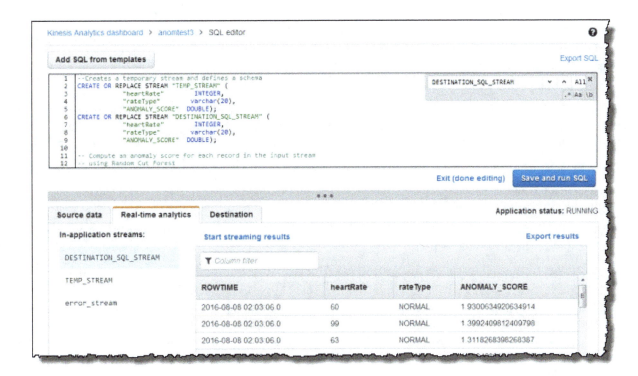

Next Step
Step 3: Configure Application Output

Step 3: Configure Application Output

After completing Step 2: Create an Application, you have application code that is reading heart rate data from a streaming source and assigning an anomaly score to each.

You can now send the application results from the in-application stream to an external destination, which is another Kinesis data stream (`OutputStreamTestingAnomalyScores`). You can then analyze the anomaly scores and determine which heart rate is anomalous. You can then extend this application further to generate alerts.

Follow these steps to configure application output:

1. Open the Amazon Kinesis Data Analytics console. In the SQL editor, choose either **Destination** or **Add a destination** in the application dashboard.

2. On the **Connect to destination** page, choose the `OutputStreamTestingAnomalyScores` stream you created in the preceding section.

   Now you have an external destination, where Amazon Kinesis Data Analytics persists any records your application writes to the in-application stream `DESTINATION_SQL_STREAM`.

3. You can optionally configure AWS Lambda to monitor the `OutputStreamTestingAnomalyScores` stream and send you alerts. For instructions, see Preprocessing Data Using a Lambda Function. If you don't set alerts, you can review the records that Kinesis Data Analytics writes to the external destination, which is the Kinesis data stream `OutputStreamTestingAnomalyScores`, as described in the next step in this example.

Next Step
Step 4: Verify Output

Step 4: Verify Output

After configuring the application output in Step 3: Configure Application Output, use the following AWS CLI commands to read records in the destination stream that is written by the application:

1. Run the `get-shard-iterator` command to get a pointer to data on the output stream.

```
1 aws kinesis get-shard-iterator \
2 --shard-id shardId-000000000000 \
3 --shard-iterator-type TRIM_HORIZON \
4 --stream-name OutputStreamTestingAnomalyScores \
5 --region us-east-1 \
6 --profile adminuser
```

You get a response with a shard iterator value, as shown in the following example response:

```
1 {
2     "ShardIterator":
3     "shard-iterator-value"   }
```

Copy the shard iterator value.

2. Run the AWS CLI `get-records` command.

```
1 aws kinesis get-records \
2 --shard-iterator shared-iterator-value \
3 --region us-east-1 \
4 --profile adminuser
```

The command returns a page of records and another shard iterator that you can use in the subsequent `get-records` command to fetch the next set of records.

Example: Detecting Data Anomalies and Getting an Explanation (RANDOM_CUT_FOREST_WITH_EXPLANATION Function)

Amazon Kinesis Data Analytics provides the `RANDOM_CUT_FOREST_WITH_EXPLANATION` function, which assigns an anomaly score to each record based on values in the numeric columns. The function also provides an explanation of the anomaly. For more information, see RANDOM_CUT_FOREST_WITH_EXPLANATION in the *Amazon Kinesis Data Analytics SQL Reference*.

In this exercise, you write application code to obtain anomaly scores for records in your application's streaming source. You also obtain an explanation for each anomaly.

Topics

- Step 1: Prepare the Data
- Step 2: Create an Analytics Application
- Step 3: Examine the Results

First Step
Step 1: Prepare the Data

Step 2: Create an Analytics Application

In this section, you create an Amazon Kinesis data analytics application and configure it to use the Kinesis data stream that you created as the streaming source in Step 1: Prepare the Data. You then run application code that uses the RANDOM_CUT_FOREST_WITH_EXPLANATION function.

To create an application

1. Open the Kinesis console at https://console.aws.amazon.com/kinesis.

2. Choose **Data Analytics** in the navigation pane, and then choose **Create application**.

3. Provide an application name and description (optional), and choose **Create application**.

4. Choose **Connect streaming data**, and then choose **ExampleInputStream** from the list.

5. Choose **Discover schema**, and make sure that Systolic and Diastolic appear as INTEGER columns. If they have another type, choose **Edit schema**, and assign the type INTEGER to both of them.

6. Under **Real time analytics**, choose **Go to SQL editor**. When prompted, choose to run your application.

7. Paste the following code into the SQL editor, and then choose **Save and run SQL**.

```
1  --Creates a temporary stream.
2  CREATE OR REPLACE STREAM "TEMP_STREAM" (
3          "Systolic"                INTEGER,
4          "Diastolic"               INTEGER,
5          "BloodPressureLevel"      varchar(20),
6          "ANOMALY_SCORE"           DOUBLE,
7          "ANOMALY_EXPLANATION"     varchar(512));
8
9  --Creates another stream for application output.
10 CREATE OR REPLACE STREAM "DESTINATION_SQL_STREAM" (
11          "Systolic"                INTEGER,
12          "Diastolic"               INTEGER,
13          "BloodPressureLevel"      varchar(20),
14          "ANOMALY_SCORE"           DOUBLE,
15          "ANOMALY_EXPLANATION"     varchar(512));
16
17 -- Compute an anomaly score with explanation for each record in the input stream
18 -- using RANDOM_CUT_FOREST_WITH_EXPLANATION
19 CREATE OR REPLACE PUMP "STREAM_PUMP" AS
20    INSERT INTO "TEMP_STREAM"
21      SELECT STREAM "Systolic", "Diastolic", "BloodPressureLevel", ANOMALY_SCORE,
                ANOMALY_EXPLANATION
22      FROM TABLE(RANDOM_CUT_FOREST_WITH_EXPLANATION(
23              CURSOR(SELECT STREAM * FROM "SOURCE_SQL_STREAM_001"), 100, 256, 100000, 1,
                  true));
24
25 -- Sort records by descending anomaly score, insert into output stream
26 CREATE OR REPLACE PUMP "OUTPUT_PUMP" AS
27    INSERT INTO "DESTINATION_SQL_STREAM"
28      SELECT STREAM * FROM "TEMP_STREAM"
29      ORDER BY FLOOR("TEMP_STREAM".ROWTIME TO SECOND), ANOMALY_SCORE DESC;
```

Next Step
Step 3: Examine the Results

Step 3: Examine the Results

When you run the SQL code for this example, you first see rows with an anomaly score equal to zero. This happens during the initial learning phase. Then you get results similar to the following:

```
1 ROWTIME SYSTOLIC DIASTOLIC BLOODPRESSURELEVEL ANOMALY_SCORE ANOMALY_EXPLANATION
2 27:49.0 101      66         NORMAL             0.711460417   {"Systolic":{"DIRECTION":"LOW","
    STRENGTH":"0.0922","ATTRIBUTION_SCORE":"0.3792"},"Diastolic":{"DIRECTION":"HIGH","STRENGTH
    ":"0.0210","ATTRIBUTION_SCORE":"0.3323"}}
3 27:50.0 144      123        HIGH               3.855851061   {"Systolic":{"DIRECTION":"HIGH","
    STRENGTH":"0.8567","ATTRIBUTION_SCORE":"1.7447"},"Diastolic":{"DIRECTION":"HIGH","STRENGTH
    ":"7.0982","ATTRIBUTION_SCORE":"2.1111"}}
4 27:50.0 113      69         NORMAL             0.740069409   {"Systolic":{"DIRECTION":"LOW","
    STRENGTH":"0.0549","ATTRIBUTION_SCORE":"0.3750"},"Diastolic":{"DIRECTION":"LOW","STRENGTH
    ":"0.0394","ATTRIBUTION_SCORE":"0.3650"}}
5 27:50.0 105      64         NORMAL             0.739644157   {"Systolic":{"DIRECTION":"HIGH","
    STRENGTH":"0.0245","ATTRIBUTION_SCORE":"0.3667"},"Diastolic":{"DIRECTION":"LOW","STRENGTH
    ":"0.0524","ATTRIBUTION_SCORE":"0.3729"}}
6 27:50.0 100      65         NORMAL             0.736993425   {"Systolic":{"DIRECTION":"HIGH","
    STRENGTH":"0.0203","ATTRIBUTION_SCORE":"0.3516"},"Diastolic":{"DIRECTION":"LOW","STRENGTH
    ":"0.0454","ATTRIBUTION_SCORE":"0.3854"}}
7 27:50.0 108      69         NORMAL             0.733767202   {"Systolic":{"DIRECTION":"LOW","
    STRENGTH":"0.0974","ATTRIBUTION_SCORE":"0.3961"},"Diastolic":{"DIRECTION":"LOW","STRENGTH
    ":"0.0189","ATTRIBUTION_SCORE":"0.3377"}}
```

- The algorithm in the `RANDOM_CUT_FOREST_WITH_EXPLANATION` function sees that the `Systolic` and `Diastolic` columns are numeric, and uses them as input.
- The `BloodPressureLevel` column has text data, and is therefore not taken into account by the algorithm. This column is simply a visual aide to help you quickly spot the normal, high, and low blood pressure levels in this example.
- In the `ANOMALY_SCORE` column, records with higher scores are more anomalous. The second record in this sample set of results is the most anomalous, with an anomaly score of 3.855851061.
- To understand the extent to which each of the numeric columns taken into account by the algorithm contributes to the anomaly score, consult the JSON field named `ATTRIBUTION_SCORE` in the `ANOMALY_SCORE` column. In the case of the second row in this set of sample results, the `Systolic` and `Diastolic` columns contribute to the anomaly in the ratio of 1.7447:2.1111. In other words, 45 percent of the explanation for the anomaly score is attributable to the systolic value, and the remaining attribution is due to the diastolic value.
- To determine the direction in which the point represented by the second row in this sample is anomalous, consult the JSON field named `DIRECTION`. Both the diastolic and systolic values are marked as `HIGH` in this case. To determine the confidence with which these directions are correct, consult the JSON field named `STRENGTH`. In this example, the algorithm is more confident that the diastolic value is high. Indeed, the normal value for the diastolic reading is usually 60–80, and 123 is much higher than expected.

Example: Detecting Hotspots on a Stream (HOTSPOTS Function)

Amazon Kinesis Data Analytics provides the `HOTSPOTS` function, which can locate and return information about relatively dense regions in your data. For more information, see HOTSPOTS in the *Amazon Kinesis Data Analytics SQL Reference.*

In this exercise, you write application code to locate hotspots on your application's streaming source. To set up the application, you do the following steps:

1. **Set up a streaming source** – You set up a Kinesis stream and write sample coordinate data as shown following:

```
1 {"x": 7.921782426109737, "y": 8.746265312709893, "is_hot": "N"}
2 {"x": 0.722248626528026, "y": 4.648868803193405, "is_hot": "Y"}
```

    The example provides a Python script for you to populate the stream. The x and y values are randomly generated, with some records being clustered around certain locations.

    The `is_hot` field is provided as an indicator if the script intentionally generated the value as part of a hotspot. This can help you evaluate whether the hotspot detection function is working properly.

2. **Create the application** – Using the AWS Management Console, you then create a Kinesis data analytics application. Configure the application input by mapping the streaming source to an in-application stream (`SOURCE_SQL_STREAM_001`). When the application starts, Kinesis Data Analytics continuously reads the streaming source and inserts records into the in-application stream.

    In this exercise, you use the following code for the application:

```
1 CREATE OR REPLACE STREAM "DESTINATION_SQL_STREAM" (
2     "x" DOUBLE,
3     "y" DOUBLE,
4     "is_hot" VARCHAR(4),
5     HOTSPOTS_RESULT VARCHAR(10000)
6 );
7 CREATE OR REPLACE PUMP "STREAM_PUMP" AS
8     INSERT INTO "DESTINATION_SQL_STREAM"
9     SELECT "x", "y", "is_hot", "HOTSPOTS_RESULT"
10    FROM TABLE (
11        HOTSPOTS(
12            CURSOR(SELECT STREAM * FROM "SOURCE_SQL_STREAM_001"),
13            1000,
14            0.2,
15            17)
16    );
```

    The code reads rows in the `SOURCE_SQL_STREAM_001`, analyzes it for significant hotspots, and writes the resulting data to another in-application stream (`DESTINATION_SQL_STREAM`). You use pumps to insert rows in in-application streams. For more information, see In-Application Streams and Pumps.

3. **Configure the output** – You configure the application output to send data from the application to an external destination, which is another Kinesis data stream. Review the hotspot scores and determine what scores indicate that a hotspot occurred (and that you need to be alerted). You can use an AWS Lambda function to further process hotspot information and configure alerts.

4. **Verify the output** – The example includes a JavaScript application that reads data from the output stream and displays it graphically, so you can view the hotspots that the application generates in real time.

The exercise uses the US West (Oregon) (`us-west-2`) AWS Region to create these streams and your application. If you use any other Region, update the code accordingly.

Topics

- Step 1: Create the Input and Output Streams
- Step 2: Create the Kinesis Data Analytics Application
- Step 3: Configure the Application Output
- Step 4: Verify the Application Output

Step 1: Create the Input and Output Streams

Before you create an Amazon Kinesis Data Analytics application for the Hotspots example, you create two Kinesis data streams. Configure one of the streams as the streaming source for your application, and the other stream as the destination where Kinesis Data Analytics persists your application output.

Topics

- Step 1.1: Create the Kinesis Data Streams
- Step 1.2: Write Sample Records to the Input Stream

Step 1.1: Create the Kinesis Data Streams

In this section, you create two Kinesis data streams: `ExampleInputStream` and `ExampleOutputStream`.

Create these data streams using the console or the AWS CLI.

- To create the data streams using the console:

  1. Sign in to the AWS Management Console and open the Kinesis console at https://console.aws.amazon.com/kinesis.

  2. Choose **Data Streams** in the navigation pane.

  3. Choose **Create Kinesis stream**, and create a stream with one shard named `ExampleInputStream`.

  4. Repeat the previous step, creating a stream with one shard named `ExampleOutputStream`.

- To create data streams using the AWS CLI:

  - Create streams (`ExampleInputStream` and `ExampleOutputStream`) using the following Kinesis `create-stream` AWS CLI command. To create the second stream, which the application will use to write output, run the same command, changing the stream name to `ExampleOutputStream`.

```
1  $ aws kinesis create-stream \
2  --stream-name ExampleInputStream \
3  --shard-count 1 \
4  --region us-west-2 \
5  --profile adminuser
6
7  $ aws kinesis create-stream \
8  --stream-name ExampleOutputStream \
9  --shard-count 1 \
10 --region us-west-2 \
11 --profile adminuser
```

Step 1.2: Write Sample Records to the Input Stream

In this step, you run Python code to continuously generate sample records and write to the `ExampleInputStream` stream.

```
1  {"x": 7.921782426109737, "y": 8.746265312709893, "is_hot": "N"}
2  {"x": 0.722248626580026, "y": 4.648868803193405, "is_hot": "Y"}
```

1. Install Python and `pip`.

   For information about installing Python, see the Python website.

You can install dependencies using pip. For information about installing pip, see Installation on the pip website.

2. Run the following Python code. This code does the following:

- Generates a potential hotspot somewhere in the (X, Y) plane.
- Generates a set of 1,000 points for each hotspot. Of these points, 20 percent are clustered around the hotspot. The rest are generated randomly within the entire space.
- The put-record command writes the JSON records to the stream. **Important**
  Do not upload this file to a web server because it contains your AWS credentials.

```python
import boto3
import json
import time

from random import random

# Modify this section to reflect your AWS configuration.
awsRegion = ""          # The AWS region where your Kinesis Analytics application is
    configured.
accessKeyId = ""        # Your AWS Access Key ID
secretAccessKey = ""    # Your AWS Secret Access Key
inputStream = "ExampleInputStream"      # The name of the stream being used as input into
    the Kinesis Analytics hotspots application

# Variables that control properties of the generated data.
xRange = [0, 10]        # The range of values taken by the x-coordinate
yRange = [0, 10]        # The range of values taken by the y-coordinate
hotspotSideLength = 1   # The side length of the hotspot
hotspotWeight = 0.2     # The fraction ofpoints that are draw from the hotspots


def generate_point_in_rectangle(x_min, width, y_min, height):
    """Generate points uniformly in the given rectangle."""
    return {
        'x': x_min + random() * width,
        'y': y_min + random() * height
    }


class RecordGenerator(object):
    """A class used to generate points used as input to the hotspot detection algorithm.
        With probability hotspotWeight,
    a point is drawn from a hotspot, otherwise it is drawn from the base distribution. The
        location of the hotspot
    changes after every 1000 points generated."""

    def __init__(self):
        self.x_min = xRange[0]
        self.width = xRange[1] - xRange[0]
        self.y_min = yRange[0]
        self.height = yRange[1] - yRange[0]
        self.points_generated = 0
        self.hotspot_x_min = None
        self.hotspot_y_min = None

```

```python
42      def get_record(self):
43          if self.points_generated % 1000 == 0:
44              self.update_hotspot()
45
46          if random() < hotspotWeight:
47              record = generate_point_in_rectangle(self.hotspot_x_min, hotspotSideLength,
                    self.hotspot_y_min,
48                                                  hotspotSideLength)
49              record['is_hot'] = 'Y'
50          else:
51              record = generate_point_in_rectangle(self.x_min, self.width, self.y_min, self.
                    height)
52              record['is_hot'] = 'N'
53
54          self.points_generated += 1
55          data = json.dumps(record)
56          return {'Data': bytes(data, 'utf-8'), 'PartitionKey': 'partition_key'}
57
58      def get_records(self, n):
59          return [self.get_record() for _ in range(n)]
60
61      def update_hotspot(self):
62          self.hotspot_x_min = self.x_min + random() * (self.width - hotspotSideLength)
63          self.hotspot_y_min = self.y_min + random() * (self.height - hotspotSideLength)
64
65
66  def main():
67      kinesis = boto3.client("kinesis",
68                              region_name=awsRegion,
69                              aws_access_key_id=accessKeyId,
70                              aws_secret_access_key=secretAccessKey)
71
72      generator = RecordGenerator()
73      batch_size = 10
74
75      while True:
76          records = generator.get_records(batch_size)
77          kinesis.put_records(StreamName=inputStream, Records=records)
78
79          time.sleep(0.1)
80
81
82  if __name__ == "__main__":
83      main()
```

Next Step
Step 2: Create the Kinesis Data Analytics Application

Step 2: Create the Kinesis Data Analytics Application

In this section of the Hotspots example, you create an Amazon Kinesis data analytics application as follows:

- Configure the application input to use the Kinesis data stream you created as the streaming source in Step 1.
- Use the provided application code in the AWS Management Console.

To create an application

1. Create a Kinesis data analytics application by following steps 1, 2, and 3 in the Getting Started exercise (see Step 3.1: Create an Application).

   In the source configuration, do the following:

   - Specify the streaming source you created in Step 1: Create the Input and Output Streams.
   - After the console infers the schema, edit the schema. Ensure that the x and y column types are set to DOUBLE and that the IS_HOT column type is set to VARCHAR.

2. Use the following application code (you can paste this code into the SQL editor):

```
1  CREATE OR REPLACE STREAM "DESTINATION_SQL_STREAM" (
2      "x" DOUBLE,
3      "y" DOUBLE,
4      "is_hot" VARCHAR(4),
5      HOTSPOTS_RESULT VARCHAR(10000)
6  );
7  CREATE OR REPLACE PUMP "STREAM_PUMP" AS
8      INSERT INTO "DESTINATION_SQL_STREAM"
9      SELECT "x", "y", "is_hot", "HOTSPOTS_RESULT"
10     FROM TABLE (
11         HOTSPOTS(
12             CURSOR(SELECT STREAM * FROM "SOURCE_SQL_STREAM_001"),
13             1000,
14             0.2,
15             17)
16     );
```

3. Run the SQL code and review the results.

Next Step
Step 3: Configure the Application Output

Step 3: Configure the Application Output

At this point in the Hotspots example, you have Amazon Kinesis Data Analytics application code discovering significant hotspots from a streaming source and assigning a heat score to each.

You can now send the application result from the in-application stream to an external destination, which is another Kinesis data stream (`ExampleOutputStream`). You can then analyze the hotspot scores and determine what an appropriate threshold is for hotspot heat. You can extend this application further to generate alerts.

To configure the application output

1. Open the Kinesis Data Analytics console at https://console.aws.amazon.com/kinesisanalytics.

2. In the SQL editor, choose either **Destination** or **Add a destination** in the application dashboard.

3. On the **Add a destination** page, choose **Select from your streams**, and then choose the `ExampleOutputStream` stream that you created in the preceding section.

   Now you have an external destination, where Amazon Kinesis Data Analytics persists any records your application writes to the in-application stream `DESTINATION_SQL_STREAM`.

4. You can optionally configure AWS Lambda to monitor the `ExampleOutputStream` stream and send you alerts. For more information, see Using a Lambda Function as Output. You can also review the records that Kinesis Data Analytics writes to the external destination, which is the Kinesis stream `ExampleOutputStream`, as described in Step 4: Verify the Application Output.

Next Step
Step 4: Verify the Application Output

Step 4: Verify the Application Output

In this section of the Hotspots example, you set up a web application that displays the hotspot information in a Scalable Vector Graphics (SVG) control.

1. Create a file named `index.html` with the following contents:

```html
<!doctype html>
<html lang=en>
<head>
    <meta charset=utf-8>
    <title>hotspots viewer</title>

    <style>
    #visualization {
      display: block;
      margin: auto;
    }

    .point {
      opacity: 0.2;
    }

    .hot {
      fill: red;
    }

    .cold {
      fill: blue;
    }

    .hotspot {
      stroke: black;
      stroke-opacity: 0.8;
      stroke-width: 1;
      fill: none;
    }
    </style>
    <script src="https://sdk.amazonaws.com/js/aws-sdk-2.202.0.min.js"></script>
    <script src="https://d3js.org/d3.v4.min.js"></script>
</head>
<body>
<svg id="visualization" width="600" height="600"></svg>
<script src="hotspots_viewer.js"></script>
</body>
</html>
```

2. Create a file in the same directory named `hotspots_viewer.js` with the following contents. Provide your AWS Region, credentials, and output stream name in the variables provided.

```javascript
// Visualize example output from the Kinesis Analytics hotspot detection algorithm.
// This script assumes that the output stream has a single shard.

// Modify this section to reflect your AWS configuration.
var awsRegion = "",        // The AWS Region where your Kinesis Analytics application is
    configured.
```

158

```
 6     accessKeyId = "",        // Your AWS Access Key ID.
 7     secretAccessKey = "",    // Your AWS Secret Access Key.
 8     hotspotsStream = "";     // The name of the Kinesis Stream where the output from the
          HOTSPOTS function is being written.
 9
10 // The variables in this section should reflect way input data was generated and the
       parameters that the HOTSPOTS
11 // function was called with.
12 var windowSize = 1000, // The window size used for hotspot detection.
13     minimumHeat = 20,  // A filter applied to returned hotspots before visualization.
14     xRange = [0, 10],  // The range of values to display on the x-axis.
15     yRange = [0, 10];  // The range of values to display on the y-axis.
16
17 //////////////////////////////////////////////////////////////////////////////////////////////
18 // D3 setup
19 //////////////////////////////////////////////////////////////////////////////////////////////

20
21 var svg = d3.select("svg"),
22     margin = {"top": 20, "right": 20, "bottom": 20, "left": 20},
23     graphWidth = +svg.attr("width") - margin.left - margin.right,
24     graphHeight = +svg.attr("height") - margin.top - margin.bottom;
25
26 // Return the linear function that maps the segment [a, b] to the segment [c, d].
27 function linearScale(a, b, c, d) {
28     var m = (d - c) / (b - a);
29     return function(x) {
30         return c + m * (x - a);
31     };
32 }
33
34 // Helper functions to extract the x-value from a stream record and scale it for output.
35 var xValue = function(r) { return r.x; },
36     xScale = linearScale(xRange[0], xRange[1], 0, graphWidth),
37     xMap = function(r) { return xScale(xValue(r)); };
38
39 // Helper functions to extract the y-value from a stream record and scale it for output.
40 var yValue = function(r) { return r.y; },
41     yScale = linearScale(yRange[0], yRange[1], 0, graphHeight),
42     yMap = function(r) { return yScale(yValue(r)); };
43
44 // A helper function that assigns a CSS class to a point based on whether it was generated
       as part of a hotspot.
45 var classMap = function(r) { return r.is_hot == "Y" ? "point hot" : "point cold"; };
46
47 var g = svg.append("g")
48     .attr("transform", "translate(" + margin.left + "," + margin.top + ")");
49
50 function update(records, hotspots) {
51
52     var points = g.selectAll("circle")
53         .data(records, function(r) { return r.dataIndex; });
54
```

```
55    points.enter().append("circle")
56        .attr("class", classMap)
57        .attr("r", 3)
58        .attr("cx", xMap)
59        .attr("cy", yMap);
60
61    points.exit().remove();
62
63    if (hotspots) {
64        var boxes = g.selectAll("rect").data(hotspots);
65
66        boxes.enter().append("rect")
67            .merge(boxes)
68            .attr("class", "hotspot")
69            .attr("x", function(h) { return xScale(h.minValues[0]); })
70            .attr("y", function(h) { return yScale(h.minValues[1]); })
71            .attr("width", function(h) { return xScale(h.maxValues[0]) - xScale(h.minValues
                 [0]); })
72            .attr("height", function(h) { return yScale(h.maxValues[1]) - yScale(h.
                 minValues[1]); });
73
74        boxes.exit().remove();
75    }
76 }
77
78 /////////////////////////////////////////////////////////////////////////////////////////
79 // Use the AWS SDK to pull output records from Kinesis and update the visualization.
80 /////////////////////////////////////////////////////////////////////////////////////////
81
82 var kinesis = new AWS.Kinesis({
83    "region": awsRegion,
84    "accessKeyId": accessKeyId,
85    "secretAccessKey": secretAccessKey
86 });
87
88 var textDecoder = new TextDecoder("utf-8");
89
90 // Decode an output record into an object and assign it an index value.
91 function decodeRecord(record, recordIndex) {
92    var record = JSON.parse(textDecoder.decode(record.Data));
93    var hotspots_result = JSON.parse(record.hotspots_result);
94    record.hotspots = hotspots_result.hotspots
95        .filter(function(hotspot) { return hotspot.heat >= minimumHeat});
96    record.index = recordIndex
97    return record;
98 }
99
100 // Fetch new records from the shard iterator, append them to records, and update the
        visualization.
101 function getRecordsAndUpdateVisualization(shardIterator, records, lastRecordIndex) {
102    kinesis.getRecords({
103        "ShardIterator": shardIterator
```

```
104    }, function(err, data) {
105        if (err) {
106            console.log(err, err.stack);
107            return;
108        }
109
110        var newRecords = data.Records.map(function(raw) { return decodeRecord(raw, ++
               lastRecordIndex); });
111        newRecords.forEach(function(record) { records.push(record); });
112
113        var hotspots = null;
114        if (newRecords.length > 0) {
115            hotspots = newRecords[newRecords.length - 1].hotspots;
116        }
117
118        while (records.length > windowSize) {
119            records.shift();
120        }
121
122        update(records, hotspots);
123
124        getRecordsAndUpdateVisualization(data.NextShardIterator, records, lastRecordIndex);
125    });
126 }
127
128 // Get a shard iterator for the output stream and begin updating the visualization. Note
       that this script will only
129 // read records from the first shard in the stream.
130 function init() {
131    kinesis.describeStream({
132        "StreamName": hotspotsStream
133    }, function(err, data) {
134        if (err) {
135            console.log(err, err.stack);
136            return;
137        }
138
139        var shardId = data.StreamDescription.Shards[0].ShardId;
140
141        kinesis.getShardIterator({
142            "StreamName": hotspotsStream,
143            "ShardId": shardId,
144            "ShardIteratorType": "LATEST"
145        }, function(err, data) {
146            if (err) {
147                console.log(err, err.stack);
148                return;
149            }
150            getRecordsAndUpdateVisualization(data.ShardIterator, [], 0);
151        })
152    });
153 }
154
155 // Start the visualization.
```

`init();`

3. With the Python code from the first section running, open `index.html` in a web browser. The hotspot information will display in the page.

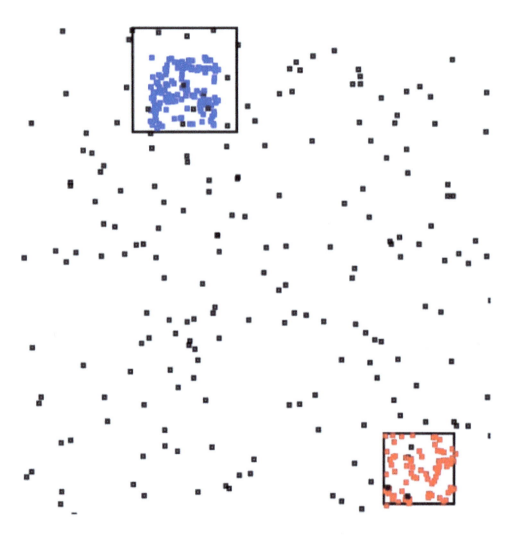

Examples: Alerts and Errors

This section provides examples of Amazon Kinesis data analytics applications that use alerts and errors. Each example provides step-by-step instructions and code to help you set up and test your Kinesis data analytics application.

Topics

- Example: Creating Simple Alerts
- Example: Creating Throttled Alerts
- Example: Exploring the In-Application Error Stream

Example: Creating Simple Alerts

In this Amazon Kinesis data analytics application, the query runs continuously on the in-application stream that is created over the demo stream. For more information, see Continuous Queries.

If any rows show a stock price change that is greater than 1 percent, those rows are inserted into another in-application stream. In the exercise, you can configure the application output to persist the results to an external destination. You can then further investigate the results. For example, you can use an AWS Lambda function to process records and send you alerts.

To create a simple alerts application

1. Create the analytics application as described in the Kinesis Data Analytics Getting Started exercise.

2. In the SQL editor in Kinesis Data Analytics, replace the application code with the following:

```
1 CREATE OR REPLACE STREAM "DESTINATION_SQL_STREAM"
2          (ticker_symbol VARCHAR(4),
3           sector        VARCHAR(12),
4           change        DOUBLE,
5           price         DOUBLE);
6
7 CREATE OR REPLACE PUMP "STREAM_PUMP" AS
8   INSERT INTO "DESTINATION_SQL_STREAM"
9      SELECT STREAM ticker_symbol, sector, change, price
10     FROM   "SOURCE_SQL_STREAM_001"
11     WHERE  (ABS(Change / (Price - Change)) * 100) > 1;
```

   The `SELECT` statement in the application code filters rows in the `SOURCE_SQL_STREAM_001` for stock price changes greater than 1 percent. It then inserts those rows into another in-application stream `DESTINATION_SQL_STREAM` using a pump. For more information about the coding pattern that explains using pumps to insert rows into in-application streams, see Application Code.

3. Choose **Save and run SQL**.

4. Add a destination. To do this, either choose the **Destination** tab in the SQL editor or choose **Add a destination** on the application details page.

   1. In the SQL editor, choose the **Destination** tab, and then choose **Connect to a destination**.

      On the **Connect to destination** page, choose **Create New**.

   2. Choose **Go to Kinesis Streams**.

   3. On the Amazon Kinesis Data Streams console, create a new Kinesis stream (for example, `gs-destination`) with one shard. Wait until the stream status is **ACTIVE**.

   4. Return to the Kinesis Data Analytics console. On the **Connect to destination** page, choose the stream that you created.

      If the stream does not appear, refresh the page.

   5. Choose **Save and continue**.

   Now you have an external destination, a Kinesis data stream, where Kinesis Data Analytics persists your application output in the `DESTINATION_SQL_STREAM` in-application stream.

5. Configure AWS Lambda to monitor the Kinesis stream you created and invoke a Lambda function.

   For instructions, see Preprocessing Data Using a Lambda Function.

Example: Creating Throttled Alerts

In this Amazon Kinesis data analytics application, the query runs continuously on the in-application stream created over the demo stream. For more information, see Continuous Queries. If any rows show that the stock price change is greater than 1 percent, those rows are inserted into another in-application stream. The application throttles the alerts such that an alert is sent immediately when the stock price changes. However, no more than one alert per minute per stock symbol is sent to the in-application stream.

To create a throttled alerts application

1. Create a Kinesis data analytics application as described in the Kinesis Data Analytics Getting Started exercise.

2. In the SQL editor in Kinesis Data Analytics, replace the application code with the following:

```
1  CREATE OR REPLACE STREAM "CHANGE_STREAM"
2          (ticker_symbol VARCHAR(4),
3           sector        VARCHAR(12),
4           change        DOUBLE,
5           price         DOUBLE);
6
7  CREATE OR REPLACE PUMP "change_pump" AS
8    INSERT INTO "CHANGE_STREAM"
9       SELECT STREAM ticker_symbol, sector, change, price
10      FROM   "SOURCE_SQL_STREAM_001"
11      WHERE  (ABS(Change / (Price - Change)) * 100) > 1;
12
13 -- ** Trigger Count and Limit **
14 -- Counts "triggers" or those values that evaluated true against the previous where clause
15 -- Then provides its own limit on the number of triggers per hour per ticker symbol to what
16 -- is specified in the WHERE clause
17
18 CREATE OR REPLACE STREAM TRIGGER_COUNT_STREAM (
19    ticker_symbol VARCHAR(4),
20    change REAL,
21    trigger_count INTEGER);
22
23 CREATE OR REPLACE PUMP trigger_count_pump AS INSERT INTO TRIGGER_COUNT_STREAM
24 SELECT STREAM ticker_symbol, change, trigger_count
25 FROM (
26    SELECT STREAM ticker_symbol, change, COUNT(*) OVER W1 as trigger_count
27    FROM "CHANGE_STREAM"
28    --window to perform aggregations over last minute to keep track of triggers
29    WINDOW W1 AS (PARTITION BY ticker_symbol RANGE INTERVAL '1' MINUTE PRECEDING)
30 )
31 WHERE trigger_count >= 1;
```

The SELECT statement in the application code filters rows in the SOURCE_SQL_STREAM_001 for stock price changes greater than 1 percent and inserts those rows into another in-application stream CHANGE_STREAM using a pump.

The application then creates a second stream named TRIGGER_COUNT_STREAM for the throttled alerts. A second query selects records from a window that hops forward every time a record is admitted into it, such that only one record per stock ticker per minute is written to the stream.

3. Choose **Save and run SQL**.

The example outputs a stream to `TRIGGER_COUNT_STREAM` similar to the following:

ROWTIME	TICKER_SYMBOL	CHANGE	TRIGGER_COUNT
2018-01-08 22:59:15.742	ASD	-1.77	1
2018-01-08 22:59:15.742	ASD	-1.77	1
2018-01-08 22:59:20.752	DFT	-3.16	1
2018-01-08 22:59:35.775	IOP	-1.88	1

Example: Exploring the In-Application Error Stream

Amazon Kinesis Data Analytics provides an in-application error stream for each application that you create. Any rows that your application cannot process are sent to this error stream. You might consider persisting the error stream data to an external destination so that you can investigate.

You perform the following exercises on the console. In these examples, you introduce errors in the input configuration by editing the schema that is inferred by the discovery process, and then you verify the rows that are sent to the error stream.

Topics

- Introducing a Parse Error
- Introducing a Divide by Zero Error

Introducing a Parse Error

In this exercise, you introduce a parse error.

1. Create a Kinesis data analytics application as described in the Kinesis Data Analytics Getting Started exercise.

2. On the application details page, choose **Connect streaming data**.

3. If you followed the Getting Started exercise, you have a demo stream (`kinesis-anlaytics-demo-stream`) in your account. On the **Connect to source** page, choose this demo stream.

4. Kinesis Data Analytics takes a sample from the demo stream to infer a schema for the in-application input stream it creates. The console shows the inferred schema and sample data in the **Formatted stream sample** tab.

5. Next, edit the schema and modify the column type to introduce the parse error. Choose **Edit schema**.

6. Change the `TICKER_SYMBOL` column type from `VARCHAR(4)` to `INTEGER`.

   Now that the column type of the in-application schema that is created is invalid, Kinesis Data Analytics can't bring in data in the in-application stream. Instead, it sends the rows to the error stream.

7. Choose **Save schema**.

8. Choose **Refresh schema samples**.

   Notice that there are no rows in the **Formatted stream** sample. However, the **Error stream** tab shows data with an error message. The **Error stream** tab shows data sent to the in-application error stream.

   Because you changed the column data type, Kinesis Data Analytics could not bring the data in the in-application input stream. It sent the data to the error stream instead.

Introducing a Divide by Zero Error

In this exercise, you update the application code to introduce a runtime error (division by zero). Notice that Amazon Kinesis Data Analytics sends the resulting rows to the in-application error stream, not to the in-application error stream where the results are supposed to be written.

1. Create a Kinesis data analytics application as described in the Kinesis Data Analytics Getting Started exercise.

   Verify the results on the **Real-time analytics** tab as follows:

   Sour

2. Update the `SELECT` statement in the application code to introduce divide by zero; for example:

```
1 SELECT STREAM ticker_symbol, sector, change, (price / 0) as ProblemColumn
2 FROM "SOURCE_SQL_STREAM_001"
3 WHERE sector SIMILAR TO '%TECH%';
```

3. Run the application.

   Because the division by zero runtime error occurs, instead of writing the results to the `DESTINATION_SQL_STREAM`, Kinesis Data Analytics sends rows to the in-application error stream. On the **Real-time analytics** tab, choose the error stream, and then you can see the rows in the in-application error stream.

Examples: Solution Accelerators

The AWS Management Console has Amazon CloudFront templates available that you can use to create complete streaming data solutions quickly.

For information about the templates that are available for creating Kinesis Data Analytics applications, see the **Related CloudFormation templates** section on the Amazon Kinesis dashboard.

Monitoring Amazon Kinesis Data Analytics

Monitoring is an important part of maintaining the reliability, availability, and performance of Amazon Kinesis Data Analytics and your Amazon Kinesis Data Analytics application. You should collect monitoring data from all of the parts of your AWS solution so that you can more easily debug a multipoint failure if one occurs. Before you start monitoring Amazon Kinesis Data Analytics, however, you should create a monitoring plan that includes answers to the following questions:

- What are your monitoring goals?
- What resources will you monitor?
- How often will you monitor these resources?
- What monitoring tools will you use?
- Who will perform the monitoring tasks?
- Who should be notified when something goes wrong?

The next step is to establish a baseline for normal Amazon Kinesis Data Analytics performance in your environment, by measuring performance at various times and under different load conditions. As you monitor Amazon Kinesis Data Analytics, you can store historical monitoring data. If you do, you can compare it with current performance data, identify normal performance patterns and performance anomalies, and devise methods to address issues.

With Amazon Kinesis Data Analytics, you monitor the application. The application processes data streams (input or output), both of which include *identifiers* which you can use to narrow your search on CloudWatch logs. For information about how Amazon Kinesis Data Analytics processes data streams, see Amazon Kinesis Data Analytics: How It Works.

The most important metric is the `millisBehindLatest`, which indicates how far behind an application is reading from the streaming source. In a typical case, the milliseconds behind should be at or near zero. It is common for brief spikes to appear, which appears as an increase in `millisBehindLatest`.

We recommend that you set up a CloudWatch alarm that triggers when the application is behind by more than an hour reading the streaming source. For some use cases that require very close to real-time processing, such as emitting processed data to a live application, you might choose to set the alarm at a lower value, such as five minutes.

For a list of metrics Amazon Kinesis Data Analytics supports, see Amazon Kinesis Data Analytics Metrics.

Topics

- Monitoring Tools
- Monitoring with Amazon CloudWatch

Monitoring Tools

AWS provides various tools that you can use to monitor Amazon Kinesis Data Analytics. You can configure some of these tools to do the monitoring for you, while some of the tools require manual intervention. We recommend that you automate monitoring tasks as much as possible.

Automated Monitoring Tools

You can use the following automated monitoring tools to watch Amazon Kinesis Data Analytics and report when something is wrong:

- **Amazon CloudWatch Alarms** – Watch a single metric over a time period that you specify, and perform one or more actions based on the value of the metric relative to a given threshold over a number of time periods. The action is a notification sent to an Amazon Simple Notification Service (Amazon SNS) topic or Amazon EC2 Auto Scaling policy. CloudWatch alarms do not invoke actions simply because they are in a particular state; the state must have changed and been maintained for a specified number of periods. For more information, see Monitoring with Amazon CloudWatch.
- **Amazon CloudWatch Logs** – Monitor, store, and access your log files from AWS CloudTrail or other sources. For more information, see Monitoring Log Files in the *Amazon CloudWatch User Guide*.
- **Amazon CloudWatch Events** – Match events and route them to one or more target functions or streams to make changes, capture state information, and take corrective action. For more information, see What is Amazon CloudWatch Events in the *Amazon CloudWatch User Guide*.
- **AWS CloudTrail Log Monitoring** – Share log files between accounts, monitor CloudTrail log files in real time by sending them to CloudWatch Logs, write log processing applications in Java, and validate that your log files have not changed after delivery by CloudTrail. For more information, see Working with CloudTrail Log Files in the *AWS CloudTrail User Guide*.

Manual Monitoring Tools

Another important part of monitoring Amazon Kinesis Data Analytics involves manually monitoring those items that the CloudWatch alarms don't cover. The Amazon Kinesis Data Analytics, CloudWatch, Trusted Advisor, and other AWS console dashboards provide an at-a-glance view of the state of your AWS environment.

- The CloudWatch home page shows the following:
  - Current alarms and status
  - Graphs of alarms and resources
  - Service health status

  In addition, you can use CloudWatch to do the following:
  - Create customized dashboards to monitor the services you care about
  - Graph metric data to troubleshoot issues and discover trends
  - Search and browse all your AWS resource metrics
  - Create and edit alarms to be notified of problems

- AWS Trusted Advisor can help you monitor your AWS resources to improve performance, reliability, security, and cost effectiveness. Four Trusted Advisor checks are available to all users. More than 50 checks are available to users with a Business or Enterprise support plan. For more information, see AWS Trusted Advisor.

Monitoring with Amazon CloudWatch

You can monitor Amazon Kinesis Data Analytics applications using CloudWatch, which collects and processes raw data from Amazon Kinesis Data Analytics into readable, near real-time metrics. These statistics are retained for a period of two weeks, so that you can access historical information and gain a better perspective on how your web application or service is performing. By default, Amazon Kinesis Data Analytics metric data is automatically sent to CloudWatch. For more information, see What Are Amazon CloudWatch, Amazon CloudWatch Events, and Amazon CloudWatch Logs? in the *Amazon CloudWatch User Guide*.

Topics

- Viewing Amazon Kinesis Data Analytics Metrics and Dimensions

Viewing Amazon Kinesis Data Analytics Metrics and Dimensions

When your Amazon Kinesis Data Analytics application processes data streams, Kinesis Data Analytics sends the following metrics and dimensions to CloudWatch. You can use the following procedures to view the metrics for Kinesis Data Analytics.

In the console, metrics are grouped first by service namespace, and then by the dimension combinations within each namespace.

For a list of metrics Amazon Kinesis Data Analytics supports, see Amazon Kinesis Data Analytics Metrics.

To view metrics using the CloudWatch console

1. Open the CloudWatch console at https://console.aws.amazon.com/cloudwatch/.

2. In the navigation pane, choose **Metrics**.

3. In the **CloudWatch Metrics by Category** pane for Amazon Kinesis Data Analytics, select a metrics category.

4. In the upper pane, scroll to view the full list of metrics.

To view metrics using the AWS CLI

- At a command prompt, use the following command.

```
1. aws cloudwatch list-metrics --namespace "AWS/KinesisAnalytics" --region region
```

Amazon Kinesis Data Analytics metrics are collected at the following levels:

- Application
- Input stream
- Output stream

Creating CloudWatch Alarms to Monitor Amazon Kinesis Data Analytics

You can create a CloudWatch alarm that sends an Amazon SNS message when the alarm changes state. An alarm watches a single metric over a time period you specify. It performs one or more actions based on the value of the metric relative to a given threshold over a number of time periods. The action is a notification sent to an Amazon SNS topic or Auto Scaling policy.

Alarms invoke actions for sustained state changes only. For a CloudWatch alarm to invoke an action, the state must have changed and been maintained for a specified amount of time.

You can set alarms using the AWS Management Console, CloudWatch CLI, or CloudWatch API, as described following.

To set an alarm using the CloudWatch console

1. Sign in to the AWS Management Console and open the CloudWatch console at https://console.aws.amazon.com/cloudwatch/.

2. Choose **Create Alarm**. The Create Alarm Wizard launches.

3. Choose **Kinesis Analytics Metrics**, and then scroll through the Amazon Kinesis Data Analytics metrics to locate the metric you want to place an alarm on.

   To display just Amazon Kinesis Data Analytics metrics, search for the file system ID of your file system. Select the metric to create an alarm for, and then choose **Next**.

4. Type values for **Name**, **Description**, and **Whenever** for the metric.

5. If you want CloudWatch to send you an email when the alarm state is reached, in the **Whenever this alarm:** field, choose **State is ALARM**. In the **Send notification to:** field, choose an existing SNS topic. If you select **Create topic**, you can set the name and email addresses for a new email subscription list. This list is saved and appears in the field for future alarms. **Note**
   If you use **Create topic** to create a new Amazon SNS topic, the email addresses must be verified before they receive notifications. Emails are only sent when the alarm enters an alarm state. If this alarm state change happens before the email addresses are verified, they do not receive a notification.

6. In the **Alarm Preview** section, preview the alarm you're about to create.

7. Choose **Create Alarm** to create the alarm.

To set an alarm using the CloudWatch CLI

- Call [mon\-put\-metric\-alarm](http://docs.aws.amazon.com/AmazonCloudWatch/latest/cli/cli-mon-put-metric-alarm.html). For more information, see the Amazon CloudWatch CLI Reference.

To set an alarm using the CloudWatch API

- Call [PutMetricAlarm](http://docs.aws.amazon.com/AmazonCloudWatch/latest/APIReference/API_PutMetricAlarm.html). For more information, see the Amazon CloudWatch API Reference.

Working with Amazon CloudWatch Logs

If an Amazon Kinesis Data Analytics application is misconfigured, it can transition to a running state during application start or update but not process any data into the in-application input stream. By adding a CloudWatch log option to the application, you can monitor for application configuration problems.

Amazon Kinesis Data Analytics can generate configuration errors under the following conditions:

- The Kinesis Stream used for input doesn't exist.
- The Amazon Kinesis Data Firehose delivery stream used for input doesn't exist.
- The Amazon S3 bucket used as a reference data source doesn't exist.
- The specified file in the reference data source in the S3 bucket doesn't exist.
- The correct resource is not defined in the AWS Identity and Access Management (IAM) role that manages related permissions.
- The correct permission is not defined in the IAM role that manages related permissions.
- Kinesis Data Analytics doesn't have permission to assume the IAM role that manages related permissions.

For more information on Amazon CloudWatch, see the CloudWatch User Guide.

Adding the PutLogEvents Policy Action

Amazon Kinesis Data Analytics needs permissions to write misconfiguration errors to CloudWatch. You can add these permissions to the IAM role that Amazon Kinesis Data Analytics assumes, as described following. For more information on using an IAM role for Amazon Kinesis Data Analytics, see Granting Amazon Kinesis Data Analytics Permissions to Access Streaming Sources (Creating an IAM Role).

Trust Policy

To grant Kinesis Data Analytics permissions to assume an IAM role, you can attach the following trust policy to the role.

```
{
  "Version": "2012-10-17",
  "Statement": [
    {
      "Effect": "Allow",
      "Principal": {
        "Service": "kinesisanalytics.amazonaws.com"
      },
      "Action": "sts:AssumeRole"
    }
  ]
}
```

Permissions Policy

To grant an application permissions to write log events to CloudWatch from an Kinesis Data Analytics resource, you can use the following IAM permissions policy.

```
{
    "Version": "2012-10-17",
    "Statement": [
        {
            "Sid": "Stmt0123456789000",
```

```
 6              "Effect": "Allow",
 7              "Action": [
 8                  "logs:PutLogEvents"
 9              ],
10              "Resource": [
11                  "arn:aws:logs:us-east-1:123456789012:log-group:my-log-group:log-stream:my-log-
                       stream*"
12              ]
13          }
14      ]
15  }
```

Adding Configuration Error Monitoring

Use the following API actions to add a CloudWatch log option to a new or existing application or change a log option for an existing application.

Note
You can currently only add a CloudWatch log option to an application by using API actions. You can't add CloudWatch log options by using the console.

Adding a CloudWatch Log Option When Creating an Application

The following code example demonstrates how to use the `CreateApplication` action to add a CloudWatch log option when you create an application. For more information on `Create_Application`, see CreateApplication.

```
 1  {
 2      "ApplicationCode": "<The SQL code the new application will run on the input stream>",
 3      "ApplicationDescription": "<A friendly description for the new application>",
 4      "ApplicationName": "<The name for the new application>",
 5      "Inputs": [ ... ],
 6      "Outputs": [ ... ],
 7      "CloudWatchLoggingOptions": [{
 8          "LogStreamARN": "<Amazon Resource Name (ARN) of the CloudWatch log stream to add to the
                new application>",
 9          "RoleARN": "<ARN of the role to use to access the log>"
10      }]
11  }
```

Adding a CloudWatch Log Option to an Existing Application

The following code example demonstrates how to use the `AddApplicationCloudWatchLoggingOption` action to add a CloudWatch log option to an existing application. For more information on `AddApplicationCloudWatchLoggingOption`, see AddApplicationCloudWatchLoggingOption.

```
 1  {
 2      "ApplicationName": "<Name of the application to add the log option to>",
 3      "CloudWatchLoggingOption": {
 4          "LogStreamARN": "<ARN of the log stream to add to the application>",
 5          "RoleARN": "<ARN of the role to use to access the log>"
 6      },
 7      "CurrentApplicationVersionId": <Version of the application to add the log to>
 8  }
```

Updating an Existing CloudWatch Log Option

The following code example demonstrates how to use the `UpdateApplication` action to modify an existing CloudWatch log option. For more information on `UpdateApplication`, see UpdateApplication.

```
1  {
2      "ApplicationName": "<Name of the application to update the log option for>",
3      "ApplicationUpdate": {
4        "CloudWatchLoggingOptionUpdates": [
5          {
6              "CloudWatchLoggingOptionId": "<ID of the logging option to modify>",
7              "LogStreamARNUpdate": "<ARN of the new log stream to use>",
8              "RoleARNUpdate": "<ARN of the new role to use to access the log stream>"
9          }
10       ],
11     },
12     "CurrentApplicationVersionId": <ID of the application version to modify>
13 }
```

Deleting a CloudWatch Log Option from an Application

The following code example demonstrates how to use the `DeleteApplicationCloudWatchLoggingOption` action to delete an existing CloudWatch log option. For more information on `DeleteApplicationCloudWatchLoggingOption`, see DeleteApplicationCloudWatchLoggingOption.

```
1  {
2      "ApplicationName": "<Name of application to delete log option from>",
3      "CloudWatchLoggingOptionId": "<ID of the application log option to delete>",
4      "CurrentApplicationVersionId": <Version of the application to delete the log option from>
5  }
```

Configuration Errors

Following, you can learn details about errors that you might see in CloudWatch logs from a misconfigured application.

Error Message Format

Error messages generated by application misconfiguration appear in the following format.

```
1  {
2  "applicationARN": "string",
3  "applicationVersionId": integer,
4  "messageType": "ERROR",
5  "message": "string",
6  "inputId": "string",
7  "referenceId": "string",
8  "errorCode": "string"
9  "messageSchemaVersion": "integer",
10 }
```

The fields in an error message contain the following information:

- *applicationARN:* The Amazon Resource Name (ARN) of the generating application, for example: `arn:aws:kinesisanalytics:us-east-1:112233445566:application/sampleApp`

- *applicationVersionId:* The version of the application at the time the error was encountered. For more information, see ApplicationDetail.

- *messageType:* The message type. Currently, this type can be only `ERROR`.

- *message:* The details of the error, for example:

```
1 There is a problem related to the configuration of your input. Please check that the
      resource exists, the role has the correct permissions to access the resource and that
      Kinesis Analytics can assume the role provided.
```

- *inputId:* ID associated with the application input. This value is only present if this input is the cause of the error. This value is not present if *referenceId* is present. For more information, see DescribeApplication.

- *referenceId:* ID associated with the application reference data source. This value is only present if this source is the cause of the error. This value is not present if *inputId* is present. For more information, see DescribeApplication.

- *errorCode:* The identifier for the error. This ID is either `InputError` or `ReferenceDataError`.

- *messageSchemaVersion:* A value that specifies the current message schema version, currently `1`. You can check this value to see if the error message schema has been updated.

Errors

The errors that might appear in CloudWatch logs for Amazon Kinesis Data Analytics include the following.

Resource Does Not Exist

If an ARN is specified for an Kinesis input stream that doesn't exist, but the ARN is syntactically correct, an error like the following is generated.

```
1 {
2 "applicationARN": "arn:aws:kinesisanalytics:us-east-1:112233445566:application/sampleApp",
3 "applicationVersionId": "5",
4  "messageType": "ERROR",
5  "message": "There is a problem related to the configuration of your input. Please check that
       the resource exists, the role has the correct permissions to access the resource and that
       Kinesis Analytics can assume the role provided.",
6  "inputId":"1.1",
7  "errorCode": "InputError",
8  "messageSchemaVersion": "1"
9 }
```

If an incorrect Amazon S3 file key is used for reference data, an error like the following is generated.

```
1 {
2 "applicationARN": "arn:aws:kinesisanalytics:us-east-1:112233445566:application/sampleApp",
3 "applicationVersionId": "5",
4  "messageType": "ERROR",
5  "message": "There is a problem related to the configuration of your reference data. Please
       check that the bucket and the file exist, the role has the correct permissions to access
       these resources and that Kinesis Analytics can assume the role provided.",
6  "referenceId":"1.1",
7  "errorCode": "ReferenceDataError",
```

```
8   "messageSchemaVersion": "1"
9 }
```

Role Does Not Exist

If an ARN is specified for an IAM input role that doesn't exist, but the ARN is syntactically correct, an error like the following is generated.

```
1 {
2   "applicationARN": "arn:aws:kinesisanalytics:us-east-1:112233445566:application/sampleApp",
3   "applicationVersionId": "5",
4   "messageType": "ERROR",
5   "message": "There is a problem related to the configuration of your input. Please check that
        the resource exists, the role has the correct permissions to access the resource and that
        Kinesis Analytics can assume the role provided.",
6   "inputId":null,
7   "errorCode": "InputError",
8   "messageSchemaVersion": "1"
9 }
```

Role Does Not Have Permissions to Access the Resource

If an input role is used that doesn't have permission to access the input resources, such as an Kinesis source stream, an error like the following is generated.

```
1 {
2   "applicationARN": "arn:aws:kinesisanalytics:us-east-1:112233445566:application/sampleApp",
3   "applicationVersionId": "5",
4   "messageType": "ERROR",
5   "message": "There is a problem related to the configuration of your input. Please check that
        the resource exists, the role has the correct permissions to access the resource and that
        Kinesis Analytics can assume the role provided.",
6   "inputId":null,
7   "errorCode": "InputError",
8   "messageSchemaVersion": "1"
9 }
```

Limits

When working with Amazon Kinesis Data Analytics, note the following limits:

- The size of a row in an in-application stream is limited to 512 KB. Kinesis Data Analytics uses up to 1 KB to store metadata. This metadata counts against the row limit.

- The SQL code in an application is limited to 100 KB.

- The service is available in specific AWS Regions. For more information, see Amazon Kinesis Data Analytics in the *AWS General Reference.*

- You can create up to 50 Kinesis Data Analytics applications per AWS Region in your account. You can create a case to request additional applications via the service limit increase form. For more information, see the AWS Support Center.

- The maximum amount of source parallelism is 64. That is, in your application input configuration, you can request the mapping of a streaming source to up to 64 in-application streams.

- The number of Kinesis processing units (KPU) is limited to eight. For instructions on how to request an increase to this limit, see **To request a limit increase** in AWS Service Limits.

  With Kinesis Data Analytics, you pay only for what you use. You are charged an hourly rate based on the average number of KPUs that are used to run your stream-processing application. A single KPU provides you with 1 vCPU and 4 GB of memory.

- Each application can have one streaming source and up to one reference data source.

- You can configure up to three destinations for your Kinesis Data Analytics application. We recommend that you use one of these destinations to persist in-application error stream data.

- The Amazon S3 object that stores reference data can be up to 1 GB in size.

- If you change the reference data that is stored in the S3 bucket after you upload reference data to an in-application table, you need to use the UpdateApplication operation (using the API or AWS CLI) to refresh the data in the in-application table. Currently, the AWS Management Console doesn't support refreshing reference data in your application.

- Currently, Kinesis Data Analytics doesn't support data generated by the Amazon Kinesis Producer Library (KPL).

Best Practices

This section describes best practices when working with Amazon Kinesis Data Analytics applications.

Topics

- Managing Applications
- Defining Input Schema
- Connecting to Outputs
- Authoring Application Code

Managing Applications

When managing Amazon Kinesis Data Analytics applications, follow these best practices:

- **Set up CloudWatch alarms** – Using the CloudWatch metrics that Amazon Kinesis Data Analytics provides, you can monitor the following:

  - Input bytes and input records (number of bytes and records entering the application)
  - Output bytes, output record
  - `MillisBehindLatest` (tracks how far behind the application is in reading from the streaming source)

  We recommend that you set up at least two CloudWatch alarms on the following metrics for your in-production applications:

  - Alarm on `MillisBehindLatest` – For most cases, we recommend that you set this alarm to trigger when your application is one hour behind the latest data, for an average of one minute. For applications with lower end-to-end processing needs, you can tune this to a lower tolerance. The alarm can help you ensure that your application is reading the latest data.

- Limit the number of production applications reading from the same Kinesis stream to two applications to avoid getting the `ReadProvisionedThroughputException` exception. **Note**
  In this case, the term *application* refers to any application that can read from the streaming source. Only an Amazon Kinesis Data Analytics application can read from a Kinesis Data Firehose delivery stream. However, many applications can read from an Kinesis stream, such as an Amazon Kinesis Data Analytics application or AWS Lambda. The recommended application limit refers to all applications that you configure to read from a streaming source.

  Amazon Kinesis Data Analytics reads a streaming source approximately once per second per application. However, an application that falls behind might read data at a faster rate to catch up. To allow adequate throughput for applications to catch up, you limit the number of applications reading the same data source.

- Limit the number of production applications reading from the same Kinesis Data Firehose delivery stream to one application.

  A Kinesis Data Firehose delivery stream can write to destinations such as Amazon S3, Amazon Redshift, and it can also be a streaming source for your Amazon Kinesis Data Analytics application. Therefore, we recommend you do not configure more than one Amazon Kinesis Data Analytics application per Kinesis Data Firehose delivery stream to make sure the delivery stream can also deliver to other destinations.

Defining Input Schema

When configuring application input in the console, you first specify a streaming source. The console then uses the discovery API (see DiscoverInputSchema) to infer a schema by sampling records on the streaming source. The schema, among other things, defines names and data types of the columns in the resulting in-application stream. The console displays the schema. We recommend you do the following with this inferred schema:

- Adequately test the inferred schema. The discovery process uses only a sample of records on the streaming source to infer a schema. If your streaming source has many record types, there is a possibility that the discovery API missed sampling one or more record types, which can result in a schema that does not accurately reflect data on the streaming source.

  When your application starts, these missed record types might result in parsing errors. Amazon Kinesis Data Analytics sends these records to the in-application error stream. To reduce these parsing errors, we recommend that you test the inferred schema interactively in the console, and monitor the in-application stream for missed records.

- The Amazon Kinesis Data Analytics API does not support specifying the NOT NULL constraint on columns in the input configuration. If you want NOT NULL constraints on columns in your in-application stream, you should create these in-application streams using your application code. You can then copy data from one in-application stream into another, and then the constraint will be enforced.

  Any attempt to insert rows with NULL values when a value is required results in an error, and Amazon Kinesis Data Analytics sends these errors to the in-application error stream.

- Relax data types inferred by the discovery process. The discovery process recommends columns and data types based on a random sampling of records on the streaming source. We recommend that you review these carefully and consider relaxing these data types to cover all of the possible cases of records in your input. This ensures fewer parsing errors across the application while it is running. For example, if inferred schema has a SMALLINT as column type, perhaps consider changing it to INTEGER.

- Use SQL functions in your application code to handle any unstructured data or columns. You may have unstructured data or columns, such as log data, in your input. For examples, see Example: Transforming DateTime Values. One approach to handling this type of data is to define the schema with only one column of type VARCHAR(N), where N is the largest possible row that you would expect to see in your stream. In your application code you can then read the incoming records, use the String and Date Time functions to parse and schematize the raw data.

- Make sure that you handle streaming source data that contains nesting more than two levels deep completely. When source data is JSON, you can have nesting. The discovery API will infer a schema that flattens one level of nesting. For two levels of nesting, the discovery API will also attempt to flatten these. Beyond two levels of nesting, there is limited support for flattening. In order to handle nesting completely, you have to manually modify the inferred schema to suite your needs. Use either of the following strategies to do this:

  - Use the JSON row path to selectively pull out only the required key value pairs for your application. A JSON row path provides a pointer to the specific key value pair you would like to bring in your application. This can be done for any level of nesting.

- Use the JSON row path to selectively pull out complex JSON objects and then use string manipulation functions in your application code to pull the specific data that you need.

Connecting to Outputs

We recommend that every application have at least two outputs. use the first destination to insert the results of your SQL queries. Use the second destination to insert the entire error stream and send it to an S3 bucket through a Amazon Kinesis Data Firehose delivery stream.

Authoring Application Code

We recommend the following:

- In your SQL statement, we recommend that you do not specify time-based window that is longer than one hour for the following reasons:
  - If an application needs to be restarted, either because you updated the application or for Amazon Kinesis Data Analytics internal reasons, all data included in the window must be read again from the streaming data source. This will take time before Amazon Kinesis Data Analytics can emit output for that window.
  - Amazon Kinesis Data Analytics must maintain everything related to the application's state, including relevant data, for the duration. This will consume significant Amazon Kinesis Data Analytics processing units.
- During development, keep window size small in your SQL statements so that you can see the results faster. When you deploy the application to your production environment, you can set the window size as appropriate.
- Instead of a single complex SQL statement, you might consider breaking it into multiple statements, in each step saving results in intermediate in-application streams. This might help you debug faster.
- When using tumbling windows, we recommend that you use two windows, one for processing time and one for your logical time (ingest time or event time). For more information, see Timestamps and the ROWTIME Column.

Troubleshooting Amazon Kinesis Data Analytics

The following can help you troubleshoot problems you have with Amazon Kinesis Data Analytics.

Get a SQL Statement to Work Correctly

If you need to figure out how to get a particular SQL statement to work correctly, you have several different resources when using Amazon Kinesis Data Analytics:

- For more information about SQL statements, see Example Applications in the *Amazon Kinesis Data Analytics Developer Guide.* This section provides a number of SQL examples that you can use.
- The Amazon Kinesis Data Analytics SQL Reference provides a detailed guide to authoring streaming SQL statements.
- If you are still running into issues, we recommend that you ask a question on the Kinesis Data Analytics Forums.

Unable to Detect or Discover My Schema

In some cases, Kinesis Data Analytics is unable to detect or discover a schema. In many of these cases, you can still use Kinesis Data Analytics.

Suppose that you have UTF-8 encoded data that doesn't use a delimiter, data that uses a format other than comma-separated value (CSV) format, or the discovery API did not discover your schema. In these cases, you can define a schema by hand or use string manipulation functions to structure your data.

To discover the schema for your stream, Kinesis Data Analytics randomly samples the latest data in your stream. If you aren't consistently sending data to your stream, Kinesis Data Analytics might not be able to retrieve a sample and detect a schema. For more information, see Using the Schema Discovery Feature on Streaming Data Using the Schema Discovery Feature and Related Editing in the *Amazon Kinesis Data Analytics Developer Guide.*

Important Application Health Parameters to Monitor

To make sure that your application is running correctly, we recommend that you monitor certain important parameters.

The most important parameter to monitor is the Amazon CloudWatch metric `MillisBehindLatest`. This metric represents how far behind the current time you are reading from the stream. This metric helps you determine whether you are processing records from the source stream fast enough.

As a rule of thumb, you should set up a CloudWatch alarm to trigger if you fall behind more than one hour. However, the amount of time depends on your use case. You can adjust it as needed.

For more information, see Best Practices in the *Amazon Kinesis Data Analytics Developer Guide. *

Invalid Code Errors When Running an Application

When you cannot save and run the SQL code for your Amazon Kinesis Data Analytics application, the following are common causes:

- **The stream was redefined in your SQL code** – After you create a stream and the pump associated with the stream, you cannot redefine the same stream in your code. For more information about creating a stream, see CREATE STREAM. For more information about creating a pump, see CREATE PUMP.

- **A GROUP BY clause uses multiple ROWTIME columns ** – You can specify only one ROWTIME column in the GROUP BY clause. For more information, see GROUP BY and ROWTIME.
- **One or more data types have an invalid casting ** – In this case, your code has an invalid implicit cast. For example, you might be casting a timestamp to a bigint in your code.
- **A stream has the same name as a service reserved stream name ** – A stream cannot have the same name as the service-reserved stream `error_stream`.

Application Doesn't Process Data After Deleting and Re-creating the Kinesis Application Input Stream or Kinesis Data Firehose Delivery Stream with the Same Name

Suppose that you delete the Kinesis stream that provides application input for a running application and create a new Kinesis stream with the same name. In this case, the application doesn't process the input data from the new stream. In addition, no data is delivered to the destination.

The same effect occurs if you delete the Kinesis Data Firehose delivery stream for a running application and create a new Kinesis Data Firehose delivery stream with the same name.

To resolve this issue, stop and restart the application through the AWS Management Console.

Insufficient Throughput or High MillisBehindLatest

If your application's MillisBehindLatest metric is steadily increasing or consistently is above 1000 (one second), it can be due to the following reasons:

- Check your application's InputBytes CloudWatch metric. If you are ingesting more than 4 MB/sec, this can cause an increase in MillisBehindLatest. To improve your application's throughput, increase the value of the `InputParallelism` parameter. For more information, see Parallelizing Input Streams for Increased Throughput.
- Check your application's output delivery Success metric for failures in delivering to your destination. Verify that you have correctly configured the output, and that your output stream has sufficient capacity.
- If your application uses an AWS Lambda function for pre-processing or as an output, check the application's InputProcessing.Duration or LambdaDelivery.Duration CloudWatch metric. If the Lambda function invocation duration is longer than 5 seconds, consider doing the following:
  - Increase the Lambda function's Memory allocation under Configuration -> Basic Settings in the Lambda console. For more information, see Configuring Lambda Functions.
  - Increase the number of shards in your input stream of the application. This will increase the number of parallel functions the application will invoke which may increase throughput.
  - Verify that the function is not making blocking calls that are impacting performance, such as synchronous requests for external resources.
  - Examine your Lambda function to see if there are other areas where you can improve performance. Check the CloudWatch Logs of the application Lambda function.For more information, see Accessing Amazon CloudWatch Metrics for AWS Lambda.
- Verify that your application is not reaching the default limit for Kinesis Processing Units (KPU). If your application is reaching this limit, you can request a limit increase. For more information, see Automatically Scaling Applications to Increase Throughput.

Authentication and Access Control for Amazon Kinesis Data Analytics

Access to Amazon Kinesis Data Analytics requires credentials. Those credentials must have permissions to access AWS resources, such as an Amazon Kinesis Data Analytics application or an Amazon Elastic Compute Cloud (Amazon EC2) instance. The following sections provide details on how you can use AWS Identity and Access Management (IAM) and Amazon Kinesis Data Analytics to help secure access to your resources.

- Authentication
- Access Control

Authentication

You can access AWS as any of the following types of identities:

- **AWS account root user** – When you first create an AWS account, you begin with a single sign-in identity that has complete access to all AWS services and resources in the account. This identity is called the AWS account *root user* and is accessed by signing in with the email address and password that you used to create the account. We strongly recommend that you do not use the root user for your everyday tasks, even the administrative ones. Instead, adhere to the best practice of using the root user only to create your first IAM user. Then securely lock away the root user credentials and use them to perform only a few account and service management tasks.

- **IAM user** – An IAM user is an identity within your AWS account that has specific custom permissions (for example, permissions to create an application in Amazon Kinesis Data Analytics). You can use an IAM user name and password to sign in to secure AWS webpages like the AWS Management Console, AWS Discussion Forums, or the AWS Support Center.

  In addition to a user name and password, you can also generate access keys for each user. You can use these keys when you access AWS services programmatically, either through one of the several SDKs or by using the AWS Command Line Interface (CLI). The SDK and CLI tools use the access keys to cryptographically sign your request. If you don't use AWS tools, you must sign the request yourself. Amazon Kinesis Data Analytics supports *Signature Version 4*, a protocol for authenticating inbound API requests. For more information about authenticating requests, see Signature Version 4 Signing Process in the *AWS General Reference*.

- **IAM role** – An IAM role is an IAM identity that you can create in your account that has specific permissions. It is similar to an *IAM user*, but it is not associated with a specific person. An IAM role enables you to obtain temporary access keys that can be used to access AWS services and resources. IAM roles with temporary credentials are useful in the following situations:

  - **Federated user access** – Instead of creating an IAM user, you can use existing user identities from AWS Directory Service, your enterprise user directory, or a web identity provider. These are known as *federated users*. AWS assigns a role to a federated user when access is requested through an identity provider. For more information about federated users, see Federated Users and Roles in the *IAM User Guide*.

  - **AWS service access** – You can use an IAM role in your account to grant an AWS service permissions to access your account's resources. For example, you can create a role that allows Amazon Redshift to access an Amazon S3 bucket on your behalf and then load data from that bucket into an Amazon

Redshift cluster. For more information, see Creating a Role to Delegate Permissions to an AWS Service in the *IAM User Guide*.

- **Applications running on Amazon EC2** – You can use an IAM role to manage temporary credentials for applications that are running on an EC2 instance and making AWS API requests. This is preferable to storing access keys within the EC2 instance. To assign an AWS role to an EC2 instance and make it available to all of its applications, you create an instance profile that is attached to the instance. An instance profile contains the role and enables programs that are running on the EC2 instance to get temporary credentials. For more information, see Using an IAM Role to Grant Permissions to Applications Running on Amazon EC2 Instances in the *IAM User Guide*.

Access Control

You can have valid credentials to authenticate your requests, but unless you have permissions you cannot create or access Amazon Kinesis Data Analytics resources. For example, you must have permissions to create an Amazon Kinesis Data Analytics application.

The following sections describe how to manage permissions for Amazon Kinesis Data Analytics. We recommend that you read the overview first.

- Overview of Managing Access Permissions to Your Amazon Kinesis Data Analytics Resources
- Using Identity-Based Policies (IAM Policies) for Amazon Kinesis Data Analytics
- Amazon Kinesis Data Analytics API Permissions: Actions, Permissions, and Resources Reference

Overview of Managing Access Permissions to Your Amazon Kinesis Data Analytics Resources

Every AWS resource is owned by an AWS account, and permissions to create or access a resource are governed by permissions policies. An account administrator can attach permissions policies to IAM identities (that is, users, groups, and roles), and some services (such as AWS Lambda) also support attaching permissions policies to resources.

Note

An *account administrator* (or administrator user) is a user with administrator privileges. For more information, see IAM Best Practices in the *IAM User Guide.*

When granting permissions, you decide who is getting the permissions, the resources they get permissions for, and the specific actions that you want to allow on those resources.

Topics

- Amazon Kinesis Data Analytics Resources and Operations
- Understanding Resource Ownership
- Managing Access to Resources
- Specifying Policy Elements: Actions, Effects, and Principals
- Specifying Conditions in a Policy

Amazon Kinesis Data Analytics Resources and Operations

In Amazon Kinesis Data Analytics, the primary resource is *an application.* In a policy, you use an Amazon Resource Name (ARN) to identify the resource that the policy applies to.

These resources have unique Amazon Resource Names (ARNs) associated with them, as shown in the following table.

Resource Type	ARN Format
Application	`arn:aws:kinesisanalytics:region:` `account-id:application/application-` `name`

Amazon Kinesis Data Analytics provides a set of operations to work with Amazon Kinesis Data Analytics resources. For a list of available operations, see Amazon Kinesis Data Analytics Actions.

Understanding Resource Ownership

The AWS account owns the resources that are created in the account, regardless of who created the resources. Specifically, the resource owner is the AWS account of the principal entity (that is, the root account, an IAM user, or an IAM role) that authenticates the resource creation request. The following examples illustrate how this works:

- If you use the root account credentials of your AWS account to create an application, your AWS account is the owner of the resource (in Amazon Kinesis Data Analytics, the resource is an application).
- If you create an IAM user in your AWS account and grant permissions to create an application to that user, the user can create an application. However, your AWS account, to which the user belongs, owns the application resource.

- If you create an IAM role in your AWS account with permissions to create an application, anyone who can assume the role can create an application. Your AWS account, to which the user belongs, owns the application resource.

Managing Access to Resources

A *permissions policy* describes who has access to what. The following section explains the available options for creating permissions policies.

Note
This section discusses using IAM in the context of Amazon Kinesis Data Analytics. It doesn't provide detailed information about the IAM service. For complete IAM documentation, see What Is IAM? in the *IAM User Guide*. For information about IAM policy syntax and descriptions, see AWS IAM Policy Reference in the *IAM User Guide*.

Policies attached to an IAM identity are referred to as *identity-based* policies (IAM polices) and policies attached to a resource are referred to as *resource-based* policies. Amazon Kinesis Data Analytics supports only identity-based policies (IAM policies).

Topics

- Identity-Based Policies (IAM Policies)
- Resource-Based Policies

Identity-Based Policies (IAM Policies)

You can attach policies to IAM identities. For example, you can do the following:

- **Attach a permissions policy to a user or a group in your account** – To grant a user permissions to create an Amazon Kinesis Data Analytics resource, such as an application, you can attach a permissions policy to a user or group that the user belongs to.

- **Attach a permissions policy to a role (grant cross-account permissions)** – You can attach an identity-based permissions policy to an IAM role to grant cross-account permissions. For example, the administrator in account A can create a role to grant cross-account permissions to another AWS account (for example, account B) or an AWS service as follows:

  1. Account A administrator creates an IAM role and attaches a permissions policy to the role that grants permissions on resources in account A.

  2. Account A administrator attaches a trust policy to the role identifying account B as the principal who can assume the role.

  3. Account B administrator can then delegate permissions to assume the role to any users in account B. Doing this allows users in account B to create or access resources in account A. The principal in the trust policy can also be an AWS service principal if you want to grant an AWS service permissions to assume the role.

  For more information about using IAM to delegate permissions, see Access Management in the *IAM User Guide*.

The following is an example policy that grants permission for the `kinesisanalytics:CreateApplication`action, which is required to create an Amazon Kinesis Data Analytics application.

Note that:

Note
This is an introductory example policy. When you attach the policy to the user, the user will be able to create an application using the AWS CLI or AWS SDK. But the user will need more permissions to configure input

and output. In addition, the user will need more permissions when using the console. The later sections provide more information.

```
1  {
2      "Version": "2012-10-17",
3      "Statement": [
4          {
5              "Sid": "Stmt1473028104000",
6              "Effect": "Allow",
7              "Action": [
8                  "kinesisanalytics:CreateApplication"
9              ],
10             "Resource": [
11                 "*"
12             ]
13         }
14     ]
15 }
```

For more information about using identity-based policies with Amazon Kinesis Data Analytics, see Using Identity-Based Policies (IAM Policies) for Amazon Kinesis Data Analytics. For more information about users, groups, roles, and permissions, see Identities (Users, Groups, and Roles) in the *IAM User Guide*.

Resource-Based Policies

Other services, such as Amazon S3, also support resource-based permissions policies. For example, you can attach a policy to an S3 bucket to manage access permissions to that bucket. Amazon Kinesis Data Analytics doesn't support resource-based policies.

Specifying Policy Elements: Actions, Effects, and Principals

For each Amazon Kinesis Data Analytics resource, the service defines a set of API operations. To grant permissions for these API operations, Amazon Kinesis Data Analytics defines a set of actions that you can specify in a policy. Some API operations can require permissions for more than one action in order to perform the API operation. For more information about resources and API operations, see Amazon Kinesis Data Analytics Resources and Operations and Amazon Kinesis Data Analytics Actions.

The following are the most basic policy elements:

- **Resource** – You use an Amazon Resource Name (ARN) to identify the resource that the policy applies to. For more information, see Amazon Kinesis Data Analytics Resources and Operations.
- **Action** – You use action keywords to identify resource operations that you want to allow or deny. For example, you can use `create` to allow users to create an application.
- **Effect** – You specify the effect, either allow or deny, when the user requests the specific action. If you don't explicitly grant access to (allow) a resource, access is implicitly denied. You can also explicitly deny access to a resource, which you might do to make sure that a user cannot access it, even if a different policy grants access.
- **Principal** – In identity-based policies (IAM policies), the user that the policy is attached to is the implicit principal. For resource-based policies, you specify the user, account, service, or other entity that you want to receive permissions (applies to resource-based policies only). Amazon Kinesis Data Analytics doesn't support resource-based policies.

To learn more about IAM policy syntax and descriptions, see AWS IAM Policy Reference in the *IAM User Guide*.

For a table showing all of the Amazon Kinesis Data Analytics API operations and the resources that they apply to, see Amazon Kinesis Data Analytics API Permissions: Actions, Permissions, and Resources Reference.

Specifying Conditions in a Policy

When you grant permissions, you can use the access policy language to specify the conditions when a policy should take effect. For example, you might want a policy to be applied only after a specific date. For more information about specifying conditions in a policy language, see Condition in the *IAM User Guide*.

To express conditions, you use predefined condition keys. There are no condition keys specific to Amazon Kinesis Data Analytics. However, there are AWS-wide condition keys that you can use as appropriate. For a complete list of AWS-wide keys, see Available Keys for Conditions in the *IAM User Guide*.

Using Identity-Based Policies (IAM Policies) for Amazon Kinesis Data Analytics

This topic provides examples of identity-based policies that demonstrate how an account administrator can attach permissions policies to IAM identities (that is, users, groups, and roles) and thereby grant permissions to perform operations on Amazon Kinesis Data Analytics resources.

Important
We recommend that you first review the introductory topics that explain the basic concepts and options available to manage access to your Amazon Kinesis Data Analytics resources. For more information, see Overview of Managing Access Permissions to Your Amazon Kinesis Data Analytics Resources.

Topics

- Permissions Required to Use the Amazon Kinesis Data Analytics Console
- AWS Managed (Predefined) Policies for Amazon Kinesis Data Analytics
- Customer Managed Policy Examples

The following shows an example of a permissions policy.

```
1  {
2      "Version": "2012-10-17",
3      "Statement": [
4          {
5              "Sid": "Stmt1473028104000",
6              "Effect": "Allow",
7              "Action": [
8                  "kinesisanalytics:CreateApplication"
9              ],
10             "Resource": [
11                 "*"
12             ]
13         }
14     ]
15 }
```

The policy has one statement:

- The first statement grants permissions for one Amazon Kinesis Data Analytics action (`kinesisanalytics:CreateApplication`) on a resource using the Amazon Resource Name (ARN) for the application. The ARN in this case specifies a wildcard character (*) to indicate that the permission is granted for any resource.

For a table showing all of the Amazon Kinesis Data Analytics API operations and the resources that they apply to, see Amazon Kinesis Data Analytics API Permissions: Actions, Permissions, and Resources Reference.

Permissions Required to Use the Amazon Kinesis Data Analytics Console

For a user to work with Amazon Kinesis Data Analytics console, you need to grant the requisite permissions. For example, if you want to grant a user permission to create an application, you need to grant permissions that will show the user the streaming sources in the account so that the user can configure input and output in the console.

We recommend the following:

- Use the AWS managed policies to grant user permissions. For available policies, see AWS Managed (Predefined) Policies for Amazon Kinesis Data Analytics.

- Create custom policies. In this case, we recommend that you review the example provided in this section. For more information, see Customer Managed Policy Examples.

AWS Managed (Predefined) Policies for Amazon Kinesis Data Analytics

AWS addresses many common use cases by providing standalone IAM policies that are created and administered by AWS. These AWS managed policies grant necessary permissions for common use cases so that you can avoid having to investigate what permissions are needed. For more information, see AWS Managed Policies in the *IAM User Guide*.

The following AWS managed policies, which you can attach to users in your account, are specific to Amazon Kinesis Data Analytics:

- **AmazonKinesisAnalyticsReadOnly** – Grants permissions for Amazon Kinesis Data Analytics actions that enable a user to list Amazon Kinesis Data Analytics applications and review input/output configuration. It also grants permissions that allow a user to view a list of Kinesis streams and Kinesis Data Firehose delivery streams. As the application is running, the user can view source data and real-time analytics results in the console.

- **AmazonKinesisAnalyticsFullAccess** – Grants permissions for all Amazon Kinesis Data Analytics actions and all other permissions that allows a user to create and manage Amazon Kinesis Data Analytics applications. However, note the following:

  - These permissions are not sufficient if the user wants to create a new IAM role in the console (these permissions allow the user to select an existing role). If you want the user to be able to create an IAM role in the console, add the `IAMFullAccess` AWS managed policy.

  - A user must have permission for the `iam:PassRole` action to specify an IAM role when configuring Amazon Kinesis Data Analytics application. This AWS managed policy grants permission for the `iam:PassRole` action to the user only on the IAM roles that start with the prefix `service-role/kinesis-analytics`.

    If the user wants to configure the Amazon Kinesis Data Analytics application with a role that does not have this prefix, you first need to explicitly grant the user permission for the `iam:PassRole` action on the specific role.

Note
You can review these permissions policies by signing in to the IAM console and searching for specific policies there.

You can also create your own custom IAM policies to allow permissions for Amazon Kinesis Data Analytics actions and resources. You can attach these custom policies to the IAM users or groups that require those permissions.

Customer Managed Policy Examples

The examples in this section provide a group of sample policies that you can attach to a user. If you are new to creating policies, we recommend that you first create an IAM user in your account and attach the policies to the user in sequence, as outlined in the steps in this section. You can then use the console to verify the effects of each policy as you attach the policy to the user.

Initially, the user doesn't have permissions and won't be able to do anything in the console. As you attach policies to the user, you can verify that the user can perform various actions in the console.

We recommend that you use two browser windows: one to create the user and grant permissions, and the other to sign in to the AWS Management Console using the user's credentials and verify permissions as you grant them to the user.

For examples that show how to create an IAM role that you can use as an execution role for your Amazon Kinesis Data Analytics application, see Creating IAM Roles in the *IAM User Guide*.

Topics

- Step 1: Create an IAM User
- Step 2: Allow the User Permissions for Actions that Are Not Specific to Amazon Kinesis Data Analytics
- Step 3: Allow the User to View a List of Applications and View Details
- Step 4: Allow the User to Start a Specific Application
- Step 5: Allow the User to Create an Amazon Kinesis Data Analytics Application
- Step 6: Allow the Application to Use Lambda Preprocessing

Step 1: Create an IAM User

First, you need to create an IAM user, add the user to an IAM group with administrative permissions, and then grant administrative permissions to the IAM user that you created. You can then access AWS using a special URL and that IAM user's credentials.

For instructions, see Creating Your First IAM User and Administrators Group in the *IAM User Guide*.

Step 2: Allow the User Permissions for Actions that Are Not Specific to Amazon Kinesis Data Analytics

First, grant a user permission for all actions that aren't specific to Amazon Kinesis Data Analytics that the user will need when working with Amazon Kinesis Data Analytics applications. These include permissions for working with streams (Amazon Kinesis Data Streams actions, Amazon Kinesis Data Firehose actions), and permissions for CloudWatch actions. Attach the following policy to the user.

You need to update the policy by providing an IAM role name for which you want to grant the `iam:PassRole` permission, or specify a wildcard character (*) indicating all IAM roles. This is not a secure practice; however you might not have a specific IAM role created during this testing.

```
1  {
2      "Version": "2012-10-17",
3      "Statement": [
4          {
5              "Effect": "Allow",
6              "Action": [
7                  "kinesis:CreateStream",
8                  "kinesis:DeleteStream",
9                  "kinesis:DescribeStream",
10                 "kinesis:ListStreams",
11                 "kinesis:PutRecord",
12                 "kinesis:PutRecords"
13             ],
14             "Resource": "*"
15         },
16         {
17             "Effect": "Allow",
18             "Action": [
19                 "firehose:DescribeDeliveryStream",
20                 "firehose:ListDeliveryStreams"
```

```
21          ],
22          "Resource": "*"
23      },
24      {
25
26          "Effect": "Allow",
27          "Action": [
28              "cloudwatch:GetMetricStatistics",
29              "cloudwatch:ListMetrics"
30          ],
31          "Resource": "*"
32      },
33      {
34          "Effect": "Allow",
35          "Action": "logs:GetLogEvents",
36          "Resource": "*"
37      },
38      {
39          "Effect": "Allow",
40          "Action": [
41              "iam:ListPolicyVersions",
42              "iam:ListRoles"
43          ],
44          "Resource": "*"
45      },
46      {
47          "Effect": "Allow",
48          "Action": "iam:PassRole",
49          "Resource": "arn:aws:iam::*:role/service-role/role-name"
50      }
51    ]
   }
```

Step 3: Allow the User to View a List of Applications and View Details

The following policy grants a user the following permissions:

- Permission for the `kinesisanalytics:ListApplications` action so the user can view a list of applications. Note that this is a service-level API call, and therefore you specify "*" as the Resource value.
- Permission for the `kinesisanalytics:DescribeApplication` action so that you can get information about any of the applications.

Add this policy to the user.

```
1  {
2      "Version": "2012-10-17",
3      "Statement": [
4          {
5              "Effect": "Allow",
6              "Action": [
7                  "kinesisanalytics:ListApplications"
8              ],
9              "Resource": "*"
10          },
11          {
12              "Effect": "Allow",
```

```
13          "Action": [
14              "kinesisanalytics:DescribeApplication"
15          ],
16          "Resource": "arn:aws:kinesisanalytics:aws-region:aws-account-id:application/*"
17      }
18   ]
19 }
```

Verify these permissions by signing into the Amazon Kinesis Data Analytics console using the IAM user credentials.

Step 4: Allow the User to Start a Specific Application

If you want the user to be able to start one of the existing Amazon Kinesis Data Analytics applications, you attach the following policy to the user, which provides the permission for `kinesisanalytics:StartApplication` action. You will need to update the policy by providing your account ID, AWS Region, and application name.

```
1 {
2      "Version": "2012-10-17",
3      "Statement": [
4          {
5          "Effect": "Allow",
6          "Action": [
7              "kinesisanalytics:StartApplication"
8          ],
9          "Resource": "arn:aws:kinesisanalytics:aws-region:aws-account-id:application/
               application-name"
10      }
11   ]
12 }
```

Step 5: Allow the User to Create an Amazon Kinesis Data Analytics Application

Now suppose you want the user to create an Amazon Kinesis Data Analytics application. You can then attach the following policy to the user. You will need to update the policy and provide an AWS Region, your account ID, and either a specific application name that you want the user to create or a "*" so the user can specify any application name (and thus the user can create multiple applications).

```
1 {
2      "Version": "2012-10-17",
3      "Statement": [
4          {
5          "Sid": "Stmt1473028104000",
6          "Effect": "Allow",
7          "Action": [
8              "kinesisanalytics:CreateApplication"
9          ],
10          "Resource": [
11              "*"
12          ]
13      },
14
15          {
16          "Effect": "Allow",
```

196

```
17      "Action": [
18          "kinesisanalytics:StartApplication",
19          "kinesisanalytics:UpdateApplication",
20          "kinesisanalytics:AddApplicationInput",
21          "kinesisanalytics:AddApplicationOutput"
22      ],
23      "Resource": "arn:aws:kinesisanalytics:aws-region:aws-account-id:application/
            application-name"
24      }
25   ]
26 }
```

Step 6: Allow the Application to Use Lambda Preprocessing

If you want the application to be able to use Lambda preprocessing, you can attach the following policy to the role. For more information on Lambda preprocessing, see Preprocessing Data Using a Lambda Function.

```
1    {
2      "Sid": "UseLambdaFunction",
3      "Effect": "Allow",
4      "Action": [
5          "lambda:InvokeFunction",
6          "lambda:GetFunctionConfiguration"
7      ],
8      "Resource": "<FunctionARN>"
9    }
```

Amazon Kinesis Data Analytics API Permissions: Actions, Permissions, and Resources Reference

When you are setting up Access Control and writing a permissions policy that you can attach to an IAM identity (identity-based policies), you can use the following table as a reference. The table lists each Amazon Kinesis Data Analytics API operation, the corresponding actions for which you can grant permissions to perform the action, and the AWS resource for which you can grant the permissions. You specify the actions in the policy's `Action` field, and you specify the resource value in the policy's `Resource` field.

You can use AWS-wide condition keys in your Amazon Kinesis Data Analytics policies to express conditions. For a complete list of AWS-wide keys, see Available Keys in the *IAM User Guide*.

Note
To specify an action, use the `kinesisanalytics` prefix followed by the API operation name (for example, `kinesisanalytics:AddApplicationInput`).

If you see an expand arrow () in the upper-right corner of the table, you can open the table in a new window. To close the window, choose the close button (**X**) in the lower-right corner.

Amazon Kinesis Data Analytics API and Required Permissions for Actions

Amazon Kinesis Data Analytics API Operations	Required Permissions (API Actions)	Resources
AddApplicationInput	kinesisanalytics:AddApplicationInput	`arn:aws:kinesisanalytics : region:accountId: application/application-name`
AddApplicationOutput	kinesisanalytics:AddApplicationOutput	`arn:aws:kinesisanalytics : region:accountId: application/application-name`
AddApplicationReferenceDataSource	kinesisanalytics:AddApplicationReferenceDataSource	`arn:aws:kinesisanalytics : region:accountId: application/application-name`
CreateApplication	kinesisanalytics:CreateApplication	`arn:aws:kinesisanalytics : region:accountId: application/application-name`
DeleteApplication	kinesisanalytics:DeleteApplication	`arn:aws:kinesisanalytics : region:accountId: application/application-name`
DeleteApplicationOutput	kinesisanalytics:DeleteApplicationOutput	`arn:aws:kinesisanalytics : region:accountId: application/application-name`
DeleteApplicationReferenceDataSource	kinesisanalytics:DeleteApplicationReferenceDataSource	`arn:aws:kinesisanalytics : region:accountId: application/application-name`
DescribeApplication	kinesisanalytics:DescribeApplication	`arn:aws:kinesisanalytics : region:accountId: application/application-name`

Amazon Kinesis Data Analytics API Operations	Required Permissions (API Actions)	Resources
DiscoverInputSchema	kinesisanalytics:DiscoverInputSchema	*
ListApplications	kinesisanalytics:ListApplications	*
StartApplication	kinesisanalytics:StartApplication	`arn:aws:kinesisanalytics : region:accountId: application/application-name`
StopApplication	kinesisanalytics:StopApplication	`arn:aws:kinesisanalytics : region:accountId: application/application-name`
UpdateApplication	kinesisanalytics:UpdateApplication	`arn:aws:kinesisanalytics : region:accountId: application/application-name`

Kinesis Data Analytics SQL Reference

For information about the SQL language elements that are supported by Amazon Kinesis Data Analytics, see Amazon Kinesis Data Analytics SQL Reference.

API Reference

You can use the AWS CLI to explore the Amazon Kinesis Data Analytics API. This guide provides Getting Started with Amazon Kinesis Data Analytics exercises that use the AWS CLI.

Topics

- Actions
- Data Types

Actions

The following actions are supported:

- AddApplicationCloudWatchLoggingOption
- AddApplicationInput
- AddApplicationInputProcessingConfiguration
- AddApplicationOutput
- AddApplicationReferenceDataSource
- CreateApplication
- DeleteApplication
- DeleteApplicationCloudWatchLoggingOption
- DeleteApplicationInputProcessingConfiguration
- DeleteApplicationOutput
- DeleteApplicationReferenceDataSource
- DescribeApplication
- DiscoverInputSchema
- ListApplications
- StartApplication
- StopApplication
- UpdateApplication

AddApplicationCloudWatchLoggingOption

Adds a CloudWatch log stream to monitor application configuration errors. For more information about using CloudWatch log streams with Amazon Kinesis Analytics applications, see Working with Amazon CloudWatch Logs.

Request Syntax

```
1 {
2    "[ApplicationName](#analytics-AddApplicationCloudWatchLoggingOption-request-ApplicationName)
        ": "string",
3    "[CloudWatchLoggingOption](#analytics-AddApplicationCloudWatchLoggingOption-request-
        CloudWatchLoggingOption)": {
4       "[LogStreamARN](API_CloudWatchLoggingOption.md#analytics-Type-CloudWatchLoggingOption-
           LogStreamARN)": "string",
5       "[RoleARN](API_CloudWatchLoggingOption.md#analytics-Type-CloudWatchLoggingOption-RoleARN)
           ": "string"
6    },
7    "[CurrentApplicationVersionId](#analytics-AddApplicationCloudWatchLoggingOption-request-
        CurrentApplicationVersionId)": number
8 }
```

Request Parameters

The request accepts the following data in JSON format.

** ApplicationName ** The Kinesis Analytics application name.
Type: String
Length Constraints: Minimum length of 1. Maximum length of 128.
Pattern: `[a-zA-Z0-9_.-]+`
Required: Yes

** CloudWatchLoggingOption ** Provides the CloudWatch log stream Amazon Resource Name (ARN) and the IAM role ARN. Note: To write application messages to CloudWatch, the IAM role that is used must have the `PutLogEvents` policy action enabled.
Type: CloudWatchLoggingOption object
Required: Yes

** CurrentApplicationVersionId ** The version ID of the Kinesis Analytics application.
Type: Long
Valid Range: Minimum value of 1. Maximum value of 999999999.
Required: Yes

Response Elements

If the action is successful, the service sends back an HTTP 200 response with an empty HTTP body.

Errors

ConcurrentModificationException
Exception thrown as a result of concurrent modification to an application. For example, two individuals attempting to edit the same application at the same time.
HTTP Status Code: 400

InvalidArgumentException
Specified input parameter value is invalid.
HTTP Status Code: 400

ResourceInUseException
Application is not available for this operation.
HTTP Status Code: 400

ResourceNotFoundException
Specified application can't be found.
HTTP Status Code: 400

See Also

For more information about using this API in one of the language-specific AWS SDKs, see the following:

- AWS Command Line Interface
- AWS SDK for .NET
- AWS SDK for C++
- AWS SDK for Go
- AWS SDK for Java
- AWS SDK for JavaScript
- AWS SDK for PHP V3
- AWS SDK for Python
- AWS SDK for Ruby V2

AddApplicationInput

Adds a streaming source to your Amazon Kinesis application. For conceptual information, see Configuring Application Input.

You can add a streaming source either when you create an application or you can use this operation to add a streaming source after you create an application. For more information, see CreateApplication.

Any configuration update, including adding a streaming source using this operation, results in a new version of the application. You can use the DescribeApplication operation to find the current application version.

This operation requires permissions to perform the `kinesisanalytics:AddApplicationInput` action.

Request Syntax

```
1  {
2     "[ApplicationName](#analytics-AddApplicationInput-request-ApplicationName)": "string",
3     "[CurrentApplicationVersionId](#analytics-AddApplicationInput-request-
          CurrentApplicationVersionId)": number,
4     "[Input](#analytics-AddApplicationInput-request-Input)": {
5        "[InputParallelism](API_Input.md#analytics-Type-Input-InputParallelism)": {
6           "[Count](API_InputParallelism.md#analytics-Type-InputParallelism-Count)": number
7        },
8        "[InputProcessingConfiguration](API_Input.md#analytics-Type-Input-
             InputProcessingConfiguration)": {
9           "[InputLambdaProcessor](API_InputProcessingConfiguration.md#analytics-Type-
                InputProcessingConfiguration-InputLambdaProcessor)": {
10             "[ResourceARN](API_InputLambdaProcessor.md#analytics-Type-InputLambdaProcessor-
                  ResourceARN)": "string",
11             "[RoleARN](API_InputLambdaProcessor.md#analytics-Type-InputLambdaProcessor-RoleARN)
                  ": "string"
12          }
13       },
14       "[InputSchema](API_Input.md#analytics-Type-Input-InputSchema)": {
15          "[RecordColumns](API_SourceSchema.md#analytics-Type-SourceSchema-RecordColumns)": [
16             {
17                "[Mapping](API_RecordColumn.md#analytics-Type-RecordColumn-Mapping)": "string",
18                "[Name](API_RecordColumn.md#analytics-Type-RecordColumn-Name)": "string",
19                "[SqlType](API_RecordColumn.md#analytics-Type-RecordColumn-SqlType)": "string"
20             }
21          ],
22          "[RecordEncoding](API_SourceSchema.md#analytics-Type-SourceSchema-RecordEncoding)": "
                string",
23          "[RecordFormat](API_SourceSchema.md#analytics-Type-SourceSchema-RecordFormat)": {
24             "[MappingParameters](API_RecordFormat.md#analytics-Type-RecordFormat-
                  MappingParameters)": {
25                "[CSVMappingParameters](API_MappingParameters.md#analytics-Type-MappingParameters
                     -CSVMappingParameters)": {
26                   "[RecordColumnDelimiter](API_CSVMappingParameters.md#analytics-Type-
                        CSVMappingParameters-RecordColumnDelimiter)": "string",
27                   "[RecordRowDelimiter](API_CSVMappingParameters.md#analytics-Type-
                        CSVMappingParameters-RecordRowDelimiter)": "string"
28                },
29                "[JSONMappingParameters](API_MappingParameters.md#analytics-Type-
                     MappingParameters-JSONMappingParameters)": {
```

```
30          "[RecordRowPath](API_JSONMappingParameters.md#analytics-Type-
                JSONMappingParameters-RecordRowPath)": "string"
31        }
32      },
33      "[RecordFormatType](API_RecordFormat.md#analytics-Type-RecordFormat-RecordFormatType
          )": "string"
34    }
35  },
36  "[KinesisFirehoseInput](API_Input.md#analytics-Type-Input-KinesisFirehoseInput)": {
37    "[ResourceARN](API_KinesisFirehoseInput.md#analytics-Type-KinesisFirehoseInput-
        ResourceARN)": "string",
38    "[RoleARN](API_KinesisFirehoseInput.md#analytics-Type-KinesisFirehoseInput-RoleARN)": "
        string"
39  },
40  "[KinesisStreamsInput](API_Input.md#analytics-Type-Input-KinesisStreamsInput)": {
41    "[ResourceARN](API_KinesisStreamsInput.md#analytics-Type-KinesisStreamsInput-
        ResourceARN)": "string",
42    "[RoleARN](API_KinesisStreamsInput.md#analytics-Type-KinesisStreamsInput-RoleARN)": "
        string"
43  },
44  "[NamePrefix](API_Input.md#analytics-Type-Input-NamePrefix)": "string"
45 }
46 }
```

Request Parameters

The request accepts the following data in JSON format.

** ApplicationName ** Name of your existing Amazon Kinesis Analytics application to which you want to add the streaming source.
Type: String
Length Constraints: Minimum length of 1. Maximum length of 128.
Pattern: [a-zA-Z0-9_.-]+
Required: Yes

** CurrentApplicationVersionId ** Current version of your Amazon Kinesis Analytics application. You can use the DescribeApplication operation to find the current application version.
Type: Long
Valid Range: Minimum value of 1. Maximum value of 999999999.
Required: Yes

** Input ** The Input to add.
Type: Input object
Required: Yes

Response Elements

If the action is successful, the service sends back an HTTP 200 response with an empty HTTP body.

Errors

CodeValidationException
User-provided application code (query) is invalid. This can be a simple syntax error.
HTTP Status Code: 400

ConcurrentModificationException

Exception thrown as a result of concurrent modification to an application. For example, two individuals attempting to edit the same application at the same time.
HTTP Status Code: 400

InvalidArgumentException

Specified input parameter value is invalid.
HTTP Status Code: 400

ResourceInUseException

Application is not available for this operation.
HTTP Status Code: 400

ResourceNotFoundException

Specified application can't be found.
HTTP Status Code: 400

See Also

For more information about using this API in one of the language-specific AWS SDKs, see the following:

- AWS Command Line Interface
- AWS SDK for .NET
- AWS SDK for C++
- AWS SDK for Go
- AWS SDK for Java
- AWS SDK for JavaScript
- AWS SDK for PHP V3
- AWS SDK for Python
- AWS SDK for Ruby V2

AddApplicationInputProcessingConfiguration

Adds an InputProcessingConfiguration to an application. An input processor preprocesses records on the input stream before the application's SQL code executes. Currently, the only input processor available is AWS Lambda.

Request Syntax

```
1  {
2      "[ApplicationName](#analytics-AddApplicationInputProcessingConfiguration-request-
          ApplicationName)": "string",
3      "[CurrentApplicationVersionId](#analytics-AddApplicationInputProcessingConfiguration-request-
          CurrentApplicationVersionId)": number,
4      "[InputId](#analytics-AddApplicationInputProcessingConfiguration-request-InputId)": "string",
5      "[InputProcessingConfiguration](#analytics-AddApplicationInputProcessingConfiguration-request
          -InputProcessingConfiguration)": {
6          "[InputLambdaProcessor](API_InputProcessingConfiguration.md#analytics-Type-
              InputProcessingConfiguration-InputLambdaProcessor)": {
7              "[ResourceARN](API_InputLambdaProcessor.md#analytics-Type-InputLambdaProcessor-
                  ResourceARN)": "string",
8              "[RoleARN](API_InputLambdaProcessor.md#analytics-Type-InputLambdaProcessor-RoleARN)": "
                  string"
9          }
10     }
11 }
```

Request Parameters

The request accepts the following data in JSON format.

** ApplicationName ** Name of the application to which you want to add the input processing configuration.
Type: String
Length Constraints: Minimum length of 1. Maximum length of 128.
Pattern: [a-zA-Z0-9_.-]+
Required: Yes

** CurrentApplicationVersionId ** Version of the application to which you want to add the input processing configuration. You can use the DescribeApplication operation to get the current application version. If the version specified is not the current version, the ConcurrentModificationException is returned.
Type: Long
Valid Range: Minimum value of 1. Maximum value of 999999999.
Required: Yes

** InputId ** The ID of the input configuration to add the input processing configuration to. You can get a list of the input IDs for an application using the DescribeApplication operation.
Type: String
Length Constraints: Minimum length of 1. Maximum length of 50.
Pattern: [a-zA-Z0-9_.-]+
Required: Yes

** InputProcessingConfiguration ** The InputProcessingConfiguration to add to the application.
Type: InputProcessingConfiguration object
Required: Yes

Response Elements

If the action is successful, the service sends back an HTTP 200 response with an empty HTTP body.

Errors

ConcurrentModificationException
Exception thrown as a result of concurrent modification to an application. For example, two individuals attempting to edit the same application at the same time.
HTTP Status Code: 400

InvalidArgumentException
Specified input parameter value is invalid.
HTTP Status Code: 400

ResourceInUseException
Application is not available for this operation.
HTTP Status Code: 400

ResourceNotFoundException
Specified application can't be found.
HTTP Status Code: 400

See Also

For more information about using this API in one of the language-specific AWS SDKs, see the following:

- AWS Command Line Interface
- AWS SDK for .NET
- AWS SDK for C++
- AWS SDK for Go
- AWS SDK for Java
- AWS SDK for JavaScript
- AWS SDK for PHP V3
- AWS SDK for Python
- AWS SDK for Ruby V2

AddApplicationOutput

Adds an external destination to your Amazon Kinesis Analytics application.

If you want Amazon Kinesis Analytics to deliver data from an in-application stream within your application to an external destination (such as an Amazon Kinesis stream, an Amazon Kinesis Firehose delivery stream, or an AWS Lambda function), you add the relevant configuration to your application using this operation. You can configure one or more outputs for your application. Each output configuration maps an in-application stream and an external destination.

You can use one of the output configurations to deliver data from your in-application error stream to an external destination so that you can analyze the errors. For more information, see Understanding Application Output (Destination).

Any configuration update, including adding a streaming source using this operation, results in a new version of the application. You can use the DescribeApplication operation to find the current application version.

For the limits on the number of application inputs and outputs you can configure, see Limits.

This operation requires permissions to perform the `kinesisanalytics:AddApplicationOutput` action.

Request Syntax

```
1  {
2     "[ApplicationName](#analytics-AddApplicationOutput-request-ApplicationName)": "string",
3     "[CurrentApplicationVersionId](#analytics-AddApplicationOutput-request-
          CurrentApplicationVersionId)": number,
4     "[Output](#analytics-AddApplicationOutput-request-Output)": {
5        "[DestinationSchema](API_Output.md#analytics-Type-Output-DestinationSchema)": {
6           "[RecordFormatType](API_DestinationSchema.md#analytics-Type-DestinationSchema-
             RecordFormatType)": "string"
7        },
8        "[KinesisFirehoseOutput](API_Output.md#analytics-Type-Output-KinesisFirehoseOutput)": {
9           "[ResourceARN](API_KinesisFirehoseOutput.md#analytics-Type-KinesisFirehoseOutput-
             ResourceARN)": "string",
10          "[RoleARN](API_KinesisFirehoseOutput.md#analytics-Type-KinesisFirehoseOutput-RoleARN)":
             "string"
11       },
12       "[KinesisStreamsOutput](API_Output.md#analytics-Type-Output-KinesisStreamsOutput)": {
13          "[ResourceARN](API_KinesisStreamsOutput.md#analytics-Type-KinesisStreamsOutput-
             ResourceARN)": "string",
14          "[RoleARN](API_KinesisStreamsOutput.md#analytics-Type-KinesisStreamsOutput-RoleARN)": "
             string"
15       },
16       "[LambdaOutput](API_Output.md#analytics-Type-Output-LambdaOutput)": {
17          "[ResourceARN](API_LambdaOutput.md#analytics-Type-LambdaOutput-ResourceARN)": "string",
18          "[RoleARN](API_LambdaOutput.md#analytics-Type-LambdaOutput-RoleARN)": "string"
19       },
20       "[Name](API_Output.md#analytics-Type-Output-Name)": "string"
21    }
22 }
```

Request Parameters

The request accepts the following data in JSON format.

** ApplicationName ** Name of the application to which you want to add the output configuration.
Type: String
Length Constraints: Minimum length of 1. Maximum length of 128.
Pattern: [a-zA-Z0-9_.-]+
Required: Yes

** CurrentApplicationVersionId ** Version of the application to which you want to add the output configuration. You can use the DescribeApplication operation to get the current application version. If the version specified is not the current version, the `ConcurrentModificationException` is returned.
Type: Long
Valid Range: Minimum value of 1. Maximum value of 999999999.
Required: Yes

** Output ** An array of objects, each describing one output configuration. In the output configuration, you specify the name of an in-application stream, a destination (that is, an Amazon Kinesis stream, an Amazon Kinesis Firehose delivery stream, or an AWS Lambda function), and record the formation to use when writing to the destination.
Type: Output object
Required: Yes

Response Elements

If the action is successful, the service sends back an HTTP 200 response with an empty HTTP body.

Errors

ConcurrentModificationException
Exception thrown as a result of concurrent modification to an application. For example, two individuals attempting to edit the same application at the same time.
HTTP Status Code: 400

InvalidArgumentException
Specified input parameter value is invalid.
HTTP Status Code: 400

ResourceInUseException
Application is not available for this operation.
HTTP Status Code: 400

ResourceNotFoundException
Specified application can't be found.
HTTP Status Code: 400

See Also

For more information about using this API in one of the language-specific AWS SDKs, see the following:

- AWS Command Line Interface
- AWS SDK for .NET
- AWS SDK for C++
- AWS SDK for Go
- AWS SDK for Java
- AWS SDK for JavaScript
- AWS SDK for PHP V3
- AWS SDK for Python

- AWS SDK for Ruby V2

AddApplicationReferenceDataSource

Adds a reference data source to an existing application.

Amazon Kinesis Analytics reads reference data (that is, an Amazon S3 object) and creates an in-application table within your application. In the request, you provide the source (S3 bucket name and object key name), name of the in-application table to create, and the necessary mapping information that describes how data in Amazon S3 object maps to columns in the resulting in-application table.

For conceptual information, see Configuring Application Input. For the limits on data sources you can add to your application, see Limits.

This operation requires permissions to perform the `kinesisanalytics:AddApplicationOutput` action.

Request Syntax

```
1  {
2     "[ApplicationName](#analytics-AddApplicationReferenceDataSource-request-ApplicationName)": "
          string",
3     "[CurrentApplicationVersionId](#analytics-AddApplicationReferenceDataSource-request-
          CurrentApplicationVersionId)": number,
4     "[ReferenceDataSource](#analytics-AddApplicationReferenceDataSource-request-
          ReferenceDataSource)": {
5        "[ReferenceSchema](API_ReferenceDataSource.md#analytics-Type-ReferenceDataSource-
             ReferenceSchema)": {
6           "[RecordColumns](API_SourceSchema.md#analytics-Type-SourceSchema-RecordColumns)": [
7              {
8                 "[Mapping](API_RecordColumn.md#analytics-Type-RecordColumn-Mapping)": "string",
9                 "[Name](API_RecordColumn.md#analytics-Type-RecordColumn-Name)": "string",
10                "[SqlType](API_RecordColumn.md#analytics-Type-RecordColumn-SqlType)": "string"
11             }
12          ],
13          "[RecordEncoding](API_SourceSchema.md#analytics-Type-SourceSchema-RecordEncoding)": "
             string",
14          "[RecordFormat](API_SourceSchema.md#analytics-Type-SourceSchema-RecordFormat)": {
15             "[MappingParameters](API_RecordFormat.md#analytics-Type-RecordFormat-
                MappingParameters)": {
16                "[CSVMappingParameters](API_MappingParameters.md#analytics-Type-MappingParameters
                   -CSVMappingParameters)": {
17                   "[RecordColumnDelimiter](API_CSVMappingParameters.md#analytics-Type-
                      CSVMappingParameters-RecordColumnDelimiter)": "string",
18                   "[RecordRowDelimiter](API_CSVMappingParameters.md#analytics-Type-
                      CSVMappingParameters-RecordRowDelimiter)": "string"
19                },
20                "[JSONMappingParameters](API_MappingParameters.md#analytics-Type-
                   MappingParameters-JSONMappingParameters)": {
21                   "[RecordRowPath](API_JSONMappingParameters.md#analytics-Type-
                      JSONMappingParameters-RecordRowPath)": "string"
22                }
23             },
24             "[RecordFormatType](API_RecordFormat.md#analytics-Type-RecordFormat-RecordFormatType
                )": "string"
25          }
26       },
```

```
27        "[S3ReferenceDataSource](API_ReferenceDataSource.md#analytics-Type-ReferenceDataSource-
              S3ReferenceDataSource)": {
28            "[BucketARN](API_S3ReferenceDataSource.md#analytics-Type-S3ReferenceDataSource-
                  BucketARN)": "string",
29            "[FileKey](API_S3ReferenceDataSource.md#analytics-Type-S3ReferenceDataSource-FileKey)":
                  "string",
30            "[ReferenceRoleARN](API_S3ReferenceDataSource.md#analytics-Type-S3ReferenceDataSource-
                  ReferenceRoleARN)": "string"
31        },
32        "[TableName](API_ReferenceDataSource.md#analytics-Type-ReferenceDataSource-TableName)": "
              string"
33    }
34 }
```

Request Parameters

The request accepts the following data in JSON format.

** ApplicationName ** Name of an existing application.
Type: String
Length Constraints: Minimum length of 1. Maximum length of 128.
Pattern: [a-zA-Z0-9_.-]+
Required: Yes

** CurrentApplicationVersionId ** Version of the application for which you are adding the reference data source.
You can use the DescribeApplication operation to get the current application version. If the version specified is
not the current version, the ConcurrentModificationException is returned.
Type: Long
Valid Range: Minimum value of 1. Maximum value of 999999999.
Required: Yes

** ReferenceDataSource ** The reference data source can be an object in your Amazon S3 bucket. Amazon
Kinesis Analytics reads the object and copies the data into the in-application table that is created. You provide
an S3 bucket, object key name, and the resulting in-application table that is created. You must also provide an
IAM role with the necessary permissions that Amazon Kinesis Analytics can assume to read the object from
your S3 bucket on your behalf.
Type: ReferenceDataSource object
Required: Yes

Response Elements

If the action is successful, the service sends back an HTTP 200 response with an empty HTTP body.

Errors

ConcurrentModificationException
Exception thrown as a result of concurrent modification to an application. For example, two individuals
attempting to edit the same application at the same time.
HTTP Status Code: 400

InvalidArgumentException
Specified input parameter value is invalid.
HTTP Status Code: 400

ResourceInUseException

Application is not available for this operation.

HTTP Status Code: 400

ResourceNotFoundException

Specified application can't be found.

HTTP Status Code: 400

See Also

For more information about using this API in one of the language-specific AWS SDKs, see the following:

- AWS Command Line Interface
- AWS SDK for .NET
- AWS SDK for C++
- AWS SDK for Go
- AWS SDK for Java
- AWS SDK for JavaScript
- AWS SDK for PHP V3
- AWS SDK for Python
- AWS SDK for Ruby V2

CreateApplication

Creates an Amazon Kinesis Analytics application. You can configure each application with one streaming source as input, application code to process the input, and up to three destinations where you want Amazon Kinesis Analytics to write the output data from your application. For an overview, see How it Works.

In the input configuration, you map the streaming source to an in-application stream, which you can think of as a constantly updating table. In the mapping, you must provide a schema for the in-application stream and map each data column in the in-application stream to a data element in the streaming source.

Your application code is one or more SQL statements that read input data, transform it, and generate output. Your application code can create one or more SQL artifacts like SQL streams or pumps.

In the output configuration, you can configure the application to write data from in-application streams created in your applications to up to three destinations.

To read data from your source stream or write data to destination streams, Amazon Kinesis Analytics needs your permissions. You grant these permissions by creating IAM roles. This operation requires permissions to perform the `kinesisanalytics:CreateApplication` action.

For introductory exercises to create an Amazon Kinesis Analytics application, see Getting Started.

Request Syntax

```
1  {
2     "[ApplicationCode](#analytics-CreateApplication-request-ApplicationCode)": "string",
3     "[ApplicationDescription](#analytics-CreateApplication-request-ApplicationDescription)": "
          string",
4     "[ApplicationName](#analytics-CreateApplication-request-ApplicationName)": "string",
5     "[CloudWatchLoggingOptions](#analytics-CreateApplication-request-CloudWatchLoggingOptions)":
          [
6        {
7           "[LogStreamARN](API_CloudWatchLoggingOption.md#analytics-Type-CloudWatchLoggingOption-
                LogStreamARN)": "string",
8           "[RoleARN](API_CloudWatchLoggingOption.md#analytics-Type-CloudWatchLoggingOption-
                RoleARN)": "string"
9        }
10    ],
11    "[Inputs](#analytics-CreateApplication-request-Inputs)": [
12       {
13          "[InputParallelism](API_Input.md#analytics-Type-Input-InputParallelism)": {
14             "[Count](API_InputParallelism.md#analytics-Type-InputParallelism-Count)": number
15          },
16          "[InputProcessingConfiguration](API_Input.md#analytics-Type-Input-
                InputProcessingConfiguration)": {
17             "[InputLambdaProcessor](API_InputProcessingConfiguration.md#analytics-Type-
                   InputProcessingConfiguration-InputLambdaProcessor)": {
18                "[ResourceARN](API_InputLambdaProcessor.md#analytics-Type-InputLambdaProcessor-
                      ResourceARN)": "string",
19                "[RoleARN](API_InputLambdaProcessor.md#analytics-Type-InputLambdaProcessor-
                      RoleARN)": "string"
20             }
21          },
22          "[InputSchema](API_Input.md#analytics-Type-Input-InputSchema)": {
23             "[RecordColumns](API_SourceSchema.md#analytics-Type-SourceSchema-RecordColumns)": [
```

```
24                {
25                    "[Mapping](API_RecordColumn.md#analytics-Type-RecordColumn-Mapping)": "string
                        ",
26                    "[Name](API_RecordColumn.md#analytics-Type-RecordColumn-Name)": "string",
27                    "[SqlType](API_RecordColumn.md#analytics-Type-RecordColumn-SqlType)": "string"
28                }
29            ],
30            "[RecordEncoding](API_SourceSchema.md#analytics-Type-SourceSchema-RecordEncoding)":
                "string",
31            "[RecordFormat](API_SourceSchema.md#analytics-Type-SourceSchema-RecordFormat)": {
32                "[MappingParameters](API_RecordFormat.md#analytics-Type-RecordFormat-
                    MappingParameters)": {
33                    "[CSVMappingParameters](API_MappingParameters.md#analytics-Type-
                        MappingParameters-CSVMappingParameters)": {
34                        "[RecordColumnDelimiter](API_CSVMappingParameters.md#analytics-Type-
                            CSVMappingParameters-RecordColumnDelimiter)": "string",
35                        "[RecordRowDelimiter](API_CSVMappingParameters.md#analytics-Type-
                            CSVMappingParameters-RecordRowDelimiter)": "string"
36                    },
37                    "[JSONMappingParameters](API_MappingParameters.md#analytics-Type-
                        MappingParameters-JSONMappingParameters)": {
38                        "[RecordRowPath](API_JSONMappingParameters.md#analytics-Type-
                            JSONMappingParameters-RecordRowPath)": "string"
39                    }
40                },
41                "[RecordFormatType](API_RecordFormat.md#analytics-Type-RecordFormat-
                    RecordFormatType)": "string"
42            }
43        },
44        "[KinesisFirehoseInput](API_Input.md#analytics-Type-Input-KinesisFirehoseInput)": {
45            "[ResourceARN](API_KinesisFirehoseInput.md#analytics-Type-KinesisFirehoseInput-
                ResourceARN)": "string",
46            "[RoleARN](API_KinesisFirehoseInput.md#analytics-Type-KinesisFirehoseInput-RoleARN)
                ": "string"
47        },
48        "[KinesisStreamsInput](API_Input.md#analytics-Type-Input-KinesisStreamsInput)": {
49            "[ResourceARN](API_KinesisStreamsInput.md#analytics-Type-KinesisStreamsInput-
                ResourceARN)": "string",
50            "[RoleARN](API_KinesisStreamsInput.md#analytics-Type-KinesisStreamsInput-RoleARN)":
                "string"
51        },
52        "[NamePrefix](API_Input.md#analytics-Type-Input-NamePrefix)": "string"
53    }
54 ],
55 "[Outputs](#analytics-CreateApplication-request-Outputs)": [
56    {
57        "[DestinationSchema](API_Output.md#analytics-Type-Output-DestinationSchema)": {
58            "[RecordFormatType](API_DestinationSchema.md#analytics-Type-DestinationSchema-
                RecordFormatType)": "string"
59        },
60        "[KinesisFirehoseOutput](API_Output.md#analytics-Type-Output-KinesisFirehoseOutput)": {
61            "[ResourceARN](API_KinesisFirehoseOutput.md#analytics-Type-KinesisFirehoseOutput-
                ResourceARN)": "string",
62            "[RoleARN](API_KinesisFirehoseOutput.md#analytics-Type-KinesisFirehoseOutput-RoleARN
```

217

```
                  )": "string"
63          },
64          "[KinesisStreamsOutput](API_Output.md#analytics-Type-Output-KinesisStreamsOutput)": {
65              "[ResourceARN](API_KinesisStreamsOutput.md#analytics-Type-KinesisStreamsOutput-
                    ResourceARN)": "string",
66              "[RoleARN](API_KinesisStreamsOutput.md#analytics-Type-KinesisStreamsOutput-RoleARN)
                    ": "string"
67          },
68          "[LambdaOutput](API_Output.md#analytics-Type-Output-LambdaOutput)": {
69              "[ResourceARN](API_LambdaOutput.md#analytics-Type-LambdaOutput-ResourceARN)": "
                    string",
70              "[RoleARN](API_LambdaOutput.md#analytics-Type-LambdaOutput-RoleARN)": "string"
71          },
72          "[Name](API_Output.md#analytics-Type-Output-Name)": "string"
73      }
74   ]
75 }
```

Request Parameters

The request accepts the following data in JSON format.

** ApplicationCode ** One or more SQL statements that read input data, transform it, and generate output. For example, you can write a SQL statement that reads data from one in-application stream, generates a running average of the number of advertisement clicks by vendor, and insert resulting rows in another in-application stream using pumps. For more information about the typical pattern, see Application Code.

You can provide such series of SQL statements, where output of one statement can be used as the input for the next statement. You store intermediate results by creating in-application streams and pumps.

Note that the application code must create the streams with names specified in the Outputs. For example, if your Outputs defines output streams named ExampleOutputStream1 and ExampleOutputStream2, then your application code must create these streams.

Type: String
Length Constraints: Minimum length of 0. Maximum length of 102400.
Required: No

** ApplicationDescription ** Summary description of the application.
Type: String
Length Constraints: Minimum length of 0. Maximum length of 1024.
Required: No

** ApplicationName ** Name of your Amazon Kinesis Analytics application (for example, sample-app).
Type: String
Length Constraints: Minimum length of 1. Maximum length of 128.
Pattern: [a-zA-Z0-9_.-]+
Required: Yes

** CloudWatchLoggingOptions ** Use this parameter to configure a CloudWatch log stream to monitor application configuration errors. For more information, see Working with Amazon CloudWatch Logs.
Type: Array of CloudWatchLoggingOption objects
Required: No

** Inputs ** Use this parameter to configure the application input.

You can configure your application to receive input from a single streaming source. In this configuration, you map this streaming source to an in-application stream that is created. Your application code can then query the in-application stream like a table (you can think of it as a constantly updating table).

For the streaming source, you provide its Amazon Resource Name (ARN) and format of data on the stream (for example, JSON, CSV, etc.). You also must provide an IAM role that Amazon Kinesis Analytics can assume to read this stream on your behalf.

To create the in-application stream, you need to specify a schema to transform your data into a schematized version used in SQL. In the schema, you provide the necessary mapping of the data elements in the streaming source to record columns in the in-app stream.

Type: Array of Input objects

Required: No

** Outputs ** You can configure application output to write data from any of the in-application streams to up to three destinations.

These destinations can be Amazon Kinesis streams, Amazon Kinesis Firehose delivery streams, AWS Lambda destinations, or any combination of the three.

In the configuration, you specify the in-application stream name, the destination stream or Lambda function Amazon Resource Name (ARN), and the format to use when writing data. You must also provide an IAM role that Amazon Kinesis Analytics can assume to write to the destination stream or Lambda function on your behalf.

In the output configuration, you also provide the output stream or Lambda function ARN. For stream destinations, you provide the format of data in the stream (for example, JSON, CSV). You also must provide an IAM role that Amazon Kinesis Analytics can assume to write to the stream or Lambda function on your behalf.

Type: Array of Output objects

Required: No

Response Syntax

```
1 {
2     "[ApplicationSummary](#analytics-CreateApplication-response-ApplicationSummary)": {
3         "[ApplicationARN](API_ApplicationSummary.md#analytics-Type-ApplicationSummary-
            ApplicationARN)": "string",
4         "[ApplicationName](API_ApplicationSummary.md#analytics-Type-ApplicationSummary-
            ApplicationName)": "string",
5         "[ApplicationStatus](API_ApplicationSummary.md#analytics-Type-ApplicationSummary-
            ApplicationStatus)": "string"
6     }
7 }
```

Response Elements

If the action is successful, the service sends back an HTTP 200 response.

The following data is returned in JSON format by the service.

** ApplicationSummary ** In response to your `CreateApplication` request, Amazon Kinesis Analytics returns a response with a summary of the application it created, including the application Amazon Resource Name (ARN), name, and status.

Type: ApplicationSummary object

Errors

CodeValidationException

User-provided application code (query) is invalid. This can be a simple syntax error.

HTTP Status Code: 400

InvalidArgumentException

Specified input parameter value is invalid.

HTTP Status Code: 400

LimitExceededException

Exceeded the number of applications allowed.

HTTP Status Code: 400

ResourceInUseException

Application is not available for this operation.

HTTP Status Code: 400

See Also

For more information about using this API in one of the language-specific AWS SDKs, see the following:

- AWS Command Line Interface
- AWS SDK for .NET
- AWS SDK for C++
- AWS SDK for Go
- AWS SDK for Java
- AWS SDK for JavaScript
- AWS SDK for PHP V3
- AWS SDK for Python
- AWS SDK for Ruby V2

DeleteApplication

Deletes the specified application. Amazon Kinesis Analytics halts application execution and deletes the application, including any application artifacts (such as in-application streams, reference table, and application code).

This operation requires permissions to perform the `kinesisanalytics:DeleteApplication` action.

Request Syntax

```
1 {
2     "[ApplicationName](#analytics-DeleteApplication-request-ApplicationName)": "string",
3     "[CreateTimestamp](#analytics-DeleteApplication-request-CreateTimestamp)": number
4 }
```

Request Parameters

The request accepts the following data in JSON format.

** ApplicationName ** Name of the Amazon Kinesis Analytics application to delete.
Type: String
Length Constraints: Minimum length of 1. Maximum length of 128.
Pattern: `[a-zA-Z0-9_.-]+`
Required: Yes

** CreateTimestamp ** You can use the `DescribeApplication` operation to get this value.
Type: Timestamp
Required: Yes

Response Elements

If the action is successful, the service sends back an HTTP 200 response with an empty HTTP body.

Errors

ConcurrentModificationException
Exception thrown as a result of concurrent modification to an application. For example, two individuals attempting to edit the same application at the same time.
HTTP Status Code: 400

ResourceInUseException
Application is not available for this operation.
HTTP Status Code: 400

ResourceNotFoundException
Specified application can't be found.
HTTP Status Code: 400

See Also

For more information about using this API in one of the language-specific AWS SDKs, see the following:

- AWS Command Line Interface
- AWS SDK for .NET

- AWS SDK for C++
- AWS SDK for Go
- AWS SDK for Java
- AWS SDK for JavaScript
- AWS SDK for PHP V3
- AWS SDK for Python
- AWS SDK for Ruby V2

DeleteApplicationCloudWatchLoggingOption

Deletes a CloudWatch log stream from an application. For more information about using CloudWatch log streams with Amazon Kinesis Analytics applications, see Working with Amazon CloudWatch Logs.

Request Syntax

```
1 {
2     "[ApplicationName](#analytics-DeleteApplicationCloudWatchLoggingOption-request-
          ApplicationName)": "string",
3     "[CloudWatchLoggingOptionId](#analytics-DeleteApplicationCloudWatchLoggingOption-request-
          CloudWatchLoggingOptionId)": "string",
4     "[CurrentApplicationVersionId](#analytics-DeleteApplicationCloudWatchLoggingOption-request-
          CurrentApplicationVersionId)": number
5 }
```

Request Parameters

The request accepts the following data in JSON format.

** ApplicationName ** The Kinesis Analytics application name.
Type: String
Length Constraints: Minimum length of 1. Maximum length of 128.
Pattern: [a-zA-Z0-9_.-]+
Required: Yes

** CloudWatchLoggingOptionId ** The CloudWatchLoggingOptionId of the CloudWatch logging option to delete. You can get the CloudWatchLoggingOptionId by using the DescribeApplication operation.
Type: String
Length Constraints: Minimum length of 1. Maximum length of 50.
Pattern: [a-zA-Z0-9_.-]+
Required: Yes

** CurrentApplicationVersionId ** The version ID of the Kinesis Analytics application.
Type: Long
Valid Range: Minimum value of 1. Maximum value of 999999999.
Required: Yes

Response Elements

If the action is successful, the service sends back an HTTP 200 response with an empty HTTP body.

Errors

ConcurrentModificationException
Exception thrown as a result of concurrent modification to an application. For example, two individuals attempting to edit the same application at the same time.
HTTP Status Code: 400

InvalidArgumentException
Specified input parameter value is invalid.
HTTP Status Code: 400

ResourceInUseException
Application is not available for this operation.
HTTP Status Code: 400

ResourceNotFoundException
Specified application can't be found.
HTTP Status Code: 400

See Also

For more information about using this API in one of the language-specific AWS SDKs, see the following:

- AWS Command Line Interface
- AWS SDK for .NET
- AWS SDK for C++
- AWS SDK for Go
- AWS SDK for Java
- AWS SDK for JavaScript
- AWS SDK for PHP V3
- AWS SDK for Python
- AWS SDK for Ruby V2

DeleteApplicationInputProcessingConfiguration

Deletes an InputProcessingConfiguration from an input.

Request Syntax

```
1 {
2    "[ApplicationName](#analytics-DeleteApplicationInputProcessingConfiguration-request-
        ApplicationName)": "string",
3    "[CurrentApplicationVersionId](#analytics-DeleteApplicationInputProcessingConfiguration-
        request-CurrentApplicationVersionId)": number,
4    "[InputId](#analytics-DeleteApplicationInputProcessingConfiguration-request-InputId)": "
        string"
5 }
```

Request Parameters

The request accepts the following data in JSON format.

** ApplicationName ** The Kinesis Analytics application name.
Type: String
Length Constraints: Minimum length of 1. Maximum length of 128.
Pattern: [a-zA-Z0-9_.-]+
Required: Yes

** CurrentApplicationVersionId ** The version ID of the Kinesis Analytics application.
Type: Long
Valid Range: Minimum value of 1. Maximum value of 999999999.
Required: Yes

** InputId ** The ID of the input configuration from which to delete the input processing configuration. You can get a list of the input IDs for an application by using the DescribeApplication operation.
Type: String
Length Constraints: Minimum length of 1. Maximum length of 50.
Pattern: [a-zA-Z0-9_.-]+
Required: Yes

Response Elements

If the action is successful, the service sends back an HTTP 200 response with an empty HTTP body.

Errors

ConcurrentModificationException
Exception thrown as a result of concurrent modification to an application. For example, two individuals attempting to edit the same application at the same time.
HTTP Status Code: 400

InvalidArgumentException
Specified input parameter value is invalid.
HTTP Status Code: 400

ResourceInUseException
Application is not available for this operation.
HTTP Status Code: 400

ResourceNotFoundException
Specified application can't be found.
HTTP Status Code: 400

See Also

For more information about using this API in one of the language-specific AWS SDKs, see the following:

- AWS Command Line Interface
- AWS SDK for .NET
- AWS SDK for C++
- AWS SDK for Go
- AWS SDK for Java
- AWS SDK for JavaScript
- AWS SDK for PHP V3
- AWS SDK for Python
- AWS SDK for Ruby V2

DeleteApplicationOutput

Deletes output destination configuration from your application configuration. Amazon Kinesis Analytics will no longer write data from the corresponding in-application stream to the external output destination.

This operation requires permissions to perform the `kinesisanalytics:DeleteApplicationOutput` action.

Request Syntax

```
1 {
2    "[ApplicationName](#analytics-DeleteApplicationOutput-request-ApplicationName)": "string",
3    "[CurrentApplicationVersionId](#analytics-DeleteApplicationOutput-request-
        CurrentApplicationVersionId)": number,
4    "[OutputId](#analytics-DeleteApplicationOutput-request-OutputId)": "string"
5 }
```

Request Parameters

The request accepts the following data in JSON format.

** ApplicationName ** Amazon Kinesis Analytics application name.
Type: String
Length Constraints: Minimum length of 1. Maximum length of 128.
Pattern: [a-zA-Z0-9_.-]+
Required: Yes

** CurrentApplicationVersionId ** Amazon Kinesis Analytics application version. You can use the DescribeApplication operation to get the current application version. If the version specified is not the current version, the `ConcurrentModificationException` is returned.
Type: Long
Valid Range: Minimum value of 1. Maximum value of 999999999.
Required: Yes

** OutputId ** The ID of the configuration to delete. Each output configuration that is added to the application, either when the application is created or later using the AddApplicationOutput operation, has a unique ID. You need to provide the ID to uniquely identify the output configuration that you want to delete from the application configuration. You can use the DescribeApplication operation to get the specific `OutputId`.
Type: String
Length Constraints: Minimum length of 1. Maximum length of 50.
Pattern: [a-zA-Z0-9_.-]+
Required: Yes

Response Elements

If the action is successful, the service sends back an HTTP 200 response with an empty HTTP body.

Errors

ConcurrentModificationException
Exception thrown as a result of concurrent modification to an application. For example, two individuals attempting to edit the same application at the same time.
HTTP Status Code: 400

InvalidArgumentException
Specified input parameter value is invalid.
HTTP Status Code: 400

ResourceInUseException
Application is not available for this operation.
HTTP Status Code: 400

ResourceNotFoundException
Specified application can't be found.
HTTP Status Code: 400

See Also

For more information about using this API in one of the language-specific AWS SDKs, see the following:

- AWS Command Line Interface
- AWS SDK for .NET
- AWS SDK for C++
- AWS SDK for Go
- AWS SDK for Java
- AWS SDK for JavaScript
- AWS SDK for PHP V3
- AWS SDK for Python
- AWS SDK for Ruby V2

DeleteApplicationReferenceDataSource

Deletes a reference data source configuration from the specified application configuration.

If the application is running, Amazon Kinesis Analytics immediately removes the in-application table that you created using the AddApplicationReferenceDataSource operation.

This operation requires permissions to perform the `kinesisanalytics.DeleteApplicationReferenceDataSource` action.

Request Syntax

```
1 {
2    "[ApplicationName](#analytics-DeleteApplicationReferenceDataSource-request-ApplicationName)":
         "string",
3    "[CurrentApplicationVersionId](#analytics-DeleteApplicationReferenceDataSource-request-
         CurrentApplicationVersionId)": number,
4    "[ReferenceId](#analytics-DeleteApplicationReferenceDataSource-request-ReferenceId)": "string
         "
5 }
```

Request Parameters

The request accepts the following data in JSON format.

** ApplicationName ** Name of an existing application.
Type: String
Length Constraints: Minimum length of 1. Maximum length of 128.
Pattern: [a-zA-Z0-9_.-]+
Required: Yes

** CurrentApplicationVersionId ** Version of the application. You can use the DescribeApplication operation to get the current application version. If the version specified is not the current version, the `ConcurrentModificationException` is returned.
Type: Long
Valid Range: Minimum value of 1. Maximum value of 999999999.
Required: Yes

** ReferenceId ** ID of the reference data source. When you add a reference data source to your application using the AddApplicationReferenceDataSource, Amazon Kinesis Analytics assigns an ID. You can use the DescribeApplication operation to get the reference ID.
Type: String
Length Constraints: Minimum length of 1. Maximum length of 50.
Pattern: [a-zA-Z0-9_.-]+
Required: Yes

Response Elements

If the action is successful, the service sends back an HTTP 200 response with an empty HTTP body.

Errors

ConcurrentModificationException
Exception thrown as a result of concurrent modification to an application. For example, two individuals

attempting to edit the same application at the same time.
HTTP Status Code: 400

InvalidArgumentException

Specified input parameter value is invalid.
HTTP Status Code: 400

ResourceInUseException

Application is not available for this operation.
HTTP Status Code: 400

ResourceNotFoundException

Specified application can't be found.
HTTP Status Code: 400

See Also

For more information about using this API in one of the language-specific AWS SDKs, see the following:

- AWS Command Line Interface
- AWS SDK for .NET
- AWS SDK for C++
- AWS SDK for Go
- AWS SDK for Java
- AWS SDK for JavaScript
- AWS SDK for PHP V3
- AWS SDK for Python
- AWS SDK for Ruby V2

DescribeApplication

Returns information about a specific Amazon Kinesis Analytics application.

If you want to retrieve a list of all applications in your account, use the ListApplications operation.

This operation requires permissions to perform the `kinesisanalytics:DescribeApplication` action. You can use `DescribeApplication` to get the current application versionId, which you need to call other operations such as `Update`.

Request Syntax

```
1 {
2    "[ApplicationName](#analytics-DescribeApplication-request-ApplicationName)": "string"
3 }
```

Request Parameters

The request accepts the following data in JSON format.

** ApplicationName ** Name of the application.
Type: String
Length Constraints: Minimum length of 1. Maximum length of 128.
Pattern: `[a-zA-Z0-9_.-]+`
Required: Yes

Response Syntax

```
1  {
2     "[ApplicationDetail](#analytics-DescribeApplication-response-ApplicationDetail)": {
3        "[ApplicationARN](API_ApplicationDetail.md#analytics-Type-ApplicationDetail-ApplicationARN
              )": "string",
4        "[ApplicationCode](API_ApplicationDetail.md#analytics-Type-ApplicationDetail-
              ApplicationCode)": "string",
5        "[ApplicationDescription](API_ApplicationDetail.md#analytics-Type-ApplicationDetail-
              ApplicationDescription)": "string",
6        "[ApplicationName](API_ApplicationDetail.md#analytics-Type-ApplicationDetail-
              ApplicationName)": "string",
7        "[ApplicationStatus](API_ApplicationDetail.md#analytics-Type-ApplicationDetail-
              ApplicationStatus)": "string",
8        "[ApplicationVersionId](API_ApplicationDetail.md#analytics-Type-ApplicationDetail-
              ApplicationVersionId)": number,
9        "[CloudWatchLoggingOptionDescriptions](API_ApplicationDetail.md#analytics-Type-
              ApplicationDetail-CloudWatchLoggingOptionDescriptions)": [
10          {
11             "[CloudWatchLoggingOptionId](API_CloudWatchLoggingOptionDescription.md#analytics-
                   Type-CloudWatchLoggingOptionDescription-CloudWatchLoggingOptionId)": "string",
12             "[LogStreamARN](API_CloudWatchLoggingOptionDescription.md#analytics-Type-
                   CloudWatchLoggingOptionDescription-LogStreamARN)": "string",
13             "[RoleARN](API_CloudWatchLoggingOptionDescription.md#analytics-Type-
                   CloudWatchLoggingOptionDescription-RoleARN)": "string"
14          }
15       ],
```

```
16    "[CreateTimestamp](API_ApplicationDetail.md#analytics-Type-ApplicationDetail-
         CreateTimestamp)": number,
17    "[InputDescriptions](API_ApplicationDetail.md#analytics-Type-ApplicationDetail-
         InputDescriptions)": [
18       {
19          "[InAppStreamNames](API_InputDescription.md#analytics-Type-InputDescription-
              InAppStreamNames)": [ "string" ],
20          "[InputId](API_InputDescription.md#analytics-Type-InputDescription-InputId)": "
              string",
21          "[InputParallelism](API_InputDescription.md#analytics-Type-InputDescription-
              InputParallelism)": {
22             "[Count](API_InputParallelism.md#analytics-Type-InputParallelism-Count)": number
23          },
24          "[InputProcessingConfigurationDescription](API_InputDescription.md#analytics-Type-
              InputDescription-InputProcessingConfigurationDescription)": {
25             "[InputLambdaProcessorDescription](API_InputProcessingConfigurationDescription.md
                 #analytics-Type-InputProcessingConfigurationDescription-
                 InputLambdaProcessorDescription)": {
26                "[ResourceARN](API_InputLambdaProcessorDescription.md#analytics-Type-
                    InputLambdaProcessorDescription-ResourceARN)": "string",
27                "[RoleARN](API_InputLambdaProcessorDescription.md#analytics-Type-
                    InputLambdaProcessorDescription-RoleARN)": "string"
28             }
29          },
30          "[InputSchema](API_InputDescription.md#analytics-Type-InputDescription-InputSchema)
              ": {
31             "[RecordColumns](API_SourceSchema.md#analytics-Type-SourceSchema-RecordColumns)":
                 [
32                {
33                   "[Mapping](API_RecordColumn.md#analytics-Type-RecordColumn-Mapping)": "
                       string",
34                   "[Name](API_RecordColumn.md#analytics-Type-RecordColumn-Name)": "string",
35                   "[SqlType](API_RecordColumn.md#analytics-Type-RecordColumn-SqlType)": "
                       string"
36                }
37             ],
38             "[RecordEncoding](API_SourceSchema.md#analytics-Type-SourceSchema-RecordEncoding)
                 ": "string",
39             "[RecordFormat](API_SourceSchema.md#analytics-Type-SourceSchema-RecordFormat)": {
40                "[MappingParameters](API_RecordFormat.md#analytics-Type-RecordFormat-
                    MappingParameters)": {
41                   "[CSVMappingParameters](API_MappingParameters.md#analytics-Type-
                       MappingParameters-CSVMappingParameters)": {
42                      "[RecordColumnDelimiter](API_CSVMappingParameters.md#analytics-Type-
                          CSVMappingParameters-RecordColumnDelimiter)": "string",
43                      "[RecordRowDelimiter](API_CSVMappingParameters.md#analytics-Type-
                          CSVMappingParameters-RecordRowDelimiter)": "string"
44                   },
45                   "[JSONMappingParameters](API_MappingParameters.md#analytics-Type-
                       MappingParameters-JSONMappingParameters)": {
46                      "[RecordRowPath](API_JSONMappingParameters.md#analytics-Type-
                          JSONMappingParameters-RecordRowPath)": "string"
47                   }
48                },
```

```
49        "[RecordFormatType](API_RecordFormat.md#analytics-Type-RecordFormat-
             RecordFormatType)": "string"
50      }
51    },
52    "[InputStartingPositionConfiguration](API_InputDescription.md#analytics-Type-
         InputDescription-InputStartingPositionConfiguration)": {
53      "[InputStartingPosition](API_InputStartingPositionConfiguration.md#analytics-Type
         -InputStartingPositionConfiguration-InputStartingPosition)": "string"
54    },
55    "[KinesisFirehoseInputDescription](API_InputDescription.md#analytics-Type-
         InputDescription-KinesisFirehoseInputDescription)": {
56      "[ResourceARN](API_KinesisFirehoseInputDescription.md#analytics-Type-
           KinesisFirehoseInputDescription-ResourceARN)": "string",
57      "[RoleARN](API_KinesisFirehoseInputDescription.md#analytics-Type-
           KinesisFirehoseInputDescription-RoleARN)": "string"
58    },
59    "[KinesisStreamsInputDescription](API_InputDescription.md#analytics-Type-
         InputDescription-KinesisStreamsInputDescription)": {
60      "[ResourceARN](API_KinesisStreamsInputDescription.md#analytics-Type-
           KinesisStreamsInputDescription-ResourceARN)": "string",
61      "[RoleARN](API_KinesisStreamsInputDescription.md#analytics-Type-
           KinesisStreamsInputDescription-RoleARN)": "string"
62    },
63    "[NamePrefix](API_InputDescription.md#analytics-Type-InputDescription-NamePrefix)":
         "string"
64  }
65  ],
66  "[LastUpdateTimestamp](API_ApplicationDetail.md#analytics-Type-ApplicationDetail-
       LastUpdateTimestamp)": number,
67  "[OutputDescriptions](API_ApplicationDetail.md#analytics-Type-ApplicationDetail-
       OutputDescriptions)": [
68    {
69      "[DestinationSchema](API_OutputDescription.md#analytics-Type-OutputDescription-
           DestinationSchema)": {
70        "[RecordFormatType](API_DestinationSchema.md#analytics-Type-DestinationSchema-
             RecordFormatType)": "string"
71      },
72      "[KinesisFirehoseOutputDescription](API_OutputDescription.md#analytics-Type-
           OutputDescription-KinesisFirehoseOutputDescription)": {
73        "[ResourceARN](API_KinesisFirehoseOutputDescription.md#analytics-Type-
             KinesisFirehoseOutputDescription-ResourceARN)": "string",
74        "[RoleARN](API_KinesisFirehoseOutputDescription.md#analytics-Type-
             KinesisFirehoseOutputDescription-RoleARN)": "string"
75      },
76      "[KinesisStreamsOutputDescription](API_OutputDescription.md#analytics-Type-
           OutputDescription-KinesisStreamsOutputDescription)": {
77        "[ResourceARN](API_KinesisStreamsOutputDescription.md#analytics-Type-
             KinesisStreamsOutputDescription-ResourceARN)": "string",
78        "[RoleARN](API_KinesisStreamsOutputDescription.md#analytics-Type-
             KinesisStreamsOutputDescription-RoleARN)": "string"
79      },
80      "[LambdaOutputDescription](API_OutputDescription.md#analytics-Type-OutputDescription
           -LambdaOutputDescription)": {
81        "[ResourceARN](API_LambdaOutputDescription.md#analytics-Type-
```

```
              LambdaOutputDescription-ResourceARN)": "string",
82            "[RoleARN](API_LambdaOutputDescription.md#analytics-Type-LambdaOutputDescription-
                 RoleARN)": "string"
83          },
84          "[Name](API_OutputDescription.md#analytics-Type-OutputDescription-Name)": "string",
85          "[OutputId](API_OutputDescription.md#analytics-Type-OutputDescription-OutputId)": "
              string"
86        }
87      ],
88      "[ReferenceDataSourceDescriptions](API_ApplicationDetail.md#analytics-Type-
            ApplicationDetail-ReferenceDataSourceDescriptions)": [
89        {
90          "[ReferenceId](API_ReferenceDataSourceDescription.md#analytics-Type-
               ReferenceDataSourceDescription-ReferenceId)": "string",
91          "[ReferenceSchema](API_ReferenceDataSourceDescription.md#analytics-Type-
               ReferenceDataSourceDescription-ReferenceSchema)": {
92            "[RecordColumns](API_SourceSchema.md#analytics-Type-SourceSchema-RecordColumns)":
                 [
93              {
94                "[Mapping](API_RecordColumn.md#analytics-Type-RecordColumn-Mapping)": "
                     string",
95                "[Name](API_RecordColumn.md#analytics-Type-RecordColumn-Name)": "string",
96                "[SqlType](API_RecordColumn.md#analytics-Type-RecordColumn-SqlType)": "
                     string"
97              }
98            ],
99            "[RecordEncoding](API_SourceSchema.md#analytics-Type-SourceSchema-RecordEncoding)
                 ": "string",
100           "[RecordFormat](API_SourceSchema.md#analytics-Type-SourceSchema-RecordFormat)": {
101             "[MappingParameters](API_RecordFormat.md#analytics-Type-RecordFormat-
                   MappingParameters)": {
102               "[CSVMappingParameters](API_MappingParameters.md#analytics-Type-
                     MappingParameters-CSVMappingParameters)": {
103                 "[RecordColumnDelimiter](API_CSVMappingParameters.md#analytics-Type-
                       CSVMappingParameters-RecordColumnDelimiter)": "string",
104                 "[RecordRowDelimiter](API_CSVMappingParameters.md#analytics-Type-
                       CSVMappingParameters-RecordRowDelimiter)": "string"
105               },
106               "[JSONMappingParameters](API_MappingParameters.md#analytics-Type-
                     MappingParameters-JSONMappingParameters)": {
107                 "[RecordRowPath](API_JSONMappingParameters.md#analytics-Type-
                       JSONMappingParameters-RecordRowPath)": "string"
108               }
109             },
110             "[RecordFormatType](API_RecordFormat.md#analytics-Type-RecordFormat-
                   RecordFormatType)": "string"
111           }
112         },
113         "[S3ReferenceDataSourceDescription](API_ReferenceDataSourceDescription.md#analytics-
              Type-ReferenceDataSourceDescription-S3ReferenceDataSourceDescription)": {
114           "[BucketARN](API_S3ReferenceDataSourceDescription.md#analytics-Type-
                 S3ReferenceDataSourceDescription-BucketARN)": "string",
115           "[FileKey](API_S3ReferenceDataSourceDescription.md#analytics-Type-
                 S3ReferenceDataSourceDescription-FileKey)": "string",
```

234

```
116            "[ReferenceRoleARN](API_S3ReferenceDataSourceDescription.md#analytics-Type-
                   S3ReferenceDataSourceDescription-ReferenceRoleARN)": "string"
117          },
118          "[TableName](API_ReferenceDataSourceDescription.md#analytics-Type-
                   ReferenceDataSourceDescription-TableName)": "string"
119        }
120     ]
121   }
122 }
```

Response Elements

If the action is successful, the service sends back an HTTP 200 response.

The following data is returned in JSON format by the service.

** ApplicationDetail ** Provides a description of the application, such as the application Amazon Resource Name (ARN), status, latest version, and input and output configuration details.
Type: ApplicationDetail object

Errors

ResourceNotFoundException
Specified application can't be found.
HTTP Status Code: 400

See Also

For more information about using this API in one of the language-specific AWS SDKs, see the following:

- AWS Command Line Interface
- AWS SDK for .NET
- AWS SDK for C++
- AWS SDK for Go
- AWS SDK for Java
- AWS SDK for JavaScript
- AWS SDK for PHP V3
- AWS SDK for Python
- AWS SDK for Ruby V2

DiscoverInputSchema

Infers a schema by evaluating sample records on the specified streaming source (Amazon Kinesis stream or Amazon Kinesis Firehose delivery stream) or S3 object. In the response, the operation returns the inferred schema and also the sample records that the operation used to infer the schema.

You can use the inferred schema when configuring a streaming source for your application. For conceptual information, see Configuring Application Input. Note that when you create an application using the Amazon Kinesis Analytics console, the console uses this operation to infer a schema and show it in the console user interface.

This operation requires permissions to perform the `kinesisanalytics:DiscoverInputSchema` action.

Request Syntax

```
1  {
2     "[InputProcessingConfiguration](#analytics-DiscoverInputSchema-request-
          InputProcessingConfiguration)": {
3        "[InputLambdaProcessor](API_InputProcessingConfiguration.md#analytics-Type-
             InputProcessingConfiguration-InputLambdaProcessor)": {
4           "[ResourceARN](API_InputLambdaProcessor.md#analytics-Type-InputLambdaProcessor-
                ResourceARN)": "string",
5           "[RoleARN](API_InputLambdaProcessor.md#analytics-Type-InputLambdaProcessor-RoleARN)": "
                string"
6        }
7     },
8     "[InputStartingPositionConfiguration](#analytics-DiscoverInputSchema-request-
          InputStartingPositionConfiguration)": {
9        "[InputStartingPosition](API_InputStartingPositionConfiguration.md#analytics-Type-
             InputStartingPositionConfiguration-InputStartingPosition)": "string"
10    },
11    "[ResourceARN](#analytics-DiscoverInputSchema-request-ResourceARN)": "string",
12    "[RoleARN](#analytics-DiscoverInputSchema-request-RoleARN)": "string",
13    "[S3Configuration](#analytics-DiscoverInputSchema-request-S3Configuration)": {
14       "[BucketARN](API_S3Configuration.md#analytics-Type-S3Configuration-BucketARN)": "string",
15       "[FileKey](API_S3Configuration.md#analytics-Type-S3Configuration-FileKey)": "string",
16       "[RoleARN](API_S3Configuration.md#analytics-Type-S3Configuration-RoleARN)": "string"
17    }
18 }
```

Request Parameters

The request accepts the following data in JSON format.

** InputProcessingConfiguration ** The InputProcessingConfiguration to use to preprocess the records before discovering the schema of the records.
Type: InputProcessingConfiguration object
Required: No

** InputStartingPositionConfiguration ** Point at which you want Amazon Kinesis Analytics to start reading records from the specified streaming source discovery purposes.
Type: InputStartingPositionConfiguration object
Required: No

** ResourceARN ** Amazon Resource Name (ARN) of the streaming source.
Type: String
Length Constraints: Minimum length of 1. Maximum length of 2048.
Pattern: `arn:.*`
Required: No

** RoleARN ** ARN of the IAM role that Amazon Kinesis Analytics can assume to access the stream on your behalf.
Type: String
Length Constraints: Minimum length of 1. Maximum length of 2048.
Pattern: `arn:aws:iam::\d{12}:role/?[a-zA-Z_0-9+=,.@\-_/]+`
Required: No

** S3Configuration ** Specify this parameter to discover a schema from data in an Amazon S3 object.
Type: S3Configuration object
Required: No

Response Syntax

```
1  {
2     "[InputSchema](#analytics-DiscoverInputSchema-response-InputSchema)": {
3        "[RecordColumns](API_SourceSchema.md#analytics-Type-SourceSchema-RecordColumns)": [
4           {
5              "[Mapping](API_RecordColumn.md#analytics-Type-RecordColumn-Mapping)": "string",
6              "[Name](API_RecordColumn.md#analytics-Type-RecordColumn-Name)": "string",
7              "[SqlType](API_RecordColumn.md#analytics-Type-RecordColumn-SqlType)": "string"
8           }
9        ],
10       "[RecordEncoding](API_SourceSchema.md#analytics-Type-SourceSchema-RecordEncoding)": "
          string",
11       "[RecordFormat](API_SourceSchema.md#analytics-Type-SourceSchema-RecordFormat)": {
12          "[MappingParameters](API_RecordFormat.md#analytics-Type-RecordFormat-MappingParameters)
             ": {
13             "[CSVMappingParameters](API_MappingParameters.md#analytics-Type-MappingParameters-
                CSVMappingParameters)": {
14                "[RecordColumnDelimiter](API_CSVMappingParameters.md#analytics-Type-
                   CSVMappingParameters-RecordColumnDelimiter)": "string",
15                "[RecordRowDelimiter](API_CSVMappingParameters.md#analytics-Type-
                   CSVMappingParameters-RecordRowDelimiter)": "string"
16             },
17             "[JSONMappingParameters](API_MappingParameters.md#analytics-Type-MappingParameters-
                JSONMappingParameters)": {
18                "[RecordRowPath](API_JSONMappingParameters.md#analytics-Type-
                   JSONMappingParameters-RecordRowPath)": "string"
19             }
20          },
21          "[RecordFormatType](API_RecordFormat.md#analytics-Type-RecordFormat-RecordFormatType)":
             "string"
22       }
23    },
24    "[ParsedInputRecords](#analytics-DiscoverInputSchema-response-ParsedInputRecords)": [
25       [ "string" ]
26    ],
27    "[ProcessedInputRecords](#analytics-DiscoverInputSchema-response-ProcessedInputRecords)": [ "
       string" ],
```

```
28    "[RawInputRecords](#analytics-DiscoverInputSchema-response-RawInputRecords)": [ "string" ]
29 }
```

Response Elements

If the action is successful, the service sends back an HTTP 200 response.

The following data is returned in JSON format by the service.

** InputSchema ** Schema inferred from the streaming source. It identifies the format of the data in the streaming source and how each data element maps to corresponding columns in the in-application stream that you can create.
Type: SourceSchema object

** ParsedInputRecords ** An array of elements, where each element corresponds to a row in a stream record (a stream record can have more than one row).
Type: Array of arrays of strings

** ProcessedInputRecords ** Stream data that was modified by the processor specified in the `InputProcessingConfiguration` parameter.
Type: Array of strings

** RawInputRecords ** Raw stream data that was sampled to infer the schema.
Type: Array of strings

Errors

InvalidArgumentException
Specified input parameter value is invalid.
HTTP Status Code: 400

ResourceProvisionedThroughputExceededException
Discovery failed to get a record from the streaming source because of the Amazon Kinesis Streams ProvisionedThroughputExceededException. For more information, see GetRecords in the Amazon Kinesis Streams API Reference.
HTTP Status Code: 400

ServiceUnavailableException
The service is unavailable. Back off and retry the operation.
HTTP Status Code: 500

UnableToDetectSchemaException
Data format is not valid. Amazon Kinesis Analytics is not able to detect schema for the given streaming source.
HTTP Status Code: 400

See Also

For more information about using this API in one of the language-specific AWS SDKs, see the following:

- AWS Command Line Interface
- AWS SDK for .NET
- AWS SDK for C++
- AWS SDK for Go
- AWS SDK for Java
- AWS SDK for JavaScript
- AWS SDK for PHP V3
- AWS SDK for Python

- AWS SDK for Ruby V2

ListApplications

Returns a list of Amazon Kinesis Analytics applications in your account. For each application, the response includes the application name, Amazon Resource Name (ARN), and status. If the response returns the `HasMoreApplications` value as true, you can send another request by adding the `ExclusiveStartApplicationName` in the request body, and set the value of this to the last application name from the previous response.

If you want detailed information about a specific application, use DescribeApplication.

This operation requires permissions to perform the `kinesisanalytics:ListApplications` action.

Request Syntax

```
1 {
2    "[ExclusiveStartApplicationName](#analytics-ListApplications-request-
         ExclusiveStartApplicationName)": "string",
3    "[Limit](#analytics-ListApplications-request-Limit)": number
4 }
```

Request Parameters

The request accepts the following data in JSON format.

** ExclusiveStartApplicationName ** Name of the application to start the list with. When using pagination to retrieve the list, you don't need to specify this parameter in the first request. However, in subsequent requests, you add the last application name from the previous response to get the next page of applications.
Type: String
Length Constraints: Minimum length of 1. Maximum length of 128.
Pattern: `[a-zA-Z0-9_.-]+`
Required: No

** Limit ** Maximum number of applications to list.
Type: Integer
Valid Range: Minimum value of 1. Maximum value of 50.
Required: No

Response Syntax

```
1 {
2    "[ApplicationSummaries](#analytics-ListApplications-response-ApplicationSummaries)": [
3       {
4          "[ApplicationARN](API_ApplicationSummary.md#analytics-Type-ApplicationSummary-
                ApplicationARN)": "string",
5          "[ApplicationName](API_ApplicationSummary.md#analytics-Type-ApplicationSummary-
                ApplicationName)": "string",
6          "[ApplicationStatus](API_ApplicationSummary.md#analytics-Type-ApplicationSummary-
                ApplicationStatus)": "string"
7       }
8    ],
9    "[HasMoreApplications](#analytics-ListApplications-response-HasMoreApplications)": boolean
10 }
```

Response Elements

If the action is successful, the service sends back an HTTP 200 response.

The following data is returned in JSON format by the service.

** ApplicationSummaries ** List of `ApplicationSummary` objects.
Type: Array of ApplicationSummary objects

** HasMoreApplications ** Returns true if there are more applications to retrieve.
Type: Boolean

See Also

For more information about using this API in one of the language-specific AWS SDKs, see the following:

- AWS Command Line Interface
- AWS SDK for .NET
- AWS SDK for C++
- AWS SDK for Go
- AWS SDK for Java
- AWS SDK for JavaScript
- AWS SDK for PHP V3
- AWS SDK for Python
- AWS SDK for Ruby V2

StartApplication

Starts the specified Amazon Kinesis Analytics application. After creating an application, you must exclusively call this operation to start your application.

After the application starts, it begins consuming the input data, processes it, and writes the output to the configured destination.

The application status must be `READY` for you to start an application. You can get the application status in the console or using the DescribeApplication operation.

After you start the application, you can stop the application from processing the input by calling the StopApplication operation.

This operation requires permissions to perform the `kinesisanalytics:StartApplication` action.

Request Syntax

```
1  {
2    "[ApplicationName](#analytics-StartApplication-request-ApplicationName)": "string",
3    "[InputConfigurations](#analytics-StartApplication-request-InputConfigurations)": [
4      {
5        "[Id](API_InputConfiguration.md#analytics-Type-InputConfiguration-Id)": "string",
6        "[InputStartingPositionConfiguration](API_InputConfiguration.md#analytics-Type-
            InputConfiguration-InputStartingPositionConfiguration)": {
7          "[InputStartingPosition](API_InputStartingPositionConfiguration.md#analytics-Type-
              InputStartingPositionConfiguration-InputStartingPosition)": "string"
8        }
9      }
10   ]
11 }
```

Request Parameters

The request accepts the following data in JSON format.

** ApplicationName ** Name of the application.
Type: String
Length Constraints: Minimum length of 1. Maximum length of 128.
Pattern: `[a-zA-Z0-9_.-]+`
Required: Yes

** InputConfigurations ** Identifies the specific input, by ID, that the application starts consuming. Amazon Kinesis Analytics starts reading the streaming source associated with the input. You can also specify where in the streaming source you want Amazon Kinesis Analytics to start reading.
Type: Array of InputConfiguration objects
Required: Yes

Response Elements

If the action is successful, the service sends back an HTTP 200 response with an empty HTTP body.

Errors

InvalidApplicationConfigurationException
User-provided application configuration is not valid.
HTTP Status Code: 400

InvalidArgumentException
Specified input parameter value is invalid.
HTTP Status Code: 400

ResourceInUseException
Application is not available for this operation.
HTTP Status Code: 400

ResourceNotFoundException
Specified application can't be found.
HTTP Status Code: 400

See Also

For more information about using this API in one of the language-specific AWS SDKs, see the following:

- AWS Command Line Interface
- AWS SDK for .NET
- AWS SDK for C++
- AWS SDK for Go
- AWS SDK for Java
- AWS SDK for JavaScript
- AWS SDK for PHP V3
- AWS SDK for Python
- AWS SDK for Ruby V2

StopApplication

Stops the application from processing input data. You can stop an application only if it is in the running state. You can use the DescribeApplication operation to find the application state. After the application is stopped, Amazon Kinesis Analytics stops reading data from the input, the application stops processing data, and there is no output written to the destination.

This operation requires permissions to perform the `kinesisanalytics:StopApplication` action.

Request Syntax

```
1 {
2     "[ApplicationName](#analytics-StopApplication-request-ApplicationName)": "string"
3 }
```

Request Parameters

The request accepts the following data in JSON format.

** ApplicationName ** Name of the running application to stop.
Type: String
Length Constraints: Minimum length of 1. Maximum length of 128.
Pattern: [a-zA-Z0-9_.-]+
Required: Yes

Response Elements

If the action is successful, the service sends back an HTTP 200 response with an empty HTTP body.

Errors

ResourceInUseException
Application is not available for this operation.
HTTP Status Code: 400

ResourceNotFoundException
Specified application can't be found.
HTTP Status Code: 400

See Also

For more information about using this API in one of the language-specific AWS SDKs, see the following:

- AWS Command Line Interface
- AWS SDK for .NET
- AWS SDK for C++
- AWS SDK for Go
- AWS SDK for Java
- AWS SDK for JavaScript
- AWS SDK for PHP V3
- AWS SDK for Python
- AWS SDK for Ruby V2

UpdateApplication

Updates an existing Amazon Kinesis Analytics application. Using this API, you can update application code, input configuration, and output configuration.

Note that Amazon Kinesis Analytics updates the `CurrentApplicationVersionId` each time you update your application.

This operation requires permission for the `kinesisanalytics:UpdateApplication` action.

Request Syntax

```
1  {
2     "[ApplicationName](#analytics-UpdateApplication-request-ApplicationName)": "string",
3     "[ApplicationUpdate](#analytics-UpdateApplication-request-ApplicationUpdate)": {
4        "[ApplicationCodeUpdate](API_ApplicationUpdate.md#analytics-Type-ApplicationUpdate-
             ApplicationCodeUpdate)": "string",
5        "[CloudWatchLoggingOptionUpdates](API_ApplicationUpdate.md#analytics-Type-
             ApplicationUpdate-CloudWatchLoggingOptionUpdates)": [
6           {
7              "[CloudWatchLoggingOptionId](API_CloudWatchLoggingOptionUpdate.md#analytics-Type-
                   CloudWatchLoggingOptionUpdate-CloudWatchLoggingOptionId)": "string",
8              "[LogStreamARNUpdate](API_CloudWatchLoggingOptionUpdate.md#analytics-Type-
                   CloudWatchLoggingOptionUpdate-LogStreamARNUpdate)": "string",
9              "[RoleARNUpdate](API_CloudWatchLoggingOptionUpdate.md#analytics-Type-
                   CloudWatchLoggingOptionUpdate-RoleARNUpdate)": "string"
10          }
11       ],
12       "[InputUpdates](API_ApplicationUpdate.md#analytics-Type-ApplicationUpdate-InputUpdates)":
              [
13          {
14             "[InputId](API_InputUpdate.md#analytics-Type-InputUpdate-InputId)": "string",
15             "[InputParallelismUpdate](API_InputUpdate.md#analytics-Type-InputUpdate-
                   InputParallelismUpdate)": {
16                "[CountUpdate](API_InputParallelismUpdate.md#analytics-Type-
                      InputParallelismUpdate-CountUpdate)": number
17             },
18             "[InputProcessingConfigurationUpdate](API_InputUpdate.md#analytics-Type-InputUpdate-
                   InputProcessingConfigurationUpdate)": {
19                "[InputLambdaProcessorUpdate](API_InputProcessingConfigurationUpdate.md#analytics
                      -Type-InputProcessingConfigurationUpdate-InputLambdaProcessorUpdate)": {
20                   "[ResourceARNUpdate](API_InputLambdaProcessorUpdate.md#analytics-Type-
                         InputLambdaProcessorUpdate-ResourceARNUpdate)": "string",
21                   "[RoleARNUpdate](API_InputLambdaProcessorUpdate.md#analytics-Type-
                         InputLambdaProcessorUpdate-RoleARNUpdate)": "string"
22                }
23             },
24             "[InputSchemaUpdate](API_InputUpdate.md#analytics-Type-InputUpdate-InputSchemaUpdate
                   )": {
25                "[RecordColumnUpdates](API_InputSchemaUpdate.md#analytics-Type-InputSchemaUpdate-
                      RecordColumnUpdates)": [
26                   {
27                      "[Mapping](API_RecordColumn.md#analytics-Type-RecordColumn-Mapping)": "
                            string",
```

```
28            "[Name](API_RecordColumn.md#analytics-Type-RecordColumn-Name)": "string",
29            "[SqlType](API_RecordColumn.md#analytics-Type-RecordColumn-SqlType)": "
                 string"
30          }
31        ],
32        "[RecordEncodingUpdate](API_InputSchemaUpdate.md#analytics-Type-InputSchemaUpdate
             -RecordEncodingUpdate)": "string",
33        "[RecordFormatUpdate](API_InputSchemaUpdate.md#analytics-Type-InputSchemaUpdate-
             RecordFormatUpdate)": {
34          "[MappingParameters](API_RecordFormat.md#analytics-Type-RecordFormat-
               MappingParameters)": {
35            "[CSVMappingParameters](API_MappingParameters.md#analytics-Type-
                 MappingParameters-CSVMappingParameters)": {
36              "[RecordColumnDelimiter](API_CSVMappingParameters.md#analytics-Type-
                   CSVMappingParameters-RecordColumnDelimiter)": "string",
37              "[RecordRowDelimiter](API_CSVMappingParameters.md#analytics-Type-
                   CSVMappingParameters-RecordRowDelimiter)": "string"
38            },
39            "[JSONMappingParameters](API_MappingParameters.md#analytics-Type-
                 MappingParameters-JSONMappingParameters)": {
40              "[RecordRowPath](API_JSONMappingParameters.md#analytics-Type-
                   JSONMappingParameters-RecordRowPath)": "string"
41            }
42          },
43          "[RecordFormatType](API_RecordFormat.md#analytics-Type-RecordFormat-
               RecordFormatType)": "string"
44        }
45      },
46      "[KinesisFirehoseInputUpdate](API_InputUpdate.md#analytics-Type-InputUpdate-
           KinesisFirehoseInputUpdate)": {
47        "[ResourceARNUpdate](API_KinesisFirehoseInputUpdate.md#analytics-Type-
             KinesisFirehoseInputUpdate-ResourceARNUpdate)": "string",
48        "[RoleARNUpdate](API_KinesisFirehoseInputUpdate.md#analytics-Type-
             KinesisFirehoseInputUpdate-RoleARNUpdate)": "string"
49      },
50      "[KinesisStreamsInputUpdate](API_InputUpdate.md#analytics-Type-InputUpdate-
           KinesisStreamsInputUpdate)": {
51        "[ResourceARNUpdate](API_KinesisStreamsInputUpdate.md#analytics-Type-
             KinesisStreamsInputUpdate-ResourceARNUpdate)": "string",
52        "[RoleARNUpdate](API_KinesisStreamsInputUpdate.md#analytics-Type-
             KinesisStreamsInputUpdate-RoleARNUpdate)": "string"
53      },
54      "[NamePrefixUpdate](API_InputUpdate.md#analytics-Type-InputUpdate-NamePrefixUpdate)
           ": "string"
55    }
56  ],
57  "[OutputUpdates](API_ApplicationUpdate.md#analytics-Type-ApplicationUpdate-OutputUpdates)
       ": [
58    {
59      "[DestinationSchemaUpdate](API_OutputUpdate.md#analytics-Type-OutputUpdate-
           DestinationSchemaUpdate)": {
60        "[RecordFormatType](API_DestinationSchema.md#analytics-Type-DestinationSchema-
             RecordFormatType)": "string"
61      },
```

```
62      "[KinesisFirehoseOutputUpdate](API_OutputUpdate.md#analytics-Type-OutputUpdate-
            KinesisFirehoseOutputUpdate)": {
63        "[ResourceARNUpdate](API_KinesisFirehoseOutputUpdate.md#analytics-Type-
            KinesisFirehoseOutputUpdate-ResourceARNUpdate)": "string",
64        "[RoleARNUpdate](API_KinesisFirehoseOutputUpdate.md#analytics-Type-
            KinesisFirehoseOutputUpdate-RoleARNUpdate)": "string"
65      },
66      "[KinesisStreamsOutputUpdate](API_OutputUpdate.md#analytics-Type-OutputUpdate-
            KinesisStreamsOutputUpdate)": {
67        "[ResourceARNUpdate](API_KinesisStreamsOutputUpdate.md#analytics-Type-
            KinesisStreamsOutputUpdate-ResourceARNUpdate)": "string",
68        "[RoleARNUpdate](API_KinesisStreamsOutputUpdate.md#analytics-Type-
            KinesisStreamsOutputUpdate-RoleARNUpdate)": "string"
69      },
70      "[LambdaOutputUpdate](API_OutputUpdate.md#analytics-Type-OutputUpdate-
            LambdaOutputUpdate)": {
71        "[ResourceARNUpdate](API_LambdaOutputUpdate.md#analytics-Type-LambdaOutputUpdate-
            ResourceARNUpdate)": "string",
72        "[RoleARNUpdate](API_LambdaOutputUpdate.md#analytics-Type-LambdaOutputUpdate-
            RoleARNUpdate)": "string"
73      },
74      "[NameUpdate](API_OutputUpdate.md#analytics-Type-OutputUpdate-NameUpdate)": "string
            ",
75      "[OutputId](API_OutputUpdate.md#analytics-Type-OutputUpdate-OutputId)": "string"
76    }
77    ],
78    "[ReferenceDataSourceUpdates](API_ApplicationUpdate.md#analytics-Type-ApplicationUpdate-
        ReferenceDataSourceUpdates)": [
79      {
80        "[ReferenceId](API_ReferenceDataSourceUpdate.md#analytics-Type-
            ReferenceDataSourceUpdate-ReferenceId)": "string",
81        "[ReferenceSchemaUpdate](API_ReferenceDataSourceUpdate.md#analytics-Type-
            ReferenceDataSourceUpdate-ReferenceSchemaUpdate)": {
82        "[RecordColumns](API_SourceSchema.md#analytics-Type-SourceSchema-RecordColumns)":
              [
83          {
84            "[Mapping](API_RecordColumn.md#analytics-Type-RecordColumn-Mapping)": "
                string",
85            "[Name](API_RecordColumn.md#analytics-Type-RecordColumn-Name)": "string",
86            "[SqlType](API_RecordColumn.md#analytics-Type-RecordColumn-SqlType)": "
                string"
87          }
88        ],
89        "[RecordEncoding](API_SourceSchema.md#analytics-Type-SourceSchema-RecordEncoding)
              ": "string",
90        "[RecordFormat](API_SourceSchema.md#analytics-Type-SourceSchema-RecordFormat)": {
91          "[MappingParameters](API_RecordFormat.md#analytics-Type-RecordFormat-
              MappingParameters)": {
92            "[CSVMappingParameters](API_MappingParameters.md#analytics-Type-
                MappingParameters-CSVMappingParameters)": {
93              "[RecordColumnDelimiter](API_CSVMappingParameters.md#analytics-Type-
                  CSVMappingParameters-RecordColumnDelimiter)": "string",
94              "[RecordRowDelimiter](API_CSVMappingParameters.md#analytics-Type-
                  CSVMappingParameters-RecordRowDelimiter)": "string"
```

```
95              },
96              "[JSONMappingParameters](API_MappingParameters.md#analytics-Type-
                   MappingParameters-JSONMappingParameters)": {
97                "[RecordRowPath](API_JSONMappingParameters.md#analytics-Type-
                     JSONMappingParameters-RecordRowPath)": "string"
98              }
99            },
100           "[RecordFormatType](API_RecordFormat.md#analytics-Type-RecordFormat-
                 RecordFormatType)": "string"
101         }
102       },
103       "[S3ReferenceDataSourceUpdate](API_ReferenceDataSourceUpdate.md#analytics-Type-
               ReferenceDataSourceUpdate-S3ReferenceDataSourceUpdate)": {
104         "[BucketARNUpdate](API_S3ReferenceDataSourceUpdate.md#analytics-Type-
               S3ReferenceDataSourceUpdate-BucketARNUpdate)": "string",
105         "[FileKeyUpdate](API_S3ReferenceDataSourceUpdate.md#analytics-Type-
               S3ReferenceDataSourceUpdate-FileKeyUpdate)": "string",
106         "[ReferenceRoleARNUpdate](API_S3ReferenceDataSourceUpdate.md#analytics-Type-
               S3ReferenceDataSourceUpdate-ReferenceRoleARNUpdate)": "string"
107       },
108       "[TableNameUpdate](API_ReferenceDataSourceUpdate.md#analytics-Type-
             ReferenceDataSourceUpdate-TableNameUpdate)": "string"
109     }
110   ]
111   },
112   "[CurrentApplicationVersionId](#analytics-UpdateApplication-request-
         CurrentApplicationVersionId)": number
113 }
```

Request Parameters

The request accepts the following data in JSON format.

** ApplicationName ** Name of the Amazon Kinesis Analytics application to update.
Type: String
Length Constraints: Minimum length of 1. Maximum length of 128.
Pattern: [a-zA-Z0-9_.-]+
Required: Yes

** ApplicationUpdate ** Describes application updates.
Type: ApplicationUpdate object
Required: Yes

** CurrentApplicationVersionId ** The current application version ID. You can use the DescribeApplication operation to get this value.
Type: Long
Valid Range: Minimum value of 1. Maximum value of 999999999.
Required: Yes

Response Elements

If the action is successful, the service sends back an HTTP 200 response with an empty HTTP body.

Errors

CodeValidationException
User-provided application code (query) is invalid. This can be a simple syntax error.
HTTP Status Code: 400

ConcurrentModificationException
Exception thrown as a result of concurrent modification to an application. For example, two individuals attempting to edit the same application at the same time.
HTTP Status Code: 400

InvalidArgumentException
Specified input parameter value is invalid.
HTTP Status Code: 400

ResourceInUseException
Application is not available for this operation.
HTTP Status Code: 400

ResourceNotFoundException
Specified application can't be found.
HTTP Status Code: 400

See Also

For more information about using this API in one of the language-specific AWS SDKs, see the following:

- AWS Command Line Interface
- AWS SDK for .NET
- AWS SDK for C++
- AWS SDK for Go
- AWS SDK for Java
- AWS SDK for JavaScript
- AWS SDK for PHP V3
- AWS SDK for Python
- AWS SDK for Ruby V2

Data Types

The following data types are supported:

- ApplicationDetail
- ApplicationSummary
- ApplicationUpdate
- CloudWatchLoggingOption
- CloudWatchLoggingOptionDescription
- CloudWatchLoggingOptionUpdate
- CSVMappingParameters
- DestinationSchema
- Input
- InputConfiguration
- InputDescription
- InputLambdaProcessor
- InputLambdaProcessorDescription
- InputLambdaProcessorUpdate
- InputParallelism
- InputParallelismUpdate
- InputProcessingConfiguration
- InputProcessingConfigurationDescription
- InputProcessingConfigurationUpdate
- InputSchemaUpdate
- InputStartingPositionConfiguration
- InputUpdate
- JSONMappingParameters
- KinesisFirehoseInput
- KinesisFirehoseInputDescription
- KinesisFirehoseInputUpdate
- KinesisFirehoseOutput
- KinesisFirehoseOutputDescription
- KinesisFirehoseOutputUpdate
- KinesisStreamsInput
- KinesisStreamsInputDescription
- KinesisStreamsInputUpdate
- KinesisStreamsOutput
- KinesisStreamsOutputDescription
- KinesisStreamsOutputUpdate
- LambdaOutput
- LambdaOutputDescription
- LambdaOutputUpdate
- MappingParameters
- Output
- OutputDescription
- OutputUpdate
- RecordColumn
- RecordFormat
- ReferenceDataSource
- ReferenceDataSourceDescription
- ReferenceDataSourceUpdate
- S3Configuration
- S3ReferenceDataSource
- S3ReferenceDataSourceDescription

- S3ReferenceDataSourceUpdate
- SourceSchema

ApplicationDetail

Provides a description of the application, including the application Amazon Resource Name (ARN), status, latest version, and input and output configuration.

Contents

ApplicationARN ARN of the application.
Type: String
Length Constraints: Minimum length of 1. Maximum length of 2048.
Pattern: `arn:.*`
Required: Yes

ApplicationCode Returns the application code that you provided to perform data analysis on any of the in-application streams in your application.
Type: String
Length Constraints: Minimum length of 0. Maximum length of 102400.
Required: No

ApplicationDescription Description of the application.
Type: String
Length Constraints: Minimum length of 0. Maximum length of 1024.
Required: No

ApplicationName Name of the application.
Type: String
Length Constraints: Minimum length of 1. Maximum length of 128.
Pattern: `[a-zA-Z0-9_.-]+`
Required: Yes

ApplicationStatus Status of the application.
Type: String
Valid Values:`DELETING | STARTING | STOPPING | READY | RUNNING | UPDATING`
Required: Yes

ApplicationVersionId Provides the current application version.
Type: Long
Valid Range: Minimum value of 1. Maximum value of 999999999.
Required: Yes

CloudWatchLoggingOptionDescriptions Describes the CloudWatch log streams that are configured to receive application messages. For more information about using CloudWatch log streams with Amazon Kinesis Analytics applications, see Working with Amazon CloudWatch Logs.
Type: Array of CloudWatchLoggingOptionDescription objects
Required: No

CreateTimestamp Time stamp when the application version was created.
Type: Timestamp
Required: No

InputDescriptions Describes the application input configuration. For more information, see Configuring Application Input.
Type: Array of InputDescription objects
Required: No

LastUpdateTimestamp Time stamp when the application was last updated.
Type: Timestamp

Required: No

OutputDescriptions Describes the application output configuration. For more information, see Configuring Application Output.
Type: Array of OutputDescription objects
Required: No

ReferenceDataSourceDescriptions Describes reference data sources configured for the application. For more information, see Configuring Application Input.
Type: Array of ReferenceDataSourceDescription objects
Required: No

See Also

For more information about using this API in one of the language-specific AWS SDKs, see the following:

- AWS SDK for C++
- AWS SDK for Go
- AWS SDK for Java
- AWS SDK for Ruby V2

ApplicationSummary

Provides application summary information, including the application Amazon Resource Name (ARN), name, and status.

Contents

ApplicationARN ARN of the application.
Type: String
Length Constraints: Minimum length of 1. Maximum length of 2048.
Pattern: `arn:.*`
Required: Yes

ApplicationName Name of the application.
Type: String
Length Constraints: Minimum length of 1. Maximum length of 128.
Pattern: `[a-zA-Z0-9_.-]+`
Required: Yes

ApplicationStatus Status of the application.
Type: String
Valid Values:`DELETING | STARTING | STOPPING | READY | RUNNING | UPDATING`
Required: Yes

See Also

For more information about using this API in one of the language-specific AWS SDKs, see the following:

- AWS SDK for C++
- AWS SDK for Go
- AWS SDK for Java
- AWS SDK for Ruby V2

ApplicationUpdate

Describes updates to apply to an existing Amazon Kinesis Analytics application.

Contents

ApplicationCodeUpdate Describes application code updates.
Type: String
Length Constraints: Minimum length of 0. Maximum length of 102400.
Required: No

CloudWatchLoggingOptionUpdates Describes application CloudWatch logging option updates.
Type: Array of CloudWatchLoggingOptionUpdate objects
Required: No

InputUpdates Describes application input configuration updates.
Type: Array of InputUpdate objects
Required: No

OutputUpdates Describes application output configuration updates.
Type: Array of OutputUpdate objects
Required: No

ReferenceDataSourceUpdates Describes application reference data source updates.
Type: Array of ReferenceDataSourceUpdate objects
Required: No

See Also

For more information about using this API in one of the language-specific AWS SDKs, see the following:

- AWS SDK for C++
- AWS SDK for Go
- AWS SDK for Java
- AWS SDK for Ruby V2

CloudWatchLoggingOption

Provides a description of CloudWatch logging options, including the log stream Amazon Resource Name (ARN) and the role ARN.

Contents

LogStreamARN ARN of the CloudWatch log to receive application messages.
Type: String
Length Constraints: Minimum length of 1. Maximum length of 2048.
Pattern: `arn:.*`
Required: Yes

RoleARN IAM ARN of the role to use to send application messages. Note: To write application messages to CloudWatch, the IAM role that is used must have the `PutLogEvents` policy action enabled.
Type: String
Length Constraints: Minimum length of 1. Maximum length of 2048.
Pattern: `arn:aws:iam::\d{12}:role/?[a-zA-Z_0-9+=,.@\-_/]+`
Required: Yes

See Also

For more information about using this API in one of the language-specific AWS SDKs, see the following:

- AWS SDK for C++
- AWS SDK for Go
- AWS SDK for Java
- AWS SDK for Ruby V2

CloudWatchLoggingOptionDescription

Description of the CloudWatch logging option.

Contents

CloudWatchLoggingOptionId ID of the CloudWatch logging option description.
Type: String
Length Constraints: Minimum length of 1. Maximum length of 50.
Pattern: `[a-zA-Z0-9_.-]+`
Required: No

LogStreamARN ARN of the CloudWatch log to receive application messages.
Type: String
Length Constraints: Minimum length of 1. Maximum length of 2048.
Pattern: `arn:.*`
Required: Yes

RoleARN IAM ARN of the role to use to send application messages. Note: To write application messages to CloudWatch, the IAM role used must have the `PutLogEvents` policy action enabled.
Type: String
Length Constraints: Minimum length of 1. Maximum length of 2048.
Pattern: `arn:aws:iam::\d{12}:role/?[a-zA-Z_0-9+=,.@\-_/]+`
Required: Yes

See Also

For more information about using this API in one of the language-specific AWS SDKs, see the following:

- AWS SDK for C++
- AWS SDK for Go
- AWS SDK for Java
- AWS SDK for Ruby V2

CloudWatchLoggingOptionUpdate

Describes CloudWatch logging option updates.

Contents

CloudWatchLoggingOptionId ID of the CloudWatch logging option to update
Type: String
Length Constraints: Minimum length of 1. Maximum length of 50.
Pattern: `[a-zA-Z0-9_.-]+`
Required: Yes

LogStreamARNUpdate ARN of the CloudWatch log to receive application messages.
Type: String
Length Constraints: Minimum length of 1. Maximum length of 2048.
Pattern: `arn:.*`
Required: No

RoleARNUpdate IAM ARN of the role to use to send application messages. Note: To write application messages to CloudWatch, the IAM role used must have the `PutLogEvents` policy action enabled.
Type: String
Length Constraints: Minimum length of 1. Maximum length of 2048.
Pattern: `arn:aws:iam::\d{12}:role/?[a-zA-Z_0-9+=,.@\-_/]+`
Required: No

See Also

For more information about using this API in one of the language-specific AWS SDKs, see the following:

- AWS SDK for C++
- AWS SDK for Go
- AWS SDK for Java
- AWS SDK for Ruby V2

CSVMappingParameters

Provides additional mapping information when the record format uses delimiters, such as CSV. For example, the following sample records use CSV format, where the records use the '$\backslash n$' as the row delimiter and a comma (",") as the column delimiter:

```
"name1", "address1"

"name2", "address2"
```

Contents

RecordColumnDelimiter Column delimiter. For example, in a CSV format, a comma (",") is the typical column delimiter.
Type: String
Length Constraints: Minimum length of 1.
Required: Yes

RecordRowDelimiter Row delimiter. For example, in a CSV format, '$\backslash n$' is the typical row delimiter.
Type: String
Length Constraints: Minimum length of 1.
Required: Yes

See Also

For more information about using this API in one of the language-specific AWS SDKs, see the following:

- AWS SDK for C++
- AWS SDK for Go
- AWS SDK for Java
- AWS SDK for Ruby V2

DestinationSchema

Describes the data format when records are written to the destination. For more information, see Configuring Application Output.

Contents

RecordFormatType Specifies the format of the records on the output stream.
Type: String
Valid Values:JSON | CSV
Required: Yes

See Also

For more information about using this API in one of the language-specific AWS SDKs, see the following:

- AWS SDK for C++
- AWS SDK for Go
- AWS SDK for Java
- AWS SDK for Ruby V2

Input

When you configure the application input, you specify the streaming source, the in-application stream name that is created, and the mapping between the two. For more information, see Configuring Application Input.

Contents

InputParallelism Describes the number of in-application streams to create.
Data from your source is routed to these in-application input streams.
(see Configuring Application Input.
Type: InputParallelism object
Required: No

InputProcessingConfiguration The InputProcessingConfiguration for the input. An input processor transforms records as they are received from the stream, before the application's SQL code executes. Currently, the only input processing configuration available is InputLambdaProcessor.
Type: InputProcessingConfiguration object
Required: No

InputSchema Describes the format of the data in the streaming source, and how each data element maps to corresponding columns in the in-application stream that is being created.
Also used to describe the format of the reference data source.
Type: SourceSchema object
Required: Yes

KinesisFirehoseInput If the streaming source is an Amazon Kinesis Firehose delivery stream, identifies the delivery stream's ARN and an IAM role that enables Amazon Kinesis Analytics to access the stream on your behalf.
Note: Either `KinesisStreamsInput` or `KinesisFirehoseInput` is required.
Type: KinesisFirehoseInput object
Required: No

KinesisStreamsInput If the streaming source is an Amazon Kinesis stream, identifies the stream's Amazon Resource Name (ARN) and an IAM role that enables Amazon Kinesis Analytics to access the stream on your behalf.
Note: Either `KinesisStreamsInput` or `KinesisFirehoseInput` is required.
Type: KinesisStreamsInput object
Required: No

NamePrefix Name prefix to use when creating an in-application stream. Suppose that you specify a prefix "MyInApplicationStream." Amazon Kinesis Analytics then creates one or more (as per the `InputParallelism` count you specified) in-application streams with names "MyInApplicationStream_001," "MyInApplicationStream_002," and so on.
Type: String
Length Constraints: Minimum length of 1. Maximum length of 32.
Pattern: `[a-zA-Z][a-zA-Z0-9_]+`
Required: Yes

See Also

For more information about using this API in one of the language-specific AWS SDKs, see the following:

- AWS SDK for C++
- AWS SDK for Go
- AWS SDK for Java

- AWS SDK for Ruby V2

InputConfiguration

When you start your application, you provide this configuration, which identifies the input source and the point in the input source at which you want the application to start processing records.

Contents

Id Input source ID. You can get this ID by calling the DescribeApplication operation.
Type: String
Length Constraints: Minimum length of 1. Maximum length of 50.
Pattern: `[a-zA-Z0-9_.-]+`
Required: Yes

InputStartingPositionConfiguration Point at which you want the application to start processing records from the streaming source.
Type: InputStartingPositionConfiguration object
Required: Yes

See Also

For more information about using this API in one of the language-specific AWS SDKs, see the following:

- AWS SDK for C++
- AWS SDK for Go
- AWS SDK for Java
- AWS SDK for Ruby V2

InputDescription

Describes the application input configuration. For more information, see Configuring Application Input.

Contents

InAppStreamNames Returns the in-application stream names that are mapped to the stream source.
Type: Array of strings
Length Constraints: Minimum length of 1. Maximum length of 32.
Pattern: `[a-zA-Z][a-zA-Z0-9_]+`
Required: No

InputId Input ID associated with the application input. This is the ID that Amazon Kinesis Analytics assigns to each input configuration you add to your application.
Type: String
Length Constraints: Minimum length of 1. Maximum length of 50.
Pattern: `[a-zA-Z0-9_.-]+`
Required: No

InputParallelism Describes the configured parallelism (number of in-application streams mapped to the streaming source).
Type: InputParallelism object
Required: No

InputProcessingConfigurationDescription The description of the preprocessor that executes on records in this input before the application's code is run.
Type: InputProcessingConfigurationDescription object
Required: No

InputSchema Describes the format of the data in the streaming source, and how each data element maps to corresponding columns in the in-application stream that is being created.
Type: SourceSchema object
Required: No

InputStartingPositionConfiguration Point at which the application is configured to read from the input stream.
Type: InputStartingPositionConfiguration object
Required: No

KinesisFirehoseInputDescription If an Amazon Kinesis Firehose delivery stream is configured as a streaming source, provides the delivery stream's ARN and an IAM role that enables Amazon Kinesis Analytics to access the stream on your behalf.
Type: KinesisFirehoseInputDescription object
Required: No

KinesisStreamsInputDescription If an Amazon Kinesis stream is configured as streaming source, provides Amazon Kinesis stream's Amazon Resource Name (ARN) and an IAM role that enables Amazon Kinesis Analytics to access the stream on your behalf.
Type: KinesisStreamsInputDescription object
Required: No

NamePrefix In-application name prefix.
Type: String
Length Constraints: Minimum length of 1. Maximum length of 32.
Pattern: `[a-zA-Z][a-zA-Z0-9_]+`
Required: No

See Also

For more information about using this API in one of the language-specific AWS SDKs, see the following:

- AWS SDK for C++
- AWS SDK for Go
- AWS SDK for Java
- AWS SDK for Ruby V2

InputLambdaProcessor

An object that contains the Amazon Resource Name (ARN) of the AWS Lambda function that is used to preprocess records in the stream, and the ARN of the IAM role that is used to access the AWS Lambda function.

Contents

ResourceARN The ARN of the AWS Lambda function that operates on records in the stream.
Type: String
Length Constraints: Minimum length of 1. Maximum length of 2048.
Pattern: `arn:.*`
Required: Yes

RoleARN The ARN of the IAM role that is used to access the AWS Lambda function.
Type: String
Length Constraints: Minimum length of 1. Maximum length of 2048.
Pattern: `arn:aws:iam::\d{12}:role/?[a-zA-Z_0-9+=,.@\-_/]+`
Required: Yes

See Also

For more information about using this API in one of the language-specific AWS SDKs, see the following:

- AWS SDK for C++
- AWS SDK for Go
- AWS SDK for Java
- AWS SDK for Ruby V2

InputLambdaProcessorDescription

An object that contains the Amazon Resource Name (ARN) of the AWS Lambda function that is used to preprocess records in the stream, and the ARN of the IAM role that is used to access the AWS Lambda expression.

Contents

ResourceARN The ARN of the AWS Lambda function that is used to preprocess the records in the stream.
Type: String
Length Constraints: Minimum length of 1. Maximum length of 2048.
Pattern: `arn:.*`
Required: No

RoleARN The ARN of the IAM role that is used to access the AWS Lambda function.
Type: String
Length Constraints: Minimum length of 1. Maximum length of 2048.
Pattern: `arn:aws:iam::\d{12}:role/?[a-zA-Z_0-9+=,.@\-_/]+`
Required: No

See Also

For more information about using this API in one of the language-specific AWS SDKs, see the following:

- AWS SDK for C++
- AWS SDK for Go
- AWS SDK for Java
- AWS SDK for Ruby V2

InputLambdaProcessorUpdate

Represents an update to the InputLambdaProcessor that is used to preprocess the records in the stream.

Contents

ResourceARNUpdate The Amazon Resource Name (ARN) of the new AWS Lambda function that is used to preprocess the records in the stream.
Type: String
Length Constraints: Minimum length of 1. Maximum length of 2048.
Pattern: `arn:.*`
Required: No

RoleARNUpdate The ARN of the new IAM role that is used to access the AWS Lambda function.
Type: String
Length Constraints: Minimum length of 1. Maximum length of 2048.
Pattern: `arn:aws:iam::\d{12}:role/?[a-zA-Z_0-9+=,.@\-_/]+`
Required: No

See Also

For more information about using this API in one of the language-specific AWS SDKs, see the following:

- AWS SDK for C++
- AWS SDK for Go
- AWS SDK for Java
- AWS SDK for Ruby V2

InputParallelism

Describes the number of in-application streams to create for a given streaming source. For information about parallelism, see Configuring Application Input.

Contents

Count Number of in-application streams to create. For more information, see Limits.
Type: Integer
Valid Range: Minimum value of 1. Maximum value of 64.
Required: No

See Also

For more information about using this API in one of the language-specific AWS SDKs, see the following:

- AWS SDK for C++
- AWS SDK for Go
- AWS SDK for Java
- AWS SDK for Ruby V2

InputParallelismUpdate

Provides updates to the parallelism count.

Contents

CountUpdate Number of in-application streams to create for the specified streaming source.
Type: Integer
Valid Range: Minimum value of 1. Maximum value of 64.
Required: No

See Also

For more information about using this API in one of the language-specific AWS SDKs, see the following:

- AWS SDK for C++
- AWS SDK for Go
- AWS SDK for Java
- AWS SDK for Ruby V2

InputProcessingConfiguration

Provides a description of a processor that is used to preprocess the records in the stream before being processed by your application code. Currently, the only input processor available is AWS Lambda.

Contents

InputLambdaProcessor The InputLambdaProcessor that is used to preprocess the records in the stream before being processed by your application code.
Type: InputLambdaProcessor object
Required: Yes

See Also

For more information about using this API in one of the language-specific AWS SDKs, see the following:

- AWS SDK for C++
- AWS SDK for Go
- AWS SDK for Java
- AWS SDK for Ruby V2

InputProcessingConfigurationDescription

Provides configuration information about an input processor. Currently, the only input processor available is AWS Lambda.

Contents

InputLambdaProcessorDescription Provides configuration information about the associated InputLambdaProcessorDescription.
Type: InputLambdaProcessorDescription object
Required: No

See Also

For more information about using this API in one of the language-specific AWS SDKs, see the following:

- AWS SDK for C++
- AWS SDK for Go
- AWS SDK for Java
- AWS SDK for Ruby V2

InputProcessingConfigurationUpdate

Describes updates to an InputProcessingConfiguration.

Contents

InputLambdaProcessorUpdate Provides update information for an InputLambdaProcessor.
Type: InputLambdaProcessorUpdate object
Required: Yes

See Also

For more information about using this API in one of the language-specific AWS SDKs, see the following:

- AWS SDK for C++
- AWS SDK for Go
- AWS SDK for Java
- AWS SDK for Ruby V2

InputSchemaUpdate

Describes updates for the application's input schema.

Contents

RecordColumnUpdates A list of `RecordColumn` objects. Each object describes the mapping of the streaming source element to the corresponding column in the in-application stream.
Type: Array of RecordColumn objects
Array Members: Minimum number of 1 item. Maximum number of 1000 items.
Required: No

RecordEncodingUpdate Specifies the encoding of the records in the streaming source. For example, UTF-8.
Type: String
Pattern: `UTF-8`
Required: No

RecordFormatUpdate Specifies the format of the records on the streaming source.
Type: RecordFormat object
Required: No

See Also

For more information about using this API in one of the language-specific AWS SDKs, see the following:

- AWS SDK for C++
- AWS SDK for Go
- AWS SDK for Java
- AWS SDK for Ruby V2

InputStartingPositionConfiguration

Describes the point at which the application reads from the streaming source.

Contents

InputStartingPosition The starting position on the stream.

- `NOW` - Start reading just after the most recent record in the stream, start at the request time stamp that the customer issued.
- `TRIM_HORIZON` - Start reading at the last untrimmed record in the stream, which is the oldest record available in the stream. This option is not available for an Amazon Kinesis Firehose delivery stream.
- `LAST_STOPPED_POINT` - Resume reading from where the application last stopped reading. Type: String Valid Values:`NOW` | `TRIM_HORIZON` | `LAST_STOPPED_POINT` Required: No

See Also

For more information about using this API in one of the language-specific AWS SDKs, see the following:

- AWS SDK for C++
- AWS SDK for Go
- AWS SDK for Java
- AWS SDK for Ruby V2

InputUpdate

Describes updates to a specific input configuration (identified by the `InputId` of an application).

Contents

InputId Input ID of the application input to be updated.
Type: String
Length Constraints: Minimum length of 1. Maximum length of 50.
Pattern: `[a-zA-Z0-9_.-]+`
Required: Yes

InputParallelismUpdate Describes the parallelism updates (the number in-application streams Amazon Kinesis Analytics creates for the specific streaming source).
Type: InputParallelismUpdate object
Required: No

InputProcessingConfigurationUpdate Describes updates for an input processing configuration.
Type: InputProcessingConfigurationUpdate object
Required: No

InputSchemaUpdate Describes the data format on the streaming source, and how record elements on the streaming source map to columns of the in-application stream that is created.
Type: InputSchemaUpdate object
Required: No

KinesisFirehoseInputUpdate If an Amazon Kinesis Firehose delivery stream is the streaming source to be updated, provides an updated stream ARN and IAM role ARN.
Type: KinesisFirehoseInputUpdate object
Required: No

KinesisStreamsInputUpdate If an Amazon Kinesis stream is the streaming source to be updated, provides an updated stream Amazon Resource Name (ARN) and IAM role ARN.
Type: KinesisStreamsInputUpdate object
Required: No

NamePrefixUpdate Name prefix for in-application streams that Amazon Kinesis Analytics creates for the specific streaming source.
Type: String
Length Constraints: Minimum length of 1. Maximum length of 32.
Pattern: `[a-zA-Z][a-zA-Z0-9_]+`
Required: No

See Also

For more information about using this API in one of the language-specific AWS SDKs, see the following:
- AWS SDK for C++
- AWS SDK for Go
- AWS SDK for Java
- AWS SDK for Ruby V2

JSONMappingParameters

Provides additional mapping information when JSON is the record format on the streaming source.

Contents

RecordRowPath Path to the top-level parent that contains the records.
Type: String
Length Constraints: Minimum length of 1.
Required: Yes

See Also

For more information about using this API in one of the language-specific AWS SDKs, see the following:

- AWS SDK for C++
- AWS SDK for Go
- AWS SDK for Java
- AWS SDK for Ruby V2

KinesisFirehoseInput

Identifies an Amazon Kinesis Firehose delivery stream as the streaming source. You provide the delivery stream's Amazon Resource Name (ARN) and an IAM role ARN that enables Amazon Kinesis Analytics to access the stream on your behalf.

Contents

ResourceARN ARN of the input delivery stream.
Type: String
Length Constraints: Minimum length of 1. Maximum length of 2048.
Pattern: `arn:.*`
Required: Yes

RoleARN ARN of the IAM role that Amazon Kinesis Analytics can assume to access the stream on your behalf. You need to make sure that the role has the necessary permissions to access the stream.
Type: String
Length Constraints: Minimum length of 1. Maximum length of 2048.
Pattern: `arn:aws:iam::\d{12}:role/?[a-zA-Z_0-9+=,.@\-_/]+`
Required: Yes

See Also

For more information about using this API in one of the language-specific AWS SDKs, see the following:

- AWS SDK for C++
- AWS SDK for Go
- AWS SDK for Java
- AWS SDK for Ruby V2

KinesisFirehoseInputDescription

Describes the Amazon Kinesis Firehose delivery stream that is configured as the streaming source in the application input configuration.

Contents

ResourceARN Amazon Resource Name (ARN) of the Amazon Kinesis Firehose delivery stream.
Type: String
Length Constraints: Minimum length of 1. Maximum length of 2048.
Pattern: `arn:.*`
Required: No

RoleARN ARN of the IAM role that Amazon Kinesis Analytics assumes to access the stream.
Type: String
Length Constraints: Minimum length of 1. Maximum length of 2048.
Pattern: `arn:aws:iam::\d{12}:role/?[a-zA-Z_0-9+=,.@\-_/]+`
Required: No

See Also

For more information about using this API in one of the language-specific AWS SDKs, see the following:

- AWS SDK for C++
- AWS SDK for Go
- AWS SDK for Java
- AWS SDK for Ruby V2

KinesisFirehoseInputUpdate

When updating application input configuration, provides information about an Amazon Kinesis Firehose delivery stream as the streaming source.

Contents

ResourceARNUpdate Amazon Resource Name (ARN) of the input Amazon Kinesis Firehose delivery stream to read.
Type: String
Length Constraints: Minimum length of 1. Maximum length of 2048.
Pattern: `arn:.*`
Required: No

RoleARNUpdate ARN of the IAM role that Amazon Kinesis Analytics can assume to access the stream on your behalf. You need to grant the necessary permissions to this role.
Type: String
Length Constraints: Minimum length of 1. Maximum length of 2048.
Pattern: `arn:aws:iam::\d{12}:role/?[a-zA-Z_0-9+=,.@\-_/]+`
Required: No

See Also

For more information about using this API in one of the language-specific AWS SDKs, see the following:

- AWS SDK for C++
- AWS SDK for Go
- AWS SDK for Java
- AWS SDK for Ruby V2

KinesisFirehoseOutput

When configuring application output, identifies an Amazon Kinesis Firehose delivery stream as the destination. You provide the stream Amazon Resource Name (ARN) and an IAM role that enables Amazon Kinesis Analytics to write to the stream on your behalf.

Contents

ResourceARN ARN of the destination Amazon Kinesis Firehose delivery stream to write to.
Type: String
Length Constraints: Minimum length of 1. Maximum length of 2048.
Pattern: `arn:.*`
Required: Yes

RoleARN ARN of the IAM role that Amazon Kinesis Analytics can assume to write to the destination stream on your behalf. You need to grant the necessary permissions to this role.
Type: String
Length Constraints: Minimum length of 1. Maximum length of 2048.
Pattern: `arn:aws:iam::\d{12}:role/?[a-zA-Z_0-9+=,.@\-_/]+`
Required: Yes

See Also

For more information about using this API in one of the language-specific AWS SDKs, see the following:

- AWS SDK for C++
- AWS SDK for Go
- AWS SDK for Java
- AWS SDK for Ruby V2

KinesisFirehoseOutputDescription

For an application output, describes the Amazon Kinesis Firehose delivery stream configured as its destination.

Contents

ResourceARN Amazon Resource Name (ARN) of the Amazon Kinesis Firehose delivery stream.
Type: String
Length Constraints: Minimum length of 1. Maximum length of 2048.
Pattern: `arn:.*`
Required: No

RoleARN ARN of the IAM role that Amazon Kinesis Analytics can assume to access the stream.
Type: String
Length Constraints: Minimum length of 1. Maximum length of 2048.
Pattern: `arn:aws:iam::\d{12}:role/?[a-zA-Z_0-9+=,.@\-_/]+`
Required: No

See Also

For more information about using this API in one of the language-specific AWS SDKs, see the following:

- AWS SDK for C++
- AWS SDK for Go
- AWS SDK for Java
- AWS SDK for Ruby V2

KinesisFirehoseOutputUpdate

When updating an output configuration using the UpdateApplication operation, provides information about an Amazon Kinesis Firehose delivery stream configured as the destination.

Contents

ResourceARNUpdate Amazon Resource Name (ARN) of the Amazon Kinesis Firehose delivery stream to write to.
Type: String
Length Constraints: Minimum length of 1. Maximum length of 2048.
Pattern: `arn:.*`
Required: No

RoleARNUpdate ARN of the IAM role that Amazon Kinesis Analytics can assume to access the stream on your behalf. You need to grant the necessary permissions to this role.
Type: String
Length Constraints: Minimum length of 1. Maximum length of 2048.
Pattern: `arn:aws:iam::\d{12}:role/?[a-zA-Z_0-9+=,.@\-_/]+`
Required: No

See Also

For more information about using this API in one of the language-specific AWS SDKs, see the following:

- AWS SDK for C++
- AWS SDK for Go
- AWS SDK for Java
- AWS SDK for Ruby V2

KinesisStreamsInput

Identifies an Amazon Kinesis stream as the streaming source. You provide the stream's Amazon Resource Name (ARN) and an IAM role ARN that enables Amazon Kinesis Analytics to access the stream on your behalf.

Contents

ResourceARN ARN of the input Amazon Kinesis stream to read.
Type: String
Length Constraints: Minimum length of 1. Maximum length of 2048.
Pattern: `arn:.*`
Required: Yes

RoleARN ARN of the IAM role that Amazon Kinesis Analytics can assume to access the stream on your behalf. You need to grant the necessary permissions to this role.
Type: String
Length Constraints: Minimum length of 1. Maximum length of 2048.
Pattern: `arn:aws:iam::\d{12}:role/?[a-zA-Z_0-9+=,.@\-_/]+`
Required: Yes

See Also

For more information about using this API in one of the language-specific AWS SDKs, see the following:

- AWS SDK for C++
- AWS SDK for Go
- AWS SDK for Java
- AWS SDK for Ruby V2

KinesisStreamsInputDescription

Describes the Amazon Kinesis stream that is configured as the streaming source in the application input configuration.

Contents

ResourceARN Amazon Resource Name (ARN) of the Amazon Kinesis stream.
Type: String
Length Constraints: Minimum length of 1. Maximum length of 2048.
Pattern: `arn:.*`
Required: No

RoleARN ARN of the IAM role that Amazon Kinesis Analytics can assume to access the stream.
Type: String
Length Constraints: Minimum length of 1. Maximum length of 2048.
Pattern: `arn:aws:iam::\d{12}:role/?[a-zA-Z_0-9+=,.@\-_/]+`
Required: No

See Also

For more information about using this API in one of the language-specific AWS SDKs, see the following:

- AWS SDK for C++
- AWS SDK for Go
- AWS SDK for Java
- AWS SDK for Ruby V2

KinesisStreamsInputUpdate

When updating application input configuration, provides information about an Amazon Kinesis stream as the streaming source.

Contents

ResourceARNUpdate Amazon Resource Name (ARN) of the input Amazon Kinesis stream to read.
Type: String
Length Constraints: Minimum length of 1. Maximum length of 2048.
Pattern: `arn:.*`
Required: No

RoleARNUpdate ARN of the IAM role that Amazon Kinesis Analytics can assume to access the stream on your behalf. You need to grant the necessary permissions to this role.
Type: String
Length Constraints: Minimum length of 1. Maximum length of 2048.
Pattern: `arn:aws:iam::\d{12}:role/?[a-zA-Z_0-9+=,.@\-_/]+`
Required: No

See Also

For more information about using this API in one of the language-specific AWS SDKs, see the following:

- AWS SDK for C++
- AWS SDK for Go
- AWS SDK for Java
- AWS SDK for Ruby V2

KinesisStreamsOutput

When configuring application output, identifies an Amazon Kinesis stream as the destination. You provide the stream Amazon Resource Name (ARN) and also an IAM role ARN that Amazon Kinesis Analytics can use to write to the stream on your behalf.

Contents

ResourceARN ARN of the destination Amazon Kinesis stream to write to.
Type: String
Length Constraints: Minimum length of 1. Maximum length of 2048.
Pattern: `arn:.*`
Required: Yes

RoleARN ARN of the IAM role that Amazon Kinesis Analytics can assume to write to the destination stream on your behalf. You need to grant the necessary permissions to this role.
Type: String
Length Constraints: Minimum length of 1. Maximum length of 2048.
Pattern: `arn:aws:iam::\d{12}:role/?[a-zA-Z_0-9+=,.@\-_/]+`
Required: Yes

See Also

For more information about using this API in one of the language-specific AWS SDKs, see the following:

- AWS SDK for C++
- AWS SDK for Go
- AWS SDK for Java
- AWS SDK for Ruby V2

KinesisStreamsOutputDescription

For an application output, describes the Amazon Kinesis stream configured as its destination.

Contents

ResourceARN Amazon Resource Name (ARN) of the Amazon Kinesis stream.
Type: String
Length Constraints: Minimum length of 1. Maximum length of 2048.
Pattern: `arn:.*`
Required: No

RoleARN ARN of the IAM role that Amazon Kinesis Analytics can assume to access the stream.
Type: String
Length Constraints: Minimum length of 1. Maximum length of 2048.
Pattern: `arn:aws:iam::\d{12}:role/?[a-zA-Z_0-9+=,.@\-_/]+`
Required: No

See Also

For more information about using this API in one of the language-specific AWS SDKs, see the following:

- AWS SDK for C++
- AWS SDK for Go
- AWS SDK for Java
- AWS SDK for Ruby V2

KinesisStreamsOutputUpdate

When updating an output configuration using the UpdateApplication operation, provides information about an Amazon Kinesis stream configured as the destination.

Contents

ResourceARNUpdate Amazon Resource Name (ARN) of the Amazon Kinesis stream where you want to write the output.
Type: String
Length Constraints: Minimum length of 1. Maximum length of 2048.
Pattern: `arn:.*`
Required: No

RoleARNUpdate ARN of the IAM role that Amazon Kinesis Analytics can assume to access the stream on your behalf. You need to grant the necessary permissions to this role.
Type: String
Length Constraints: Minimum length of 1. Maximum length of 2048.
Pattern: `arn:aws:iam::\d{12}:role/?[a-zA-Z_0-9+=,.@\-_/]+`
Required: No

See Also

For more information about using this API in one of the language-specific AWS SDKs, see the following:

- AWS SDK for C++
- AWS SDK for Go
- AWS SDK for Java
- AWS SDK for Ruby V2

LambdaOutput

When configuring application output, identifies an AWS Lambda function as the destination. You provide the function Amazon Resource Name (ARN) and also an IAM role ARN that Amazon Kinesis Analytics can use to write to the function on your behalf.

Contents

ResourceARN Amazon Resource Name (ARN) of the destination Lambda function to write to.
Type: String
Length Constraints: Minimum length of 1. Maximum length of 2048.
Pattern: `arn:.*`
Required: Yes

RoleARN ARN of the IAM role that Amazon Kinesis Analytics can assume to write to the destination function on your behalf. You need to grant the necessary permissions to this role.
Type: String
Length Constraints: Minimum length of 1. Maximum length of 2048.
Pattern: `arn:aws:iam::\d{12}:role/?[a-zA-Z_0-9+=,.@\-_/]+`
Required: Yes

See Also

For more information about using this API in one of the language-specific AWS SDKs, see the following:

- AWS SDK for C++
- AWS SDK for Go
- AWS SDK for Java
- AWS SDK for Ruby V2

LambdaOutputDescription

For an application output, describes the AWS Lambda function configured as its destination.

Contents

ResourceARN Amazon Resource Name (ARN) of the destination Lambda function.
Type: String
Length Constraints: Minimum length of 1. Maximum length of 2048.
Pattern: `arn:.*`
Required: No

RoleARN ARN of the IAM role that Amazon Kinesis Analytics can assume to write to the destination function.
Type: String
Length Constraints: Minimum length of 1. Maximum length of 2048.
Pattern: `arn:aws:iam::\d{12}:role/?[a-zA-Z_0-9+=,.@\-_/]+`
Required: No

See Also

For more information about using this API in one of the language-specific AWS SDKs, see the following:

- AWS SDK for C++
- AWS SDK for Go
- AWS SDK for Java
- AWS SDK for Ruby V2

LambdaOutputUpdate

When updating an output configuration using the UpdateApplication operation, provides information about an AWS Lambda function configured as the destination.

Contents

ResourceARNUpdate Amazon Resource Name (ARN) of the destination Lambda function.
Type: String
Length Constraints: Minimum length of 1. Maximum length of 2048.
Pattern: `arn:.*`
Required: No

RoleARNUpdate ARN of the IAM role that Amazon Kinesis Analytics can assume to write to the destination function on your behalf. You need to grant the necessary permissions to this role.
Type: String
Length Constraints: Minimum length of 1. Maximum length of 2048.
Pattern: `arn:aws:iam::\d{12}:role/?[a-zA-Z_0-9+=,.@\-_/]+`
Required: No

See Also

For more information about using this API in one of the language-specific AWS SDKs, see the following:

- AWS SDK for C++
- AWS SDK for Go
- AWS SDK for Java
- AWS SDK for Ruby V2

MappingParameters

When configuring application input at the time of creating or updating an application, provides additional mapping information specific to the record format (such as JSON, CSV, or record fields delimited by some delimiter) on the streaming source.

Contents

CSVMappingParameters Provides additional mapping information when the record format uses delimiters (for example, CSV).
Type: CSVMappingParameters object
Required: No

JSONMappingParameters Provides additional mapping information when JSON is the record format on the streaming source.
Type: JSONMappingParameters object
Required: No

See Also

For more information about using this API in one of the language-specific AWS SDKs, see the following:

- AWS SDK for C++
- AWS SDK for Go
- AWS SDK for Java
- AWS SDK for Ruby V2

Output

Describes application output configuration in which you identify an in-application stream and a destination where you want the in-application stream data to be written. The destination can be an Amazon Kinesis stream or an Amazon Kinesis Firehose delivery stream.

For limits on how many destinations an application can write and other limitations, see Limits.

Contents

DestinationSchema Describes the data format when records are written to the destination. For more information, see Configuring Application Output.
Type: DestinationSchema object
Required: Yes

KinesisFirehoseOutput Identifies an Amazon Kinesis Firehose delivery stream as the destination.
Type: KinesisFirehoseOutput object
Required: No

KinesisStreamsOutput Identifies an Amazon Kinesis stream as the destination.
Type: KinesisStreamsOutput object
Required: No

LambdaOutput Identifies an AWS Lambda function as the destination.
Type: LambdaOutput object
Required: No

Name Name of the in-application stream.
Type: String
Length Constraints: Minimum length of 1. Maximum length of 32.
Pattern: [a-zA-Z][a-zA-Z0-9_]+
Required: Yes

See Also

For more information about using this API in one of the language-specific AWS SDKs, see the following:

- AWS SDK for C++
- AWS SDK for Go
- AWS SDK for Java
- AWS SDK for Ruby V2

OutputDescription

Describes the application output configuration, which includes the in-application stream name and the destination where the stream data is written. The destination can be an Amazon Kinesis stream or an Amazon Kinesis Firehose delivery stream.

Contents

DestinationSchema Data format used for writing data to the destination.
Type: DestinationSchema object
Required: No

KinesisFirehoseOutputDescription Describes the Amazon Kinesis Firehose delivery stream configured as the destination where output is written.
Type: KinesisFirehoseOutputDescription object
Required: No

KinesisStreamsOutputDescription Describes Amazon Kinesis stream configured as the destination where output is written.
Type: KinesisStreamsOutputDescription object
Required: No

LambdaOutputDescription Describes the AWS Lambda function configured as the destination where output is written.
Type: LambdaOutputDescription object
Required: No

Name Name of the in-application stream configured as output.
Type: String
Length Constraints: Minimum length of 1. Maximum length of 32.
Pattern: `[a-zA-Z][a-zA-Z0-9_]+`
Required: No

OutputId A unique identifier for the output configuration.
Type: String
Length Constraints: Minimum length of 1. Maximum length of 50.
Pattern: `[a-zA-Z0-9_.-]+`
Required: No

See Also

For more information about using this API in one of the language-specific AWS SDKs, see the following:

- AWS SDK for C++
- AWS SDK for Go
- AWS SDK for Java
- AWS SDK for Ruby V2

OutputUpdate

Describes updates to the output configuration identified by the `OutputId`.

Contents

DestinationSchemaUpdate Describes the data format when records are written to the destination. For more information, see Configuring Application Output.
Type: DestinationSchema object
Required: No

KinesisFirehoseOutputUpdate Describes an Amazon Kinesis Firehose delivery stream as the destination for the output.
Type: KinesisFirehoseOutputUpdate object
Required: No

KinesisStreamsOutputUpdate Describes an Amazon Kinesis stream as the destination for the output.
Type: KinesisStreamsOutputUpdate object
Required: No

LambdaOutputUpdate Describes an AWS Lambda function as the destination for the output.
Type: LambdaOutputUpdate object
Required: No

NameUpdate If you want to specify a different in-application stream for this output configuration, use this field to specify the new in-application stream name.
Type: String
Length Constraints: Minimum length of 1. Maximum length of 32.
Pattern: `[a-zA-Z][a-zA-Z0-9_]+`
Required: No

OutputId Identifies the specific output configuration that you want to update.
Type: String
Length Constraints: Minimum length of 1. Maximum length of 50.
Pattern: `[a-zA-Z0-9_.-]+`
Required: Yes

See Also

For more information about using this API in one of the language-specific AWS SDKs, see the following:

- AWS SDK for C++
- AWS SDK for Go
- AWS SDK for Java
- AWS SDK for Ruby V2

RecordColumn

Describes the mapping of each data element in the streaming source to the corresponding column in the in-application stream.

Also used to describe the format of the reference data source.

Contents

Mapping Reference to the data element in the streaming input of the reference data source.
Type: String
Required: No

Name Name of the column created in the in-application input stream or reference table.
Type: String
Pattern: `[a-zA-Z_][a-zA-Z0-9_]*`
Required: Yes

SqlType Type of column created in the in-application input stream or reference table.
Type: String
Length Constraints: Minimum length of 1.
Required: Yes

See Also

For more information about using this API in one of the language-specific AWS SDKs, see the following:

- AWS SDK for C++
- AWS SDK for Go
- AWS SDK for Java
- AWS SDK for Ruby V2

RecordFormat

Describes the record format and relevant mapping information that should be applied to schematize the records on the stream.

Contents

MappingParameters When configuring application input at the time of creating or updating an application, provides additional mapping information specific to the record format (such as JSON, CSV, or record fields delimited by some delimiter) on the streaming source.
Type: MappingParameters object
Required: No

RecordFormatType The type of record format.
Type: String
Valid Values:`JSON | CSV`
Required: Yes

See Also

For more information about using this API in one of the language-specific AWS SDKs, see the following:

- AWS SDK for C++
- AWS SDK for Go
- AWS SDK for Java
- AWS SDK for Ruby V2

ReferenceDataSource

Describes the reference data source by providing the source information (S3 bucket name and object key name), the resulting in-application table name that is created, and the necessary schema to map the data elements in the Amazon S3 object to the in-application table.

Contents

ReferenceSchema Describes the format of the data in the streaming source, and how each data element maps to corresponding columns created in the in-application stream.
Type: SourceSchema object
Required: Yes

S3ReferenceDataSource Identifies the S3 bucket and object that contains the reference data. Also identifies the IAM role Amazon Kinesis Analytics can assume to read this object on your behalf. An Amazon Kinesis Analytics application loads reference data only once. If the data changes, you call the UpdateApplication operation to trigger reloading of data into your application.
Type: S3ReferenceDataSource object
Required: No

TableName Name of the in-application table to create.
Type: String
Length Constraints: Minimum length of 1. Maximum length of 32.
Pattern: [a-zA-Z][a-zA-Z0-9_]+
Required: Yes

See Also

For more information about using this API in one of the language-specific AWS SDKs, see the following:

- AWS SDK for C++
- AWS SDK for Go
- AWS SDK for Java
- AWS SDK for Ruby V2

ReferenceDataSourceDescription

Describes the reference data source configured for an application.

Contents

ReferenceId ID of the reference data source. This is the ID that Amazon Kinesis Analytics assigns when you add the reference data source to your application using the AddApplicationReferenceDataSource operation.
Type: String
Length Constraints: Minimum length of 1. Maximum length of 50.
Pattern: `[a-zA-Z0-9_.-]+`
Required: Yes

ReferenceSchema Describes the format of the data in the streaming source, and how each data element maps to corresponding columns created in the in-application stream.
Type: SourceSchema object
Required: No

S3ReferenceDataSourceDescription Provides the S3 bucket name, the object key name that contains the reference data. It also provides the Amazon Resource Name (ARN) of the IAM role that Amazon Kinesis Analytics can assume to read the Amazon S3 object and populate the in-application reference table.
Type: S3ReferenceDataSourceDescription object
Required: Yes

TableName The in-application table name created by the specific reference data source configuration.
Type: String
Length Constraints: Minimum length of 1. Maximum length of 32.
Pattern: `[a-zA-Z][a-zA-Z0-9_]+`
Required: Yes

See Also

For more information about using this API in one of the language-specific AWS SDKs, see the following:

- AWS SDK for C++
- AWS SDK for Go
- AWS SDK for Java
- AWS SDK for Ruby V2

ReferenceDataSourceUpdate

When you update a reference data source configuration for an application, this object provides all the updated values (such as the source bucket name and object key name), the in-application table name that is created, and updated mapping information that maps the data in the Amazon S3 object to the in-application reference table that is created.

Contents

ReferenceId ID of the reference data source being updated. You can use the DescribeApplication operation to get this value.
Type: String
Length Constraints: Minimum length of 1. Maximum length of 50.
Pattern: `[a-zA-Z0-9_.-]+`
Required: Yes

ReferenceSchemaUpdate Describes the format of the data in the streaming source, and how each data element maps to corresponding columns created in the in-application stream.
Type: SourceSchema object
Required: No

S3ReferenceDataSourceUpdate Describes the S3 bucket name, object key name, and IAM role that Amazon Kinesis Analytics can assume to read the Amazon S3 object on your behalf and populate the in-application reference table.
Type: S3ReferenceDataSourceUpdate object
Required: No

TableNameUpdate In-application table name that is created by this update.
Type: String
Length Constraints: Minimum length of 1. Maximum length of 32.
Pattern: `[a-zA-Z][a-zA-Z0-9_]+`
Required: No

See Also

For more information about using this API in one of the language-specific AWS SDKs, see the following:

- AWS SDK for C++
- AWS SDK for Go
- AWS SDK for Java
- AWS SDK for Ruby V2

S3Configuration

Provides a description of an Amazon S3 data source, including the Amazon Resource Name (ARN) of the S3 bucket, the ARN of the IAM role that is used to access the bucket, and the name of the Amazon S3 object that contains the data.

Contents

BucketARN ARN of the S3 bucket that contains the data.
Type: String
Length Constraints: Minimum length of 1. Maximum length of 2048.
Pattern: `arn:.*`
Required: Yes

FileKey The name of the object that contains the data.
Type: String
Length Constraints: Minimum length of 1. Maximum length of 1024.
Required: Yes

RoleARN IAM ARN of the role used to access the data.
Type: String
Length Constraints: Minimum length of 1. Maximum length of 2048.
Pattern: `arn:aws:iam::\d{12}:role/?[a-zA-Z_0-9+=,.@\-_/]+`
Required: Yes

See Also

For more information about using this API in one of the language-specific AWS SDKs, see the following:

- AWS SDK for C++
- AWS SDK for Go
- AWS SDK for Java
- AWS SDK for Ruby V2

S3ReferenceDataSource

Identifies the S3 bucket and object that contains the reference data. Also identifies the IAM role Amazon Kinesis Analytics can assume to read this object on your behalf.

An Amazon Kinesis Analytics application loads reference data only once. If the data changes, you call the UpdateApplication operation to trigger reloading of data into your application.

Contents

BucketARN Amazon Resource Name (ARN) of the S3 bucket.
Type: String
Length Constraints: Minimum length of 1. Maximum length of 2048.
Pattern: `arn:.*`
Required: Yes

FileKey Object key name containing reference data.
Type: String
Length Constraints: Minimum length of 1. Maximum length of 1024.
Required: Yes

ReferenceRoleARN ARN of the IAM role that the service can assume to read data on your behalf. This role must have permission for the `s3:GetObject` action on the object and trust policy that allows Amazon Kinesis Analytics service principal to assume this role.
Type: String
Length Constraints: Minimum length of 1. Maximum length of 2048.
Pattern: `arn:aws:iam::\d{12}:role/?[a-zA-Z_0-9+=,.@\-_/]+`
Required: Yes

See Also

For more information about using this API in one of the language-specific AWS SDKs, see the following:

- AWS SDK for C++
- AWS SDK for Go
- AWS SDK for Java
- AWS SDK for Ruby V2

S3ReferenceDataSourceDescription

Provides the bucket name and object key name that stores the reference data.

Contents

BucketARN Amazon Resource Name (ARN) of the S3 bucket.
Type: String
Length Constraints: Minimum length of 1. Maximum length of 2048.
Pattern: `arn:.*`
Required: Yes

FileKey Amazon S3 object key name.
Type: String
Length Constraints: Minimum length of 1. Maximum length of 1024.
Required: Yes

ReferenceRoleARN ARN of the IAM role that Amazon Kinesis Analytics can assume to read the Amazon S3 object on your behalf to populate the in-application reference table.
Type: String
Length Constraints: Minimum length of 1. Maximum length of 2048.
Pattern: `arn:aws:iam::\d{12}:role/?[a-zA-Z_0-9+=,.@\-_/]+`
Required: Yes

See Also

For more information about using this API in one of the language-specific AWS SDKs, see the following:

- AWS SDK for C++
- AWS SDK for Go
- AWS SDK for Java
- AWS SDK for Ruby V2

S3ReferenceDataSourceUpdate

Describes the S3 bucket name, object key name, and IAM role that Amazon Kinesis Analytics can assume to read the Amazon S3 object on your behalf and populate the in-application reference table.

Contents

BucketARNUpdate Amazon Resource Name (ARN) of the S3 bucket.
Type: String
Length Constraints: Minimum length of 1. Maximum length of 2048.
Pattern: `arn:.*`
Required: No

FileKeyUpdate Object key name.
Type: String
Length Constraints: Minimum length of 1. Maximum length of 1024.
Required: No

ReferenceRoleARNUpdate ARN of the IAM role that Amazon Kinesis Analytics can assume to read the Amazon S3 object and populate the in-application.
Type: String
Length Constraints: Minimum length of 1. Maximum length of 2048.
Pattern: `arn:aws:iam::\d{12}:role/?[a-zA-Z_0-9+=,.@\-_/]+`
Required: No

See Also

For more information about using this API in one of the language-specific AWS SDKs, see the following:

- AWS SDK for C++
- AWS SDK for Go
- AWS SDK for Java
- AWS SDK for Ruby V2

SourceSchema

Describes the format of the data in the streaming source, and how each data element maps to corresponding columns created in the in-application stream.

Contents

RecordColumns A list of `RecordColumn` objects.
Type: Array of RecordColumn objects
Array Members: Minimum number of 1 item. Maximum number of 1000 items.
Required: Yes

RecordEncoding Specifies the encoding of the records in the streaming source. For example, UTF-8.
Type: String
Pattern: `UTF-8`
Required: No

RecordFormat Specifies the format of the records on the streaming source.
Type: RecordFormat object
Required: Yes

See Also

For more information about using this API in one of the language-specific AWS SDKs, see the following:
- AWS SDK for C++
- AWS SDK for Go
- AWS SDK for Java
- AWS SDK for Ruby V2

Document History for Amazon Kinesis Data Analytics

The following table describes the important changes to the documentation since the last release of Amazon Kinesis Data Analytics.

- **API version: 2015-08-14**
- **Latest documentation update:** May 18, 2018

Change	Description	Date
Example applications for pre-processing data	Additional code samples for REGEX_LOG_PARSE, REGEX_REPLACE, and DateTime operators. For more information, see Examples: Transforming Data .	May 18, 2018
Increase in size of returned rows and SQL code	The limit for the size for a returned row is increased to 512 KB, and the limit for the size of the SQL code in an application is increased to 100 KB. For more information, see Limits.	May 2, 2018
AWS Lambda function examples in Java and .NET	Code samples for creating Lambda functions for preprocessing records and for application destinations. For more information, see Creating Lambda Functions for Preprocessing and Creating Lambda Functions for Application Destinations.	March 22, 2018
New HOTSPOTS function	Locate and return information about relatively dense regions in your data. For more information, see Example: Detecting Hotspots on a Stream (HOTSPOTS Function).	March 19, 2018
Lambda function as a destination	Send analytics results to a Lambda function as a destination. For more information, see Using a Lambda Function as Output.	December 20, 2017
New RANDOM_CUT_FOREST_WITH_EXPLANATION function	Get an explanation of what fields contribute to an anomaly score in a data stream. For more information, see Example: Detecting Data Anomalies and Getting an Explanation (RANDOM_CUT_FOREST_WITH_EXPLANATION Function).	November 2, 2017

Change	Description	Date
Schema discovery on static data	Run schema discovery on static data stored in an Amazon S3 bucket. For more information, see Using the Schema Discovery Feature on Static Data.	October 6, 2017
Lambda preprocessing feature	Preprocess records in an input stream with AWS Lambda before analysis. For more information, see Preprocessing Data Using a Lambda Function.	October 6, 2017
Auto scaling applications	Automatically increase the data throughput of your application with auto scaling. For more information, see Automatically Scaling Applications to Increase Throughput.	September 13, 2017
Multiple in-application input streams	Increase application throughput with multiple in-application streams. For more information, see Parallelizing Input Streams for Increased Throughput.	June 29, 2017
Guide to using the AWS Management Console for Kinesis Data Analytics	Edit an inferred schema and SQL code using the schema editor and SQL editor in the Kinesis Data Analytics console. For more information, see Step 4 (Optional) Edit the Schema and SQL Code Using the Console.	April 7, 2017
Public release	Public release of the Amazon Kinesis Data Analytics Developer Guide.	August 11, 2016
Preview release	Preview release of the Amazon Kinesis Data Analytics Developer Guide.	January 29, 2016

AWS Glossary

For the latest AWS terminology, see the AWS Glossary in the *AWS General Reference.*

www.ingramcontent.com/pod-product-compliance
Lightning Source LLC
LaVergne TN
LVHW082037050326
832904LV00005B/211